PENGUIN LIFE

FINANCE FOR THE PEOPLE

Paco de Leon is an author, an illustrator, a musician and
the founder of The Hell Yeah Group, a financial firm dedicated to inspiring creatives to engage with their personal
and business finances. Her career experiences in banking,
business consulting, financial planning and wealth management have informed her financial philosophies. She is
a TED speaker and her work has been published or fea-
tured in *The New York Times*, *Forbes*, *Bloomberg*, *Vice*, and
other publications, and on NPR. She lives in Los Angeles
with her wife.

# FINANCE
## FOR THE PEOPLE

## GETTING A GRIP ON
## YOUR FINANCES

Paco de Leon

life

PENGUIN BOOKS
An imprint of Penguin Random House LLC
penguinrandomhouse.com

A Penguin Life Book

LIBRARY OF CONGRESS CATALOGING-IN-PUBLICATION DATA

Names: de Leon, Paco, author.
Title: Finance for the people: getting a grip on your finances / Paco de Leon.
Description: New York: Penguin Life [2022] | Includes bibliographical references.
Identifiers: LCCN 2021026464 | ISBN 9780143136255 (paperback) |
ISBN 9780525507840 (ebook)
Subjects: LCSH: Finance, Personal. | Money.
Classification: LCC HG179 .D3835 2022 | DDC 332.024—dc23
LC record available at https://lccn.loc.gov/2021026464

Printed in the United States of America
5th Printing

Set in Chaparral Pro
Designed by Sabrina Bowers

This publication is designed to provide accurate and authoritative information in regard to the subject matter covered. It is sold with the understanding that the publisher is not engaged in rendering legal, accounting, or other professional services. If you require legal advice or other expert assistance, you should seek the services of a competent professional.

While the author has made every effort to provide accurate telephone numbers, internet addresses, and other contact information at the time of publication, neither the publisher nor the author assumes any responsibility for errors or for changes that occur after publication. Further, the publisher does not have any control over and does not assume any responsibility for author or third-party websites or their content.

*To my sweet wife, Jenn,*
*for always believing in me,*
*and to my former fifteen-year-old self, and*
*to you, the reader, whose potential for*
*creativity and change is unlimited*

# Contents

## PART 1

### *Get a Grip*

## PART 2

### *The Fundamentals of Finance:*
### *Earning, Saving and Decision-making*

# *Introduction*

Money is a proxy for power, and I believe, like so many humans in the modern world, that when you have money you have power. The most obvious way we think about this is that people who have a great deal of money tend to have a great deal of power. But, of course, the opposite is also true. And I'm convinced that's why so many of us also carry such deep emotional associations to money. I once had a therapist who told me that the feeling I dread the most is the feeling of powerlessness. When I learned this about myself, I was able to see so many of my behaviors in a new light. My career in money made perfect sense when seen through this lens. To struggle with money, to feel you don't have enough, to feel like you don't have control over your financial life, is at its essence a terrifying feeling of powerlessness—for me, for you, for everyone.

Power gets a bad rap; some people who seek it do so in order to wield it over others. I want to have power because I don't want it wielded over me. Becoming empowered in a society that doesn't want me to be empowered is one of the single most radical actions I can take. A close second is writing this book.

I didn't write this book because of my white-hot passion for personal finance. In fact, I *don't* have a white-hot passion for personal finance. What I do care about is helping people connect to their personal power because once you come into it, it's like a bell that cannot be un-rung. Coming into your power gives you clarity. It changes your world subtly and forever. It shows you that you will always have options, but you have to learn how to see them.

I wrote this book for practical reasons; it's valuable to understand how to navigate the financial system from someone who knows the twists and turns. It's also incredibly practical to use processes and systems to help you reach financial milestones. Much of the practical knowledge I share in this book comes from my experience working with clients as a financial planner, a bookkeeper, a small business consultant, a collections agent, a failed salesperson and a person owning and running small businesses. This book is different from other personal finance books for a few reasons. While it's incredibly practical, it's also much more than that. This book will help you think about money in a different way. Much like my realization with my relationship to power, I want to help you see your relationship with money in a new light.

Just to be clear, I'm not sharing what I've learned from the perspective of someone in the financial industry who benefits from it and wants to maintain the status quo. Fuck the status quo. This book is about setting information free.

I approached my decision to study finance and economics the same way a lot of people approach their financial decisions: I was haphazardly following conventional wisdom in an attempt to be practical, and to not screw up my life.

Before my last semester, when I examined what options a finance degree would grant me, I decided I would either become a financial planner or a business consultant. As I understood it, financial planners helped people with their money, and business consultants helped businesses with theirs. I figured it was the same kind of work, but for different types of clients.

A couple of months after graduating, and through a series of fortunate events, I found gainful employment with a boutique business consulting firm in Los Angeles. But here's what felt like a cosmic joke: the consulting firm sublet an office and a few cubicles inside the office of a financial planning firm. Weirdly, I had gotten both of the things that I wanted.

My first day of work at the consulting firm was in August 2008, right around the time that the housing crisis was starting to heat up. The financial planning firm we shared space with was having a staff meeting in the conference room next door. I could overhear them talking about the beginnings of the housing meltdown; clients were panicking, and they were coming up with a plan to help them remain calm. I already knew that I wanted to be in that conference room, sitting at that table, hearing those conversations. And I knew why.

What was happening in the financial world seemed like an exciting, once-in-a-lifetime event. I wanted to sit shotgun as the financial world burned. I know that makes me sound messed up, but I was twenty-two and had my whole boring career ahead of me. I thought this was as exciting as the world of finance could get. Two years later, I ended up working for that financial planning firm. I made it into the conference room. I got a seat at that table.

In Monday morning staff meetings in that room, I heard economists, journalists and fund managers speak and teach us how this world worked. I sat across from clients. I learned about how power and money worked in the real world—and learned that I didn't have either of those things. I learned how to create financial plans and navigate clients' family dynamics. More seasoned financial planners shared their wisdom with me. They taught me that if you want to know the whole story, you have to follow the money; that the most dangerous combination in a client (or in anyone, really) is ignorance and arrogance, and as professional investors, they'd choose having luck over skill any day of the week.

After I stopped feeling so lucky and grateful to have secured a seat at this literal table, I wondered why I was able to get that seat. Why was I fortunate enough to have this insight into how the financial world works? Why me and not some other brown, gay kid who went to an unremarkable state college and luckily stumbled into that office? Why did I get this access that so many others were denied? Why was I learning the kind of stuff that only got shared behind the closed doors of financial planning firms and the closed doors of homes in America's wealthiest zip codes? After a long battle of trying to get my intuition to shut up, I finally surrendered. I realized I had to take what I've learned and share it with as many people as possible. I needed to share it with the people who needed this information the most but were the ones least likely to be able to afford it. I needed to share it with all the people who have felt ignored, unserved and underserved by the personal finance industry.

My experience of being an outsider on the inside have informed the philosophies I share throughout this book, but I'm also deeply influenced by other disciplines. Of course, I look at money through the lens of economics, but I also look at money through the stories we tell ourselves in our personal and collective histories. I look at the role that our emotions play in making rational decisions. And how things like trauma and stress cannot be compartmentalized and divorced from our financial lives. To understand our relationship with money, this book, unlike most personal finance books, doesn't ignore the issues inherent in our system. It also doesn't offer solutions to these deep-rooted problems—that's a whole different kind of book. But this book recognizes the reality and looks at how the origin of money, debt and financial products have reached through space and time to shape our modern lives today. This book is about doing what we can with what we've got.

Although we can use practical, modern tools in an attempt to control the outcome, this kind of holistic approach goes beyond that. It's also about feeling less fragile by implementing practices to help us cope and let go of the things outside our control.

Think of this book as a skeleton key to a better relationship with money. I'm not going to teach you anything advanced like how to make money day-trading foreign currencies or encourage you to save 50 percent of your mid-six-figure salary so you can be financially independent at thirty-two years old. But, if you're just starting to care about your finances, this is a very solid, comprehensive start.

One of the most fascinating observations I've made throughout my years of working with clients and writing about finance is the disconnect people have between what they want and how they act; especially with folks who are starting to navigate their finances for the first time. Folks want to save more, but they don't. Folks want to invest, but another year goes by and they haven't started. Folks need to make more money, but they resign themselves to accepting what's given to them.

So I've tried to address why human beings, myself included, have had gaps between our intentions and our behaviors. Sometimes it's circumstances; other times it's beliefs. The majority of the time, it's the overlap between circumstances, intentions and behaviors. I hope that these struggles resonate with your own, whatever their causes may be. And if they don't, perhaps they can help you discover what yours are. Ultimately, this excavation is a necessary part of getting to a place where you choose to focus on your agency and not what you cannot control.

Even though this book details specific strategies you can implement in your financial life, I don't subscribe to the idea that just because I am an expert, I know exactly what's right for you. I learned this firsthand. As more people asked me to give them advice, I realized that each person knows what's right for them; they just need to develop their sense of listening to their own voice.

So a big part of the work you'll do throughout reading this book are self-inquiry exercises that foster your ability to listen to your own voice, your desires and your intuition. Once your inner guide is informed by the hard facts and reality of the world, you can come into your own genius. I don't mean genius like Einstein; I mean genius as in feeling like you are in charge of your life.

The first observation I invite you to make is the one universal assumption that we are all weird about money and we must first address how and why we are weird. Addressing this weirdness can give us clarity that prescriptive advice cannot because we're all weird in our own unique, special ways.

Our understanding of how money works in the world comes from a cocktail of conflicting perspectives, incentives, stories and beliefs. Even though money is supposed to be a system of social agreement that expresses what we as a society and as individuals value, not everyone values what our systems reward and punish. It's easy to be misaligned with what you value and what you *should* be doing.

Understanding why we're weird about money is the first step in having the power to be less weird about it. This work is bringing the unconscious into the conscious; it's turning the light on in a dark room. It gives us a new perspective. It gives us options and shows us new ways to take action—from our daily habits to how we relate to others to the policies we vote for.

I've had to put years of consistent work into undoing a lot of the ideas and beliefs I have internalized about myself and my worth. Ideas that are tangibly reflected in the world around me through things like the wage gap and the revenue gap between women-of-color-owned businesses and non-minority-women-owned businesses. Ideas that have made me internalize the belief that I am not worthy of things that other people inherently deserve. I've had to take responsibility for my own internalization of these beliefs, which is just another layer of the mind-fuck, weird-about-money cake.

A huge part of this book rests upon this framework because when we know the things shaping us, we have a chance to change our shape. When we realize our power to change, we stop feeling like a victim and become someone who feels empowered and free.

Becoming that person doesn't require Herculean strength. What it does require is your willingness to be open. Sometimes even your willingness to suspend your current beliefs because they may be preventing you from seeing things differently.

Think of it like this: Have you ever tried to explain how a mango tastes to someone who's never tasted one? Or tried to imagine a color you've never seen before? That's how it might feel to think about being great with money, or just better with it than you are.

Reality is funny like that. It's hard to imagine anything different than what you've already encountered because you don't have past experience as a frame of reference. But that's why you have to be open to trying to see what you haven't yet seen. Being open is a way to feel free because you aren't holding tight to expectations. When you relax that grip, you can see other ways to win.

This book is my small contribution to the personal finance industry—an industry that hasn't exactly been awesome over the years. It's my attempt to try to make it a little bit better by being honest and real about what I've seen firsthand: how bad behavior within the industry is incentivized and becomes systemic, and how, in the face of that reality, people can come into their power and learn to take control of their financial situations. Part of keeping it real and honest is by approaching the world not as we think it should be but as it currently is. So while I won't tell you not to buy lattes or avocado toast, I will also refrain from arguing at every opportunity what should be done to make things fair. I'm not against things being fair, but the reality is that even if things could be equal, we'd all still face different problems because life is a shit show. Misfortune is real—really real. And since I don't have any experiences where I felt I could rely on a government or any other institution to fight for my share of fair, I've come to believe that part of being empowered is accepting that we can't expect that someone is coming to save us.

Each person in every generation has had their shit sandwich—some were drafted into a war that altered the course of their lives, many accepted student loans without fully understanding the terms, some people bought houses at the peak of the market, then there were the folks who were supposed to retire but the 2008 crash decimated their nest egg, and just around the corner we have the threat of automation and robots coming to take our jobs. Some people got really sick and the cost to get healthy was an amount that they may never be able to pay back. And at the time of this writing, we're all figuring out how to navigate the COVID economy. Each financial shock creates a crisis that some people never recover from. Many of us are victims of inequality and many are trying to make a life in a city where rising rents aren't keeping up with stagnant wages. There have been generations of economic, educational, legal, health and housing policies that have held folks back because of their class or race or both. I wish I had solutions for that, but I don't. How can everyone pull themselves up by their bootstraps when not everyone can afford to buy bootstraps? See, this is the part of the metaphor that should be emphasized: someone else makes the boots and the straps. We need each other. Humanity progresses because we help each other.

# LIFE'S DIFFERENT SHIT SANDWICHES

DRAFTED INTO A WAR

DIDN'T UNDERSTAND STUDENT LOANS

BOUGHT A HOUSE AT THE PEAK OF THE MARKET

RETIREMENT ACCOUNT WRECKED A YEAR BEFORE RETIREMENT

FIRST-GEN COLLEGE GRAD GRADUATED DURING A GLOBAL PANDEMIC

This book is just one form of help. While I wish I was equipped to write a book that provides a prescriptive solution to deep-seated inequality through an equitable redistributing of wealth, I definitely don't have the answers to fixing a system that I myself struggle within.

What I do know is that teaching as many people as I can about how the current system works is a single step towards change. We cannot work on changing something we don't know about, but the more we learn, the better equipped we are to challenge the system. Knowing the rules to the game is important because whether you recognize it or not, you're a player in it. For most of us, the system we're participating in was something we were born into and by making a choice to not opt out, we are opting in. Once you learn the rules, you can choose the way you're playing the game. You can opt out. You can give others a seat at the table.

This book is about encouraging you to take your relationship with your money seriously and giving you the tools to do it. It's about helping you unearth the reasons within yourself for giving a damn. It is about what you can do with what you've got to make a real difference in your life and the lives of those around you. It's simple, but not always easy. Trust the process.

## How to Use This Book

**T**his book is an invitation to change how you think about money, how you feel about money and what you do with your money.

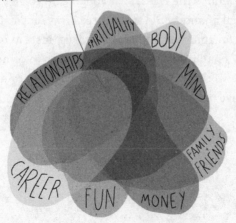

THE AREAS OF YOUR LIFE THAT MAKE YOUR LIFE FEEL LIKE YOUR LIFE

SPIRITUALITY · BODY · MIND · RELATIONSHIPS · FAMILY & FRIENDS · CAREER · FUN · MONEY

All of the parts of our lives are connected; they overlap and form how we feel about ourselves. So, the feelings you have about money aren't something that you can compartmentalize. You carry those feelings with you into your relationships and your everyday life. How you feel about yourself impacts the choices you make. And all the choices you make create who you are, what you're able to do and who you will allow yourself to be.

I'm inviting you to do something very hard: to learn the rules of an unfair game, attempt to play it, trust that the process will help you learn about yourself and the world around you and realize if you want to help change the system at large, you've got to start with first changing yourself. You can't expect to change anything outside of you if you aren't willing or able to change yourself from the inside first.

## THE PYRAMID OF FINANCIAL AWESOMENESS

Every good field guide should give you a clear, 50,000-foot view of the world into which you'll descend. Ours is called the Pyramid of Financial Awesomeness. It's the map for your hero's journey. It's the forest that contains the trees. It's a tool meant to give you a sense of the personal finance world at a glance. A way for you to see all the components, in approachable broad strokes, instead of intimidating jargon in small print. It's my way of trying to communicate to you that this world is a lot smaller and more figure-outable than you might have realized.

## HOW TO USE THE PYRAMID—
## THEORY AND PRACTICE

Each brick within the Pyramid of Financial Awesomeness represents both a financial concept for you to learn and actions for you to take. The idea being that, in a perfectly frictionless world, you can simply learn each concept, then take action implementing what you learned and, voila!, you magically become financially awesome.

The base of the pyramid is made up of foundational and fundamental building blocks, a solid starting point. The level of bricks in the pyramid ascends in order of priority. So if you want to read this book like a choose-your-own-adventure book, reader beware: there is a rhyme and reason for how these ideas are presented. The fundamentals, like knowing how much money you can spend, will drive the decision-making in later chapters—like how much you should save or how much life insurance you need.

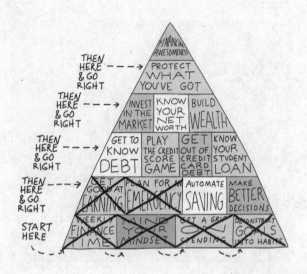

There are some concepts you might have already begun to tackle. For example, you might have already learned about retirement and are contributing to a 401(k). Don't worry if that's the case—now you can go back and fill in the gaps. If you need to make changes to things you've already started, you can take it as it comes.

Even though everyone will use the same field guide, the actual journey is going to look different for each person.

## New Level, New Devil

With every level of the Pyramid of Financial Awesomeness, there is a new devil you must face. It's like *Super Mario Bros.* As you progress, each boss you face is bigger, with more hammers being rained down on you. Winning the next level might require a technique different from the level before it. Your devil could be your limiting beliefs that prevent you from taking the steps to earning more money. It could be your struggle to reconcile your participation in the financialization of the world and its larger impact on workers. Knowing that this is part of what your own progress looks like will make it easier to spot and deal with it when it confronts you. When you feel yourself stuck, remind yourself that the mindset and the actions you took that got you to where you are right now might be different than the mindset and the actions required to get to the next level of progress.

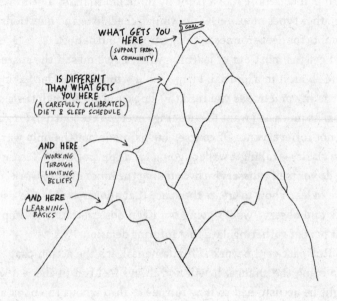

## Motion vs. Action: Learning About the Work vs. Doing the Work

In *Atomic Habits* by James Clear, he explains that motion is all the things you can do without really taking action on something. It's research, it's reading, it's learning, it's thinking, it's developing awareness. And action, well, action is doing the damn thing. The motion is watching YouTube tutorials, flipping through cookbooks and bookmarking bread recipes. The action is proofing the yeast and kneading the dough.

Each chapter of this book will dive into concepts and theories so you can get an initial grasp on the fundamentals of personal finance—the motion. And within each chapter there will be opportunities for you to take action on what you've learned and to practice and apply it through different exercises.

Some exercises will involve the mathematics of your personal finances. It's not hard math, and I break each step down so the math is much more like a paint by numbers than an algebra test. The other types of exercises are simple checklists and questions or prompts for deeper inner inquiry through journaling.

I get the most out of learning when I give myself the space to write about it in a journal. I hope you'll strongly consider having a journaling practice as you read this book and go through the exercises. As much as I want to encourage everyone to journal, I realize it's not for everyone. Of course, journaling is not the only way to gain clarity—taking a walk or going for a run works too. Please do not do yourself a disservice by avoiding the inner inquiry work. You have to learn how to create the space that allows you to take a step back and observe what's going on. Keen observation is an important part of gathering data that informs decisions.

This part of the work is fundamental. It's the action that will help bring the change. It will not always feel fun in the way you might be accustomed to how fun feels. Throughout the book and through the exercises, I'm going to challenge you, your beliefs and your assumptions. But being challenged is part of the fun.

## Type 2 Fun

One year, over a Thanksgiving holiday with some friends, I met a guy who had just finished filming an episode of the reality television show *Naked and Afraid*. You know the show. Two people, usually a man and a woman (or in this particular episode, a group of people), get dropped off in the middle of a sprawling parcel of wilderness and have to figure out how to survive for twenty-one days. And they're naked! That part just seems cruel.

So, on the first night of my holiday, I find myself sitting across the table from this guy. We're having beers at a lovely country-western bar. As he's picking at everyone's leftovers, he tells me that he just got back from being naked in a jungle for twenty-one days. While he can't reveal details of his most recent excursion because of a nondisclosure agreement, he tells us about the first time he was on the show.

He describes to his captive audience the day that a yellow jacket stung him on his penis. He also tells us about the kinds of conversations he had with his fellow contestants. Two very different but very important types of conversations dominated their discussions because they were integral to their survival: They would frequently ask each other about the details of their bowel movements to monitor one another's health. And they would have deep, descriptive conversations about recipes and the general deliciousness of cookies and baked goods.

As I realize he's describing my worst nightmare, he's saying all of this with a huge smile on his face. At one point he even admits to missing being naked in the jungle and can't wait to do it again. So of course I have to ask him the most obvious question that you are asking yourself right now, "So then, was this fun for you?"

And he then explains to me the concept of type 2 fun. Type 1 fun is enjoyable while it's happening. It's cold beers on the beach, a stroll in the park, easy, simple fun. Type 2 fun is the kind of fun that is miserable while it's happening but you're excited to look back and value it as a character-building experience.

While I personally think trying to survive naked in nature is not anywhere near fun, doing the work of learning about yourself and challenging your beliefs so you can change your financial life isn't anywhere close to being as terrifying, dangerous and challenging.

I'm not a proponent of comparing each another's suffering, but I will say this; if this guy could look back on an experience that included him getting stung on the tippy top of his penis and genuinely say he had fun, then you can read this book, do the work, change or come into who you fundamentally believe yourself to be and look back at what a fun challenge it was. Right?

## Schedule Weekly Finance Time

Setting aside a block of time each week to care about your finances is one of the most important things you can do to improve your financial life. If there is one thing you take away from this book it's this: when you give your financial life space, in the form of time, you give it room to expand. It's one of the simplest actions you can take to start immediately improving this part of your life. I can personally attest to its effectiveness.

Weekly finance time can be anywhere from thirty minutes to an hour that you set aside each week to give your finances the care and attention they require. When you set aside the time, you are committing to yourself in advance. You are prioritizing your financial life and not letting your other obligations or desires encroach on this important time. Each time you show up, you learn how to trust yourself a little bit more. You build confidence in your ability to change and build new habits.

Growing up, I never internalized the idea that hard work leads to success. What I did internalize was that consistency leads to good habits that can compound over time. Showing up consistently can be its own success because of who you become through that commitment, regardless of the outcome.

Weekly finance time feels like a silly and simple recommendation, but often the most effective things we implement in our lives can be boiled down to simple, consistent acts in the face of an uncertain, uncontrollable world.

Committing to showing up works because it's a single relatively easy act. It's much easier to psychologically commit to showing up once a week than it is to commit to a big lofty goal like paying off all

your debt and letting yourself transform into the debt-free person you
know you truly are. Just build the
easy habit of showing up each week;
the rest will follow. It's like the common exercise advice to commit to
changing into your running clothes
and shoes every other day instead of
committing to running four days a
week. It's much easier to commit to
changing your clothes. And once

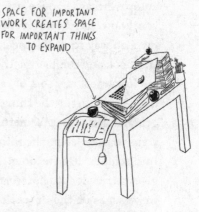

SPACE FOR IMPORTANT
WORK CREATES SPACE
FOR IMPORTANT THINGS
TO EXPAND

you change into them, more often than not, it's the trigger that
leads you to go out for a run whether or not you feel like it.

What you do during your weekly finance time can vary. It's a
space for you to contemplate big financial decisions—like switch-
ing jobs, starting a new business or what you'll need to do to financially prepare for starting a family. During weekly finance time you
can do research and have the space to initiate your cognitive brain
in decision-making. Freelancers and business owners might dedicate a good amount of their finance time to managing and reviewing
their business finances—things like sending new invoices, following up on outstanding ones, paying invoices, running payroll and
doing bookkeeping.

Here are some other ways you can use the time: You can call
your cell phone service provider to find out if there is a plan that is
cheaper and better suits your needs. You can take a look at your
credit card pay-off plan to celebrate being one payment closer to
being out of credit card debt. You can organize your tax documents
and get prepared to file your taxes way before the deadline. You can
call your old employer and roll over your old 401(k). You can decide
that your weekly finance time will be a time for you and your partner to discuss financial decisions. You can transfer a year-end bonus
into a savings or investment account. You can set up your bills on

autopay because you're using a spending plan that you trust and you know you won't overdraft. An excellent and highly recommended way to utilize weekly finance time is to spend it reading this book and completing the exercises.

If you feel any sort of resistance to scheduling your weekly finance time, here's the thing about our financial system and life in general: sometimes something that we think holds us back and traps us can also be the thing that helps us find a way to freedom. In discipline lies freedom. The discipline of weekly finance time gives us freedom to not worry about our finances because we know we've set aside the time to deal with them. We're giving it its own space so that it doesn't need to take up space in our minds when we don't want to it to. Weekly finance time is a small act of freedom.

## The Circles of Control and Concern

One last concept that will be helpful for using this book and navigating your finances are the circles of control and circles of concern. Stephen Covey, the author of the best-selling book *The 7 Habits of Highly Effective People*, coined these tools to help demonstrate that while we can look at all of the things that concern us, we can also realize that we have more power than we think over things that feel out of our control.

As the name suggests, things that are within our circle of control are things we have direct control over: who we buy from, what we read, what skills we learn, the attitude we choose and where we invest our money. Things within this circle are not only within our control but also have a direct impact on how our lives feel, and can have an impact on the world around us.

Things within our circles of concern may or may not impact our lives, but they are things we have no control over. Stock prices, how celebrities spend their money, your old co-worker's Instagram profile of only vacation photos and the economy at large are all things that may or may not be within your circle of concern, but they are certainly outside of your circle of control.

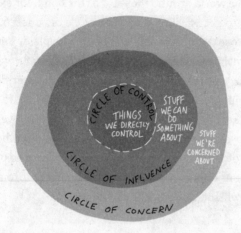

In moments of powerlessness, I try to expand my circle of control by focusing on the things within it. For example, when I'm feeling anxious about my financial future, I first control what I'm focusing on: my breath and the feeling of anxiety in my body. Once I feel less reactive, I can understand what's behind the feeling. It could be that a big potential client has decided not to sign with our company, a large unexpected expense has come up or the stock market has taken a downward tumble. In each instance, here's how I focus on the things within my circle of control. When missing out on a big client, I can refocus on marketing and understanding why we didn't get the job so we can improve our close rate. With an unexpected expense, I focus on budgeting for the month: where can I divert money to cover the expense? A tumbling stock market might mean I need to stop looking at my investment portfolio for a few days and remind myself that the market is just doing what it does and in the long run, I'll be fine. By expanding my circle of control, I get to choose not to be reactive. Reducing reactivity means I can be more thoughtful about how I spend my energy within my circle of control. Using my energy to impact the things I can control has a drastic impact on my daily life. These things can also have a larger impact on the world around me—take this book, for example.

It's easy to get consumed by your circle of concern. You can go into a comatose doom scrolling and feeling helpless. But while your power lies within your circle of control, so does your vulnerability. It can be scary to take responsibility for your power despite all of the things outside of your control that impact your life. Sometimes it can feel like a wave throwing you around. But in every moment, we can choose to fight and find our footing. We can be concerned and critical of the world around us but still choose to put the great majority of our energy towards taking actions that impact our circles of control. The world needs this of us.

## "USE THIS TOOL" PROMPTS

Throughout this book I've included some tools that I have personally found extremely helpful on my journey to getting right with my money and getting my money right. Some of these tools may be classified as weird and esoteric. But money is weird and esoteric. Its value is based on our collective imagination. It doesn't get any weirder than that.

---

**DO THE WORK**

### Set Up Your Weekly Finance Time

☐ **STEP 1. Listen to [insert a motivational song of your choice here] while looking at yourself in the mirror and decide you want to change. You think I'm joking about this step; I'm not.**

☐ **STEP 2. Whatever you use for your calendar, open it up.**

☐ **STEP 3. Find an hour in your week that can be blocked off as a standing weekly meeting with yourself.**

☐ **STEP 4. Schedule it as your weekly finance time.**

☐ **STEP 5. Make yourself unavailable for meetings, calls or anything that isn't your weekly finance time. Guard this time aggressively, but sometimes, like when you're on vacation, it's understandable to compromise.**

☐ **STEP 6. When you sit down to do weekly finance time, pick an area of concern and spend it reading the corresponding chapter in this book and doing the exercises.**

☐ **STEP 7. Keep showing up for yourself. Like, for years. Like, forever.**\*

☐ **STEP 8. Watch what happens and let me know. Seriously, I want to know.**

DO THE WORK

### Draw Your Own Pyramid

**Time to put your feet into the cold sea-foam and put the theory into practice by creating your own personal Pyramid of Financial Awesomeness.**

☐ **STEP 1. Use this Pyramid of Financial Awesomeness to keep track of your progress. (Trace the Pyramid and infuse your creativity to make it into your own style.)**

---

\* This is the critical step. This is the step that separates professionals from amateurs. This is the step that compounds itself and changes your life. It's easy to do anything inconsistently. It's easy to go to one Pilates class and then never show up again. Don't be inconsistent.

☐ **STEP 2. Share it with us on social media.**

☐ **STEP 3. Be sure to tag #financeforthepeople**

# PART 1

# *Get a Grip*

The story of money is whatever story you tell yourself: Money is valuable because we all believe it's valuable. We take it for granted that we're all willing participants in an elaborate game of make believe that has become our reality. I couldn't write a book about money without first examining how we write our stories about what money means in our lives.

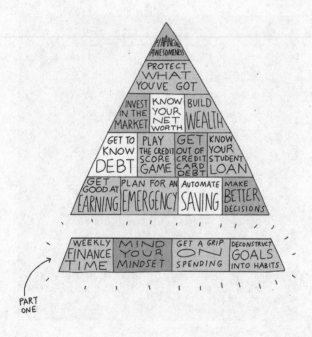

In this part, we will dive deep into why we are all weird about money. We'll spend time considering all the various events, factors and conditions that have set the stage for the modern consumer's relationship to spending. We'll learn how to construct a system of managing spending that protects you from yourself. We'll also explore how to set financial goals that are in alignment with your values and desires.

**CHAPTER 1**

# Why We're Weird About Money

My very first job in financial services was as a debt collector for a bank in the summer of 2006. I'd sit in a call center located in sunny Brea, California, speaking to customers who were late making their car payments. I didn't have an uncle who could get me an internship at Goldman Sachs, so this was my attempt at getting experience in the "finance industry."

At first, I felt rude and awkward. Not only was I a twenty-year-old who had never been responsible for a car payment—or for much of anything—I was also this disembodied voice on the phone asking people very personal questions. This put a spotlight on my own feelings about money. I was raised to believe that people only confronted the details of their financial transgressions and misfortunes in dark, shameful solitude—not through casual openness with strangers. I learned how to talk to total strangers about money. But not in a superficial way like a store clerk telling you your purchase total. No—I had to ask *every single* customer I spoke to why their car payment would be late. Besides learning how to speak casually about money and how loans and credit scores worked, my time at the bank taught me some things that impacted my view of the world forever.

## THE RECIPE FOR WHY YOU ARE WEIRD ABOUT MONEY

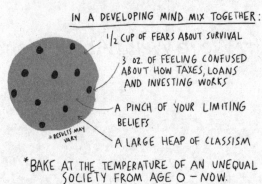

IN A DEVELOPING MIND MIX TOGETHER:

½ CUP OF FEARS ABOUT SURVIVAL

3 OZ. OF FEELING CONFUSED ABOUT HOW TAXES, LOANS AND INVESTING WORKS

A PINCH OF YOUR LIMITING BELIEFS

*RESULTS MAY VARY

A LARGE HEAP OF CLASSISM

*BAKE AT THE TEMPERATURE OF AN UNEQUAL SOCIETY FROM AGE 0 – NOW.

## BEING WEIRD IS UNIVERSAL

In my career thus far, I've spoken to thousands of people about money. One common thread regardless of gender, race, sexual identity, political affiliation and socioeconomic background is that people are weird about money. I'm sure you're not shocked by this, of course. The recipe is perfect: negative emotions + gaps in information about the world of money and our own minds x inequality = weirdness and problems. That's basically a formula for your own personal financial soap opera.

And all that weirdness can contribute to our financial decision-making in the very few areas where we have control.

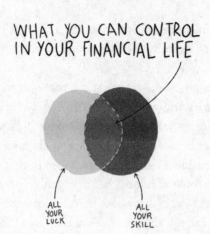

WHAT YOU CAN CONTROL
IN YOUR FINANCIAL LIFE

ALL
YOUR
LUCK

ALL
YOUR
SKILL

From a psychological perspective, our external and internal environments, our past behaviors and how much skill we perceive we have shape and are shaped by how we think about money, what we believe about money, what we value and the kinds of people we identify ourselves as.

I once spoke to a woman who had large sums of inherited wealth but perceived herself to be the kind of person who stood against economic, racial and wealth inequality. Her two identities were in complete conflict with one another and caused her great suffering and pain. She was so uncomfortable with her inherited wealth and privilege that she seemed to spend her money quickly, as if to get rid of it. Every month she received a trust fund distribution and spent all of it before the next one arrived; which resulted in her struggling between each distribution—in essence, living the way many people live paycheck to paycheck. She was struggling to deal with her conflicting identities and her feelings of guilt, shame and perhaps worth. Psychologically, our brains want to reconcile the conflicts within ourselves by restructuring our beliefs, our identities or our behaviors. Oftentimes the behaviors that we choose end up looking like self-sabotage, like this woman. The greatest budgeting app in the world is not going to be the thing that helps her. She needs to examine her weirdness about money. That's the first step.

Another woman I spoke to told me that she grew up wealthy and was used to having people do everything for her. So paying her bills and opening up her mail was challenging because of the environment she was brought up in, her lack of skills in managing her bills and who she identified herself to be—a part of the bourgeois class that had people to handle her mail and pay her bills for her. Since money was never an issue for her, she never paid much attention to it, even though she knew she needed to. Of course, this resulted in a lot of oversights. She needlessly paid late fees and had a general blindness and ignorance to her personal economics even despite her relative wealth. Having money doesn't make you immune to being weird about it—there's even a chance it might make you weirder because you might not have been taught the skills to practically deal with money. And if you were taught that it's gauche or taboo to talk about money, you might never ask for help when you need it.

I've seen a lot of folks who grew up in environments of poverty, scarcity and unpredictability who are traumatized but who also strongly *identify* as people who are traumatized and victimized. Beyond the actual external obstacles traumatized people face, there is another layer of internal obstacles. When someone strongly identifies as traumatized and victimized but wants financial stability, sometimes the behaviors that get that person to stability are in conflict with the traumatized person's identity. This conflict, like so many others, results in the battle between who they believe they are and how they behave. To reconcile the conflict, they can heal their trauma and work towards finding ways to identify less with their trauma or behave in a way that confirms their identity of being victimized, which again often looks like self-sabotage.

If we don't understand the various psychological frameworks

for why people are weird about money, it could look to us like they are acting outside of their best interests because they don't have education or willpower. This is why so much traditional financial advice from experts is so flawed. It's surface level at best because it tends to only address skills and behaviors. It ignores the role of external and internal environments that shape and are shaped by our values, beliefs, identity and the painful conflict that all these factors create whenever there is misalignment.

## CAPITALISM AND CONSUMERISM MAKE US WEIRD ABOUT MONEY

Sigmund Freud was an Austrian neurologist and founder of the practice of psychoanalysis, a method to treat mental illness and to understand human behavior. Freud postulated that events and experiences we had during early development greatly shape our personality and influence our adult lives. He believed the brain had various layers of consciousness—the conscious mind, the subconscious and the unconscious. He believed that human behaviors, which we might believe are motivated by conscious, rational choices, are often motivated by our subconscious and unconscious minds.

Edward Bernays, Freud's nephew, was the first person to use Freud's ideas about humanity to manipulate the masses through what we now know as modern marketing and advertising.[1] He got his start during World War I, using media to help the Woodrow Wilson administration promote the U.S. war effort at home and abroad. After attending the peace conference at the end of the war, Bernays saw firsthand how effective propaganda was and wondered how it might be used to control and manipulate the masses during peacetime. When he got back to America, he established a company that would create propaganda, which he renamed as "public relations."

Bernays, using his uncle's insights, developed an approach he named "engineering consent." It was based on the idea that it's possible to manipulate people through their unconscious, irrational emotions and influence them to behave in a certain way. He sold the means to "control and regiment the masses according to our will without their knowing about it."[2] Bernays thought that irrelevant objects could create symbols for how you want people to see you; that it was possible to get people to act irrationally if you link products to their emotional desires and feelings. Prior to the large-scale adoption of this kind of advertising, most forms of marketing were focused on the practicality of the product's features. Bernays's approach appealed not to what you need but what you unconsciously desire. It's not that you think you *need* that new piece of clothing, it's that you'll *feel better* with that new piece of clothing.

One of the most notable and successful campaigns Bernays produced was a demonstration at the 1929 Easter Parade in New York City. He had been approached by George W. Hill, president of the American Tobacco Company, to solve the problem of getting women to smoke on the street as opposed to only indoors. Bernays looked to psychological theories and consulted with the psychiatrist A. A. Brill, a pupil of Sigmund Freud, asking him what the psychological basis was for a woman's desire to smoke. Brill advised that cigarettes symbolized men and smoking them was a way to feel equal to a man. Cigarettes were about freedom and equality. So Bernays staged a dramatic public display of women smoking during the Easter Parade and told the press to expect woman suffragists to be lighting "torches of freedom." The next day, on April 1, 1929, the front page of the *New York Times* read "Group of Girls Puff at Cigarettes as a Gesture of 'Freedom'." And the rest is, as they say, history.

After that successful stunt, corporations began to follow suit and Wall Street soon after. A leading Wall Street banker Paul Mauzr of Lehman Brothers said in a 1927 issue of *Harvard Business Review*,

"We must shift America from a needs, to a desires culture. People must be trained to desire, to want new things, even before the old had been entirely consumed. We must shape a new mentality in America. Man's desires must overshadow his needs." This cultural shift led to a boom in consumption that created a stock market boom of which Bernays was also directly involved in by crafting the idea that regular people should own stocks and shares.

Corporations craft modern marketing messaging based on psychological theories of how our minds quietly deceive us. We are being manipulated to make irrational decisions to buy things we do not need, to spend money we could be saving, to go into debt even when we know it's not in our best interests. These messages driving us to consume are inescapable and appeal to our emotions and minds in ways most people are unaware of.

It's hard to believe this story because it seems so blatantly deceitful. But the American economy is so strong precisely because of the insatiable desire of the consumer to consume. This one thing alone makes us weird about money, but of course, it's just one of many invisible factors.

## MISTAKING SOCIAL PROBLEMS FOR PERSONAL FINANCIAL PROBLEMS MAKES US WEIRD ABOUT MONEY

Life in societies where there are large gaps between the rich and the poor create ongoing psychological and social stress. Researchers and scientists have been able to trace how external inequality has a physiological connection to our bodies through chronic inflammation, chromosomal aging and brain function.[3]

Not only can the stress of inequality grind down into our bodies at the cellular level, creating health issues and negatively impacting our immune systems, it can impact our brains and our ability to make sound decisions. We see this when people who are living in poverty spend some of the little bit of extra cash they have on lottery tickets instead of saving it. We see this when people take out payday loans at criminal interest rates and terms so terrible that it's nearly inevitable they'll get caught in a trap of constantly borrowing and constantly owing. Obviously, a rational person knows they shouldn't buy lottery tickets and take out payday loans. But the decision to do it anyway is not necessarily a decision made with the cognitive, rational decision-making part of the brain. What happens to a brain under constant economic stressors is a cycle where the cognitive parts of our brain—the prefrontal cortex, responsible for sound decision-making, long-term planning like goal setting and impulse control—experience less activity; essentially it shuts down and our primitive mind takes over. Neurologically, the connections between neurons and myelination, the process that insulates cables between neurons and thus helps them pass signals faster, is impaired. Practically, this results in lousy, impulsive decision-making. And with a less active prefrontal cortex, it's harder for the brain to choose long-term health over immediate pleasure.

Societies that have more inequality have higher rates of crime, homicide, incarceration, higher rates of kids being bullied, more teen pregnancies, lower literacy, more psychiatric problems, higher rates of alcoholism, drug abuse and less social mobility. All of these stressors create trauma in minds, bodies and brains. The constant stressors can create a trap where those who are at the lowest end of socioeconomic strata can get stuck in a cycle of financial decision-making that doesn't engage their cognitive thinking.

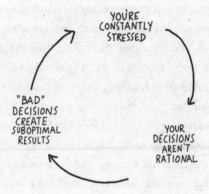

THE CYCLE OF DECISIONS
BROUGHT TO YOU BY
THE STRESS OF INEQUALITY

YOU'RE CONSTANTLY STRESSED

YOUR DECISIONS AREN'T RATIONAL

"BAD" DECISIONS CREATE SUBOPTIMAL RESULTS

Inequality has a kind of compounding effect that is bad for society overall. We have to first be able to see its true impact on financial health and people's ability to make financial decisions in the few areas where they can exercise control. When financial experts blame behavioral issues on willpower, when they simplify a solution through financial literacy and when they use shame and moral judgments, it helps no one and harms all of society. It's not just awkward and uncomfortable when personal finance experts don't see that some financial problems are social problems in disguise. A narrow perspective fosters solutions that are also narrow.

It's not only our external environment and things outside of our control that make us weird about money. There are plenty of things within our control or that we can change that contribute to the weirdness.

Let's explore some of those things.

## WE ARE WHAT WE TELL OURSELVES—OUR INTERNAL ENVIRONMENT AND OUR IDENTITY

Being weird about money can result from the stories we've been told and continue to tell ourselves consciously and unconsciously. Those stories come from what we learn from others, what we experience ourselves and how we interpret the world. When we're young, we learn these stories from the people who take care of us: our parents, grandparents, aunts, uncles, cousins, friends and that random older kid on your block who you used to go bike riding with. We also learn stories from places like the police, the legal system, teachers, media, marketing, articles, books, music, movies, social media and the internet at large. We draw conclusions and make connections because of those stories and they become our beliefs and reinforce our mindset.

Everything we experience gets poured in, shaken up and becomes our understanding of how the world works. Even the things that you choose not to believe will shape you. Everything is connected.

Let's take an example of a young boy who witnesses his father's lifelong frustration with being outearned by his wife. This boy will have his own interpretation of the arguments and fights he witnesses his parents having about money. Instead of thinking it has to do with his father's inherited beliefs about a man's role in a marriage or his father's general insecurity and ego, the young boy may simplify the explanation: talking about money causes fighting. Fighting makes me feel unsafe. Talking about money is unsafe. And when he feels unsafe, he gets defensive and isolates himself. We all have experiences like this and we all interpret them differently.

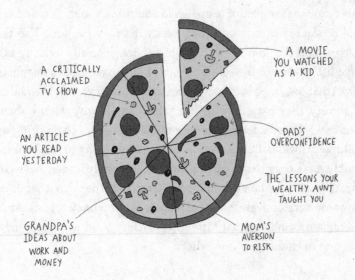

What makes us even weirder about money is the decision we continue to make to be aggressively silent about the matter of money as a society. For example, how many of us have worked in environments where we were not allowed to talk about our salary with our co-workers? And I'm sure most of us were never encouraged to talk about money with our families. We may have witnessed arguments about money, but we've probably not seen the resolution of those conflicts. When we constantly suppress any desire to talk about money, chances are high that when we finally do, it's not done in the most calm or straightforward way, but in an emotional outburst. If we don't practice talking about money, we probably suck at talking about money.

In an age where you can use a dating app on your phone to openly solicit sex and where it's now even more common to freely disclose political affiliation in the bios of those apps, it's amazing that the classic "talking about money is taboo" belief is still so strongly ingrained in our society's collective belief system. To me, this taboo makes a lot of sense when you think about class and the role of slavery in economic prosperity. History has long had the "haves" and the "have-nots." The haves are generally wealthy and have little concern in regard to money. The have-nots struggle to have their basic needs met or, in the case of the extreme inequality of slavery, they have nothing. So, yes, I can see why talking about money while considering the dire straits of others could bring up feelings of awkwardness, shame and guilt by having to confront inequality. It's easy to see why talking about money under those circumstances was labeled inappropriate. But the idea that it is inappropriate or even shameful to talk about money regardless of circumstance has seeped into all of society. And we're only now starting to challenge these beliefs.

## YOUR SUBCONSCIOUS BELIEFS ARE JUST BELOW THE SURFACE

Experiences bury themselves like seeds into your subconscious and grow into beliefs that shape your mindset: the actions you take, the jobs you apply for, the places you feel like you're allowed to belong; all of these things first start out as ideas in your mind. If you don't take your worldview apart to see how the beliefs got programmed, if you never decide what stays and what goes, you're letting a bunch of other people's rules subconsciously dictate how you deal with money and how you think it works in the world—from your job, to how you spend your paycheck, to how money impacts your relationships. These beliefs construct your mindset around money.

Did your parents tell you that only lazy people accept unemployment? Did your grandma always tell you that money is dirty? Did you watch your dad sacrifice all of his free time and give up his leisure because the greatest pursuit in life is the almighty dollar?

Have you thought about how these stories have wormed deep into your mind and made you who you are? Would you like to have different beliefs? Who would you be with different beliefs? The kind of person who confidently negotiates their salary? The kind of person who saves money with every paycheck? The kind of person who doesn't think it's hard to earn money? This is why it's so important to be critical of your beliefs and how they came to be. It gives you insight and it frees you from the hopes, dreams and fears of those who came before you, and that allows you to have the power to change.

Not all shifts in your belief systems happen in one fell swoop. Some shifts will happen gradually over time. My mindset around money evolved over many years of insightful moments and epiphanies. The person I am today, the one writing a book to help people with their finances, was built and not born. And when I step back to look at the first step I took to get here, it started by looking within my own mind and examining my thinking patterns. Our whole experience of our lives is truly only lived out between our two ears. We have to start there, by recognizing the stories we've been playing on loop and then rewriting the ones that have been holding us back.

While addressing your beliefs can feel like a confrontation, it doesn't have to be contentious. It can simply be letting go of the things that got you to where you are today but cannot get you where you want to be tomorrow. Like trading in your ninth grade algebra book for your tenth grade geometry book. The math book as a tool could only get you as far as passing algebra. You have to upgrade your tools to pass geometry.

## Necessary, but Not Sufficient

Before we go any further on beliefs, I just want to quickly address that I'm not so naive that I think changing your beliefs will be sufficient enough to eliminate all of your financial struggles. Of course, there are other factors that have a real impact, like the actions you take, the state of the job market, your environment, systemic racism and inequality. There are real-ass, practical things we are up against. But regardless of the circumstances, the right set of beliefs is still a necessary part of accomplishing anything. In other words, belief alone won't get you to where you're going, but not having the right ones could prevent you from taking the first step.

## Unearth Your Beliefs

You might think you already know what you believe. Your conscious mind can rattle off your list of values. But if you've ever done something or said something that feels out of character, something that made you reflect and wonder what motivated you to behave in such a way, then you are probably not entirely aware of how your subconscious beliefs are influencing your everyday behavior. You're on autopilot. If you want to change, you have to stop being on autopilot and become aware of not just how you're behaving, but why.

You do this by diving into your subconscious mind to discover what's there. Our subconscious mind is like a basement or attic. It's a place where emotional baggage gets stored, where we dump stuff instead of processing it and letting it go. Where we've filed away our ideas and beliefs about how the world works. Unless we've spent time exploring it, we aren't entirely sure what is inhabiting the dark corners. So, of course, it's natural to want to avoid the dark, creepy unknown.

But just like a basement or attic, the fear of the unknown is really what scares us. Once we turn on the lights, we're able to see that what we were afraid of was the idea of fear itself.

YOUR BOLD
CREATIVE SELF
THAT YOU HIDE
FROM THE WORLD

THINGS
YOU'RE
AFRAID
TO CONFRONT

EMOTIONAL
BAGGAGE

THE SUBCONSCIOUS MIND IS LIKE A DARK ATTIC

There are lots of different methods you can use to access your subconscious. There are various forms of therapy, meditation, coaching, hypnosis and lucid dreaming, to name a few. There is no one right path to take. Depending on your personal and financial circumstances and history of mental health, you may want to work with a licensed therapist or other professional to help you explore this kind of work.

## OUR FRACTURED FEELINGS MAKE US WEIRD ABOUT MONEY

Each person is a multitude of desires and fears. We are one person made up of many "I's" that all have their own wants. This can often create an oppositional force within us. One part of us might know we need something, yet another part of us might despise what we need. One part of you wants to invest your money while the other part of you is in conflict with the ethics of investing. One part of you wants to work for yourself while the other part of you fears risk and uncertainty. One part of you wants to get in control of your spending, while the other part of you hates feeling restricted.

It's completely normal to have these conflicts. Problems arise when we don't know how to integrate our conflicting selves and we try to reject certain parts. As we grow up, we get signals from our environment that tell us how we should act and who we should be in order to be loved and not rejected. Any desires, feelings or parts of us outside of what we think will be acceptable threaten our sense of belonging. In order to preserve our safety, we subconsciously reject and hide those parts of us. Some psychiatrists call these hidden aspects of ourselves the shadow self.

I first learned about the psychological concept of the shadow self from one of my personal development coaches, Kristan Sargeant. But the concept is credited to the psychiatrist and psychotherapist Carl Gustav Jung. Jung proposed that the shadow self is the unconscious part of us that our ego doesn't identify with, or actively rejects. Our shadow self is the unknown, subconscious dark side of our personality. It's the parts of ourselves we don't want to look at—qualities we deem unattractive, try to push away, downplay or hide beneath the surface because we think society or our family will not find these parts of us acceptable.

If you've ever heard a parent say that caring about money makes you greedy, power hungry, materialistic or immoral, then you might try to subconsciously hide or disown those parts of you that desire power or possessions. And this fracturing of yourself could lead to you having a difficult time accepting and asking for things, like a well-paying job, a promotion, a raise or even seeing opportunities to invest your money. It might make you dodge or not take opportunities, or you might reject the ideas of your upbringing and secretly accumulate a bunch of crap you don't need or become unhealthily preoccupied with accumulating money. Every person will have a unique response to help them cope with feelings they struggle to reconcile.

The only real way to truly cope with our financial behaviors, negative feelings and past traumas is to get to the root of them and work on integrating them into our lives. In our society, negative feelings don't have a place. We're never taught how to deal with them. This extends to our consumerist culture. If we have negative feelings, marketing messages encourage us to buy something to make those bad feelings go away because if they don't go away something is wrong with us. When we continue to evade our negative feelings, we just guarantee that they'll continue to pop up in our lives and we'll continue to feel troubled for not being able to resolve them. We'll keep trying to use consumption to fix something that consumption can't fix. Then we can begin to feel negatively about our negative feelings—we might start to feel shame and guilt, which are pretty common feelings associated with money.

Every person who feels shame around money will have a story or memory behind that shame that they've held on to so tightly that they've created a rule or belief about it. One person might feel shame if they think they don't deserve to have money because they haven't worked hard enough for it—a rule they may have created by witnessing their parents grind for their keep. Another person's shame might be keeping them from spending money on themselves because they don't think they deserve it. The same experience might make you overspend because you think having money makes you a bad person. We might feel shame when we think about our debt, and it can keep us from making a plan to pay it off faster. Shame might keep you from having a hard conversation about money, or you might unwittingly project your shame into the conversation. If your shame makes you feel like wanting more money is not a good quality in a person then that shame could be keeping you from finding a better opportunity to earn income, like through entrepreneurship or studying negotiation so you can be more effective the next time you're up for a raise.

Guilt is another common feeling associated with money. It can come up when we venture outside the boundaries of what is expected of us or what we should and shouldn't be doing. Going into debt, taking the risk of starting a business instead of finding a steady job or pursuing a career that might not be lucrative are great examples of how we can feel guilty when we venture outside of expectations. When we're told we shouldn't do something, guilt keeps us within parameters that are presumed acceptable. It helps us resist doing things that could harm or disturb our collective and individual interests.

All these negative feelings come together in a unique combination for each of us. Guilt and shame might keep someone in a job that doesn't pay them enough, while guilt and shame might compel someone else to sacrifice their life to achieving material success. I was once told a story about a woman whose earliest memory of money was intertwined with addiction, physical abuse and trauma. A parent would get a paycheck, use it to get drunk and then come home and abuse this woman's mother. She witnessed this regularly and began to associate money with danger. As she got older, she avoided looking at her finances and often spent whatever money she had because of her subconscious, unspoken rules about what money represented. When she was finally able to bring this painful memory into her consciousness, she could get to the root of her money issues.

Jung wrote, "Everyone carries a shadow and the less it is embodied in the individual's conscious life, the blacker and denser it is. If an inferiority is conscious, one always has a chance to correct it. . . . But if it is repressed and isolated from consciousness, it never gets corrected."[4]

Waking up to the power of your subconscious and unconscious minds allows us to actively integrate parts of ourselves that we've rejected and fractured. This work is imperative; when you don't do it, you're unconsciously allowing old rules to reach across space and time to dictate how you behave today.

## WHAT DO YOU BELIEVE ABOUT MONEY?

Changing your relationship with money starts by unearthing your beliefs about money.

To rebuild my relationship with money I had to understand where I learned my ideas about worth and worthiness. I had to confront and accept some of the feelings, ideas and parts of myself that I rejected in order to feel safe or to have a sense of belonging. I had to

call in these rejected parts of myself and confront why I didn't believe I deserved what other people deserved. I had to get to the root of why I didn't see myself worthy of stability or feeling ease in my financial life. I had to try to understand where my belief that I had to suffer to earn my keep came from. And I needed to understand why I thought putting myself before others made me feel selfish.

I got to the root of my beliefs, rules about money and how I'd rejected parts of myself through open-ended journaling, therapy and working with a personal development coach who specialized in shadow work. Through these various processes, I was able to clearly see the things about myself that I was most ashamed or afraid of. By finding my vulnerabilities, I could begin healing, accepting and calling in (instead of calling out and rejecting) my whole self.

Today, when I face my negative feelings, it's painful in the moment but I'm able to move through it and use my emotions as data. I've learned to turn down work, push back in negotiating, and raise my prices without feeling guilty. In moments when I feel doubt about spending money on things that bring me comfort, joy or buy me time, I check in with myself to make sure the doubt does not come from me thinking I'm not worth it. Integrating and allowing negative feelings is an ongoing process.

Ultimately, accepting ourselves, warts and all, is a way to achieve unwavering self-confidence, which directly impacts our feelings of self-worth. It's a way to take our power back because we aren't blindly accepting other people's rejection of who we truly are. To accept yourself when other people don't is kind of the ultimate fuck you. That's why it's so powerful to do this.

Carl Jung said when we fully accept our shadow self we can access the wisdom it contains. Fear can become an opportunity for courage. Pain can be catalyzed into resilience. Your challenges are opportunities for growth and change.

If you want to be less weird about money, if you want to stop repeating patterns, you have to confront how you got weird in the first place. Learn to process the pain, allow yourself to heal and to accept yourself. Carl Jung said, "Until you make the unconscious conscious, it will direct your life and you will call it fate."

**DO THE WORK**

## "Whose Line Is It Anyway?"

**First you ask and then you listen. Accessing your subconscious and connecting with your shadow self is a beautifully simple process that can be done through journaling. Answer the following questions:**

- **Give an example from your childhood where you've witnessed people in your life feeling stressed about money. How has this experience informed your personal relationship with money?**

- **Who did you feel you had to be in your family in order to be seen, loved, known and valued? Give an example of this experience from your childhood.**

- **Growing up, what were some stories that you learned from your family about the way money operates? What were the unspoken and spoken messages about money?**

- **Give an example of an experience you had growing up where you sensed negative and disapproving ideas about money.**

- **Give an example of an experience you had growing up where you learned negative or disapproving ideas about power and abundance.**

- **Give an example of an experience you had growing up where you witnessed people feeling shame about money.**

- **Did you feel treasured growing up? How? Did you not feel treasured growing up? How?**

- **Do you have desires about money, abundance and power that you feel like you have to disown in order to feel accepted by your family, friends or society?**

**CHAPTER 2**

# How to Think About Spending

Imagine yourself on a Monday morning with big plans and ambitions about how you will spend your time. You've got a to-do list and you're chasing the high of crossing shit off that list. Your boss might unexpectedly call a meeting or someone might call in sick, so you have to step in to handle some tasks you weren't planning to. "That's okay," you think, "I still have enough time." You try to dive into your task list and an emergency happens. You need to put out a fire. You eat a sad desk lunch to try to stay on task. And just when you think you are actually going to have a chance to spend your time how you want to spend it, one of your co-workers needs your help with the new program that you helped implement two weeks ago. The day ends and you've spent all your time on things you didn't want to spend it on. Sometimes the way we spend our money feels a lot like a chaotic Monday at work. Our efforts can feel unfocused and disconnected, and no matter how we try to plan, there is never enough time.

Of course, just like with time, feeling like you have enough money is a function of actually having enough money, something I'll dive deeper into in Chapter 5. But it's also largely a function of how we feel about what we have, spend and keep. For many of us what will make us feel better about how we spend our money is figuring out how to feel like we have enough and creating a system to ensure how we spend our money takes into account how we will feel about those actions later. Before we get into the systems you can set up for managing your spending, let's first unpack the very prickly feeling of not having enough.

Our brains are like a junk drawer with old processes and new processes running concurrently. There are two old processes in particular that work in concert to make us feel like we don't have enough. The first process is how our brains naturally scan for and seek out danger. This is an old process that in the past was necessary for our survival. When life for humans was much more dangerous and sketchy, our survival depended on our ability to perceive things like when food or water was scarce. Our brains evolved to favor paying attention to dangerous things in our environment over positive things.

When your mind is occupied with scarcity, you're focused on what you lack and you're filled with feelings of stress, anxiety and fear. When you're in this state of stress, it's hard to make good decisions, financially and otherwise. Being in this state helped humans survive when they were literally starving, but today, it prevents us from using cognition to make decisions. Today, it creates a false positive when we aren't in actual danger.

The other process human brains adapted in order to survive is our preoccupation with comparing ourselves to one another.[1] This makes sense since the ability to adequately size up one's competition can impact a group's survival. And within a group, comparing ourselves to others can ensure we're keeping up and earning our place within the safety of that group.

There aren't as many real reasons today to be so preoccupied with comparison or danger, but we often still feel ourselves dealing with these feelings. Today a preoccupation with danger can look like worry over money, fear of illness, or feeling scared about an uncertain future. Comparison looks like scrolling social media and feeling bad when you see yet another vacation photo of an old co-worker. You might think, "How can she even afford to go on vacation that much?" You might go to a friend's house and see a beautiful new lamp and think, "I want to be the kind of person who owns that kind of lamp." You might see a photo of a celebrity and compare your body to their body. You might see that a colleague just published a book and wonder why you haven't achieved that same thing. While these instincts may have once served humans very well, in today's world they can act as an impediment.

## WE'VE BEEN GROOMED TO CONSUME

Unfortunately, these adapted human quirks are often exploited. In Chapter 1, I told the story of Edward Bernays, the invention of modern marketing and how he discovered that desires can be manufactured by tapping into the subconscious and unconscious mind. Marketing goes even further in the age of social media.

Social media is a magnifier for the comparisons we already do and it can exacerbate the pain of not fitting into the group. Instead of learning how to integrate and move through our feelings, a consumer-driven culture tells us that we can always buy something to ease our discomfort, and that we should. On social media, the ads are integrated into the same feed that has made us feel bad. Social media creates the problem and offers the solution in the same feed. It's Machiavellian! It's diabolical! It so brilliant that I almost can't hate on how genius it is, but then I realize how it's super messed up that a lot of people don't realize how this vulnerability is being exploited.

There are two ways that you can defend yourself against these vulnerabilities in our old-ass brains. The first one is to use the tools that allow you to feel like you *do* have enough—that is, address your feelings. And the second is to introduce systems that help reduce the likelihood that you'll fall victim to this predatory system.

## CONSCIOUSLY UNCOUPLE FROM THE SCARCITY MINDSET

There are few universal principles in life, but this is definitely one of them: practicing gratitude will make you aware of all the ways in which life is abundant. The antidote to scarcity is gratitude. As much as that sounds like a bunch of nonsense, let me just drop the science.

Practicing gratitude and simply being appreciative or grateful can measurably improve your overall well-being.[2] Practicing gratitude can rewire your prefrontal cortex so that you tend to appreciate and remember positive experiences and cultivate the resiliency needed to deal with adversity. The more you practice gratitude, the stronger your neural pathways will become. These strong neural pathways are linked to increased happiness, reduced depression and strengthened resiliency. It's also linked to lower blood pressure, reduced chronic pain, increased energy and even living longer. People who practice gratitude tend to have higher self-esteem than those who don't. People who think grateful thoughts before bed sleep better than those who don't.

When we feel gratitude for what we have or towards someone who has helped us, our brain stem releases dopamine. Dopamine makes us feel good and fosters positive emotions and prosocial behavior like camaraderie. When we reflect or write down things that we are grateful for in our lives, our brains release serotonin. Serotonin enhances our mood, motivation and willpower. And the more you practice activating these neural pathways, the less effort it takes to activate these pathways the next time.

There is a very simple tool you can use every day that will allow you to dampen your feelings of scarcity and amplify your feelings of abundance. Think of this tool like an app or a process that you run on the operating system of your body and brain every day. I encourage you to try it right now before you get into the actual weeds of creating your own spending plan.

## Use This Tool: Grateful Flow

One of my coaches introduced me to an exercise called grateful flow created by Phil Stutz, MD, and Barry Michels, JD, LCSW. It only takes a minute or less to do. Here's how you practice grateful flow:

1. Begin by closing your eyes and taking a few deep breaths. I like to put my hand on my heart and remember that being able to breathe and having a heartbeat are gifts given to all of us. They are unconditional gifts that we never had to ask for. Having this moment allows me to get into the space where I can find other gifts to be grateful for.

2. Think of one thing you are grateful for that you'd normally take for granted. It can be as simple as the chair supporting your body, but the key is to really allow yourself to feel grateful for that one thing. Focus on the feelings and physical sensations of gratitude in your body. You might feel warmth, lightness, your heart beating or your lips turning up into a smile. Let yourself open up to this presence and power.

3. Focus on something else you are grateful for. Go through the feelings, the sensations in your body, and relax into this presence.

4. Find a third thing to feel gratitude for and go through the same exploration of your feelings and bodily sensations.

Each time you do this exercise, push yourself to find a new thing you are grateful for. Here are some examples of what I've been thankful for over the last few days.

The sound of the palm trees outside my window.

Seeing a family of blue jays on my neighbor's roof.

A cool shower on a hot day.

The weird and unique sensation that sparkling water gives my nose and throat.

Seeing a juicy heirloom tomato I grew in my garden.

Feeling the cool breeze on my skin.

It's a really simple, easily implemented tool that is surprisingly impactful. You might even consider starting your weekly finance time with a grateful flow practice. It's an experiment I highly recommend you try running. It only costs you a few moments in your day but has the potential to dramatically improve your experience in life. If you want to feel better about money, you can start by feeling better in general.

Now that we're primed, it's time to create a spending plan.

Setting up a spending plan that works for you requires some reframing, some reverse engineering and a bit of up-front intentional work.

## HOW MUCH MONEY DO YOU NEED?

By going through a spending plan, we are hoping to answer the question: how much money do you need? This isn't the normal approach to spending. Traditionally in personal finance, when we think about spending, we tend to think in terms of budgeting. Budgeting starts with how much we make, and dividing that paycheck accordingly; it's all about asking questions like, "What can I afford?," "What *should* I be spending my money on?" and "Am I living below my means?" While these are all normal ways to think about spending, this approach uses language that invokes scarcity. Budgeting is rooted in lack.

A spending plan is a very different perspective. It's a way to reverse-engineer a desired outcome. It's exploring the answers to an open-ended question. That openness can temporarily lift limitations to entertain possibilities. It's a different way of thinking that can provide different solutions. Asking yourself how much you need is an expansive, abundant way of thinking about spending. Instead of letting your income dictate how much you *can* spend, you can consider what income you would need to match what you need and want to spend. As much as you might not believe it, what you earn is not a circumstance that you must passively and willingly accept. There are ways you can have agency over your earnings. This is something we'll explore more in Chapter 5, but this idea is present in the exercise of creating your spending plan.

By thinking about what you need, you can determine the compensation that would make you not resent your job. The numbers in a spending plan will show you that truth; they'll show you what you need to earn to feel like you are a human who is paid a wage that allows you to feel respected. You can do the math to figure out what you need and work backwards to figure out how to earn it. If you're just entering the workforce, a spending plan can help you find out what your starting salary requirements should be.

Thinking about what you need can also open up a deeper dialogue about how you're currently spending. When you think about what you need, you allow yourself to question how that expense relates to your life. You reflect on what you value and if that is being reflected in how you spend your money and change accordingly.

## THE PLAN TO CREATE A SPENDING PLAN

Creating your spending plan will require you to think about your spending by classifying your expenses into three broad groups. There's the Bills & Life group for essentials, the Fun & BS group for nonessentials and then the Future & Goals group, a broad category for all the various things you are saving for, including what you put into investment accounts.

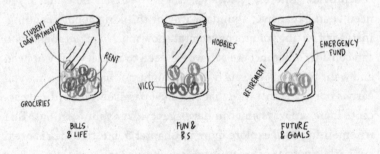

Thinking about your spending in these groups makes it easier to understand how much money you need for what is essential (bills and life), what is not essential but is life-giving (fun and BS) and what your future self will need (future and goals). It allows you to create a repeatable process to ensure that your essential costs are accounted for, you're saving a portion of everything you earn and that you have money you can spend freely.

These broad categories make understanding your spending easier to handle inside of your brain. They are specifically helpful when you need to reduce your spending in a pinch or during a crisis because you can scale back on the nonessentials. And for anyone who isn't earning enough money to meet all their needs, they can look at the categories as stepping-stones or thresholds that need to be met.

## A Quick Note About Your Future & Goals Group

The Future & Goals group is not just one savings account. It's a category that will include all of the various things you're saving for in the future that you can't pay for all at once, like retirement, an emergency fund, a wedding, an adorable puppy or baby (or both!).

I know what you're thinking, "Does this mean you'll have more than one savings account?" Yes! I recommend it! For example, if you want to buy a car and you'll need a down payment or a plan to buy it outright (without borrowing money). Set up a separate savings account that you put money into each month. There might even be a time (I hope) where you have multiple investment accounts too.

The reason why you'd have more than one savings account is so you can easily see where you are in relation to your goal, as opposed to having to do the mental math of figuring out how much of your savings is for your emergency fund versus your new car versus your someday-baby (or adorable puppy) fund.

We'll talk more about investing in Part 4.

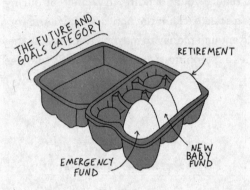

THE FUTURE AND GOALS CATEGORY
ENCOMPASSES VARIOUS SAVINGS
AND INVESTMENT ACCOUNTS

## Why a Spending Plan Works Better Than a Budget

When you begin to put your spending plan together, it resembles a budget because it requires you to review your expenses and understand how you are spending your money. The difference between a spending plan and budget lies in its execution, something I'll dive more into in the next chapter.

Folks who keep track using a budget often do it out of necessity. In other words, there is very little flexibility and slack in how much they have and how much they can spend. If this is where you are now, you might still need to keep a close eye on your daily expenditures, but I still think the framework of a spending plan is more beneficial than traditional budgeting.

Traditional budgeting is tedious because it requires you to either track all of your expenses each month to make sure you're within budget or else do the mental math and juggling of knowing how much money you could spend after you subtract rent and account for groceries and the spontaneous sushi lunch you had two days ago. It also requires way too much unnecessary decision-making about nonessential spending. With a spending plan, you've created a repeatable process with rules that silo your expenses so you can eliminate unnecessary decisions. When you eliminate these unnecessary decisions, you reduce the potential for making a crappy decision.

Traditional budgeting enforces scarcity in your life because your nonessential spending is always filtered through the question, "Can I afford this?" By separating out the money you'll spend in a Fun & BS account, you're giving yourself permission to spend that money as you wish. The question goes from "Can I afford this?" to "How do I want to spend this?"

One of the biggest benefits I've experienced in my own life with a spending plan is that it allows partners to have their own separate Fun & BS accounts. This makes managing joint finances a lot easier. The autonomy over how you get to spend money for nonessential items helps reduce points of friction in how we want to personally enjoy our money. While my idea of fun money well spent is to save it all up for a musical instrument or to buy some cryptocurrency, my wife would rather spend her fun money on a personal face steamer. Since we already have to make financial decisions together for our joint finances, it's nice to have autonomy over some of our money.

## First, Take Stock of What You Spent

Before you can figure out how much you need to spend, you first need to look at how much you have actually spent. Knowing how much money you've spent makes knowing how much money you need much easier to understand. It gives you a starting point and a frame of reference. When you go to make changes, seeing how you recently spent your money can give you an idea of what's realistic for you. If you're creating a spending plan based on an imagined future, because you're starting a new job and moving to a new city, you can estimate costs by researching.

In the same way looking back at how your formative experiences have shaped you, looking back at how you spent your money can inform your behavior going forward. If you need to have that moment of reckoning, the come-to-Jesus moment, the epiphany that you want to make some changes, going through how you've spent your money will help you have that moment of clarity. If you're feeling shame, guilt or any other negative feelings check in with those feelings. It's okay to feel them but remember the money narratives you've uncovered in your journaling. Remember that power that comes with truly accepting yourself and taking personal responsibility.

If you've noticed some of your fixed expenses like internet and cell phone bills have slowly crept up, looking at your expenses can bring this to your attention and prompt you to contact your service providers to find ways to bring these costs back down.

## Get the Data Together

In order to look back on past expenses, you'll want to use your bank and credit card statements as a reference to help you figure out how much you've spent and how much you need. It's a good rule of thumb to look at the last three months of your spending. The last three months is recent enough to show you a range for costs that vary month to month, like a cell phone or grocery bill. I hope that you don't use eleven different credit cards each month because it'll make this exercise annoying. But if you do, I'm sure you'll quickly see why you may want to change that.

## Make [Your Name Here]'s Spending Plan

I encourage you to use a pencil with an eraser because as you read this book, you will likely go back and make changes. Using the last three months as a guideline, enter what you project to spend each month in each category.

You can find the average for costs that vary month to month. To calculate the average cost, you add the total monthly cost for a category and divide the total by the number of months, which would be three. For example, if you spent $350, $415 and $397 on groceries, the average monthly cost is $387 because ($350 + $415 + $397) ÷ 3 = $387. Alternatively, you can take a maximalist approach and choose the largest number over the last three months. If we take the same figures from our example, the maximalist approach is allocating $415 a month for groceries.

You can organize the last three months of data manually (calculator, pen and paper, a pile of paper statements), with a spreadsheet, with an app or with any kind of tool you'd like to use. Please pick the tool that works best for you.

Here are some tips for completing your spending plan:

- When referencing your account statements, don't get too bogged down in the details, but don't just gloss over the numbers.

- Be honest with yourself. But, if you start to judge yourself, try to shift to listening instead of judging. Remember judgment is rejection. Try to find out what's causing you to reject yourself. Now is the time to honor your values and make a promise to yourself to continue to honor them.

- Try to accept your past spending behavior and when you feel your body tensing or you begin to have negative thoughts pop up, slow down and take a deep breath in and a deep exhale. Just because something is easy and simple, like taking a breath, doesn't mean that it's not effective in helping you process your feelings.

- You can use this exercise to feel gratitude for all the things you have been able to enjoy in your life. Spending money is not inherently bad. There is nothing wrong with enjoying it responsibly.

- Don't forget to think about the non-monthly expenses. Account for them as a monthly expense to make sure they don't get overlooked in your spending plan. For example, a registration fee for an automobile is usually an annual fee of $120. To make that annual cost into a monthly one we divide it by 12 because there are twelve months in one year. The auto registration fee is $10 a month.

- Consider giving yourself a buffer to account for variable expenses like groceries or a utility bill that isn't fixed. A buffer is the cost of feeling secure and the amount you choose for your buffer will depend on what you feel comfortable with and what you can afford. For some a $500 buffer is plenty, while others may only be able to afford a smaller amount to start.

- You can dream here. If you can't fantasize about a delightful life in the privacy of these book pages, then where can you? Don't be afraid of what you want, but stay centered in your values.

- Traditional financial wisdom says a good rule of thumb for how much you should be saving and investing for the future is to save 10 to 30 percent of your take-home (after-tax) pay. This might feel like a lot because it is a lot. This is the ideal and it's okay if you are not able to save this much now—we'll go deeper into savings in future chapters. This is something to work towards. Until then, save as much as you reasonably and responsibly can.

- I recommend revisiting your spending plan when you expect
  or have a life change externally, like a new job, or internally,
  like if you've felt your beliefs and values shifting. Addition-
  ally, revisiting it at least once a year is also a great practice.
  January is often a natural inflection point, but your spending during the holidays might be different than the rest of
  the year, so be mindful of that detail.

# BILLS & LIFE

RENT / MORTGAGE $ _____
PROPERTY TAXES $ _____
HOME / RENTERS $ _____
   INSURANCE

TRANSPORTATION $ _____

MEDICAL & $ _____
INSURANCE

PET $ _____

DEBT $ _____

OTHER ESSENTIALS $ _____
$ _____

PHONE $ _____

HOUSEHOLD SUPPLIES $ _____
REPAIRS & MAINTENANCE $ _____

FOOD @ HOME $ _____

UTILITIES $ _____

KIDS $ _____

HEALTH $ _____

MONTHLY TOTAL : _____

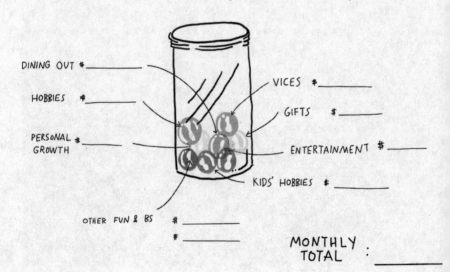

# FUN & BS

DINING OUT $ _____

HOBBIES $ _____

PERSONAL $ _____
GROWTH

OTHER FUN & BS $ _____
$ _____

VICES $ _____

GIFTS $ _____

ENTERTAINMENT $ _____

KIDS' HOBBIES $ _____

MONTHLY TOTAL : _____

# FUTURE & GOALS

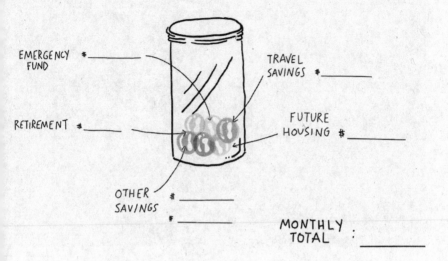

EMERGENCY FUND    # _____

TRAVEL SAVINGS    # _____

RETIREMENT    # _____

FUTURE HOUSING    # _____

OTHER SAVINGS    # _____

# _____

MONTHLY TOTAL : _____

# YOUR MONTHLY SPENDING PLAN

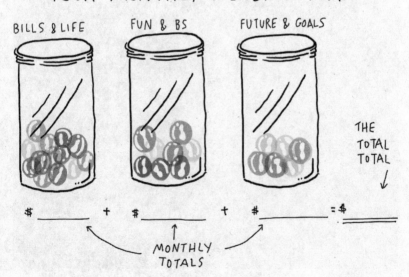

BILLS & LIFE        FUN & BS        FUTURE & GOALS

THE TOTAL TOTAL

# _____ + # _____ + # _____ = $ _____

MONTHLY TOTALS

**CHAPTER 3**

# Protect Yourself from Yourself

## Get a Grip on Spending

Now that you've looked back at your spending and projected forward with a plan, the next step is to set up a system and a process to help you stay on budget without actually having to budget. If you're skeptical because you've never been able to find a system that works for you, I get it. I have failed at many a budgeting attempt.

The spending plan in action relies on a system of separate accounts to delineate how you spend your money. It's designed to protect you from yourself, your irrational decisions and your particular weirdness around spending, kind of like bumpers on a bowling lane.

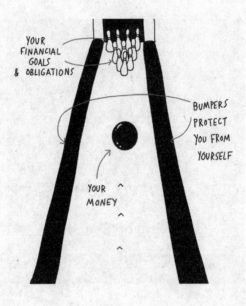

## PACO'S LAW

I'm sure you've heard of Murphy's law, an old adage that states "anything that can go wrong, will go wrong." And then there is Parkinson's law, which basically boils down to: work expands to fill the time available for its completion.

Now I'd like to introduce you to Paco's law.

Paco's law says that "your spending will equal what you have available to spend." This isn't true for every person out there but the amount of people I have personally encountered who are struggling with getting a grip on their spending is so huge that there should be a law for it.

Here's a weird yet helpful way to look at Paco's law. Have you ever had to take liquid medicine, like antibiotics or a cough syrup? Chances are you have, and chances are you used that little cup it comes with to take the medication instead of just pouring some out into a large cup and hoping you'd take the right dose. Paco's law is basically a way for you to pour a specific amount of something (money) into a container (a checking account) in order to ensure you only consume (spend) a certain amount.

HOW TO ENSURE THE OVERCONSUMPTION OF COUGH SYRUP

USE A DRINKING GLASS

TAKE SWIGS FROM THE BOTTLE

USE A MEASURING CUP WITH THE WRONG UNITS

USE A GIANT LADLE

Knowing about Paco's law is the first step to not becoming a victim of it. How do you know if you're overspending? Look out for the signs:

- You save less than 5 percent of your income
- Your credit card balances aren't going down
- You credit score is below 600
- You have no emergency fund
- You've never made a budget
- You've paid an overdraft fee

Even if you're pretty good with your money, separating your spending could help you boost your savings or refocus your spending in a way that is more aligned with your values.

ANOTHER WAY TO LOOK AT PACO'S LAW

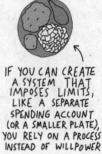

WHEN YOU DON'T PUT
ARTIFICIAL LIMITATIONS
ON HOW MUCH YOU CAN
CONSUME, YOU HAVE
TO RELY ON WILLPOWER

IF YOU CAN CREATE
A SYSTEM THAT
IMPOSES LIMITS,
LIKE A SEPARATE
SPENDING ACCOUNT
(OR A SMALLER PLATE),
YOU RELY ON A PROCESS
INSTEAD OF WILLPOWER

### The Anti-Budget:
### A Separate Spending System

Here's how the separate spending system works:

- Set up two separate checking accounts—one checking account for all the Bills & Life expenses and one checking account for all the Fun & BS expenses.

- Fund each account with how much you need (more on exactly how later)

- Separate your spending. Only pay for Bills & Life expenses out of the Bills & Life account and only use the Fun & BS account for the nonessentials in your life. This system only works if you make sure that you adopt this rule as a part of the operating process.

Separating your Fun & BS spending will allow you to impose a cut-off amount to your nonessential spending. If you don't separate it, you'll need to keep track of your Fun & BS spending to always make sure you know how much of your money is safe to spend considering your bills and life. And if you have had trouble keeping track in the past, chances are you will have trouble in the future unless you change something about the method you're using. This is a pretty good change that you could try.

This method doesn't require tedious tracking, but it does require you to look at your account balances. During your weekly finance time, give your Bills & Life account some attention to make sure things look normal. For example, if you have a $1,000 buffer, check in to make sure that you haven't dipped below that buffer. If you have, you can investigate further. You'll also need to look at your Fun & BS account balance before you actually go out or spend your money. Looking at your account balances is like the bare minimum of getting your finances in order. In the health and fitness world, it's the equivalent of not sitting on your couch all day. I'm not asking you to be a marathon runner or come up with solutions for world peace—I'm literally asking you to do the bare minimum. Please, look at your Fun & BS account balance whenever you plan on spending money from that account and look your Bills & Life balance during your weekly finance time.

## HOW TO FUND YOUR ACCOUNTS

Actually implementing the system means that each time you get paid, you'll need to split your paycheck into each account. There are two different methods you can use to fund your Bills & Life, Fun & BS and savings from your paychecks.

Here are your options:

## Option 1: Automate It

If you can set up your direct deposit to go into multiple accounts, this might be the easiest because you don't have to worry about transfers. For example, you get paid $1,150 after taxes, every other week and your employer allows you to set up multiple direct deposits. One option is to set aside $150 automatically for retirement, then break up the remaining net paycheck:

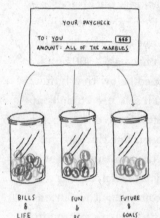

- $650 gets deposited into your Bills & Life checking account
- $150 gets deposited into your Fun & BS checking account
- $200 gets deposited into your emergency fund savings account (for your Future & Goals)

## Option 2: Do It Your Damn Self

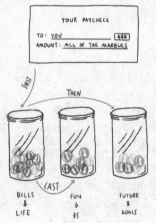

The other option is to manually transfer money after your paycheck has been deposited.

This is the most time-intensive method, but I don't hate it because it forces you to look at your finances regularly. And regularly looking at them is one way to feel engaged with them. This method is usually good for freelancers who don't have a set paycheck and are just getting their footing with their finances. It's a big reason why I'm a proponent of weekly finance time.

Depending on how much money you currently have and when your bills are due, it might take some financial finessing to get a smooth system on track.

## HERE ARE SOME PRO TIPS
## TO MAKE SURE YOU STAY ON TRACK

### *Tip No. 1: Build a Buffer*

It's nice to have a buffer in your Bills & Life account. We all have a bunch of bills that get paid throughout the month, and a buffer will be helpful if there are any weird timing issues, like having the bulk of your bills due at the beginning of the month. An ideal buffer is an entire month's worth of expenses, but less works too. You can slowly build up your buffer by adding a little bit more in your Bills & Life account until you have a month's worth of expenses on hand. A faster but more austere method to building a buffer is to drastically cut or completely cut your Fun & BS spending for a month or three. I don't love deprivation, but in short spurts it can work. It's like a sprint.

If you don't have enough of a buffer, you might need to spend some time figuring out a schedule for paying your bills. Usually you can call and have the due dates changed. Yes, you have to sit down and make phone calls and it's annoying, but the effort is worth feeling confident that your system is set up to work properly.

### *Tip No. 2: Don't Bring Your Bills & Life Debit Card to a Fun & BS Situation*

If you're going out for a night of fun and BS, leave your responsible Bills & Life debit card at home. Don't tempt yourself with it. When you've had a few libations, are feeling full of emotion and want to buy drinks for everyone at the bar, it's best not to have the temptation present. Remember that the quality of your decisions can be drastically improved by avoiding an environment where you will be tempted to make bad decisions.

## Tip No. 3: Mind the Hedonic Treadmill

The hedonic treadmill, sometimes called hedonic adaptation, is a concept that says humans will keep relatively stable levels of happiness despite positive or negative events. Someone who is on the hedonic treadmill is trying to find happiness by constantly seeking pleasure as opposed to seeking a different kind of well-being through a meaningful life of self-expression, recognizing and fulfilling your true potential.

Imagine a talented young athlete who dreams of becoming a professional snowboarder. Throughout junior high school they excel, but they get injured in their first year of high school. The injury is so severe that the young athlete will never be able to compete professionally.

Their crushed dreams of pro snowboarding might sting at first, but over time they find joy in cross-country skiing and helping injured athletes. Before long, the idea of being a pro athlete gets replaced with the dream of being a sports trainer, having a family and enjoying holidays in the snow. This shift is an example of the remarkable adaptability of human beings.

But here's the flip side. Imagine a young person who grew up poor and working class. When they're younger they imagine having an apartment to call their own. They think that's all they will need to feel happy. This person does everything right and the circumstances are on their side. At twenty-two, they've finished college, secured employment and got that apartment of their own. This person is happy.

But in two years, their friends move from a rented apartment to a rented house and suddenly that apartment of their own is lackluster in comparison. They work hard, get a promotion and can finally afford to rent a house. Exciting at first, but a year later, their friends buy the house next door. They make improvements, and now this person's expectations of what they thought would make them happy have just gotten more expensive.

There isn't anything inherently wrong with growth and improvement. There is nothing wrong with setting goals, achieving them and then setting higher ones. But the constant drive for more can become damaging when you are not conscious of your motivation or of the fact that you're even on the hedonic treadmill.

If we think that our well-being and happiness can only come from external pleasure, we will be trapped on the hedonic treadmill and no matter how much money we make, how much power and status we have, we'll never feel like we have enough. Donald Trump is the perfect example of this. Even as the president of the United States, he still did not have enough power or status to satisfy him. He will probably go to the grave never feeling like he has enough money, no matter how much he has. Of course, this is an extreme example.

Feeling better about spending less starts with recognizing the reality of being on the hedonic treadmill. Part of this reality is the false belief that satisfying our desires will lead to ongoing positive feelings like happiness and pleasure. This is the trap of consumerism. Some purchases might make you feel better in the long run, but a lot of them will not.

An alternative to the hedonic approach to happiness is called the eudaemonic approach. It can be summarized as an approach to well-being through six dimensions: "(1) self-discovery, (2) perceived development of one's best potentials, (3) a sense of purpose and meaning in life, (4) investment of significant effort in pursuit of excellence, (5) intense involvement in activities, and (6) enjoyment of activities as personally expressive."[1] What I love about this approach is that it's personal. It is not one size fits all. It's a lot more work than buying crap that was advertised to you on Instagram, but it's a much more sustainable approach to happiness and a radical act in a consumer-driven society. The good news is that the first dimension, self-discovery, is something I will continue to encourage throughout the pages of this book. You're on your way to fostering your own eudaemonic approach to happiness and well-being.

Two very practical ways to mind the hedonic treadmill are to step off it temporarily by choosing not to buy nonessentials for a period of time. Try thirty days, or if you're feeling wacky, a few months or a whole year!

Another method that might keep you on the treadmill but in a trickster sort of way is keeping a buy list for nonessentials. Create a list of all the things you want to buy. Feel free to go full nerd on this list. Do research, make notes, make it a handsome list. And any time you want to buy something, put it on the list. Make a rule for how long things need to be on the list before you buy them. It could be twenty-four hours or a few months. Making yourself wait for any length is a good way to train your brain to get used to delayed gratification.

## Tip No. 4: Get a Global Perspective

Let's look at some statistics from the World Bank to give you a global snapshot of other people's personal economics.

In 2017, 24.1 percent of the world lived on less than $3.20 a day and 43.6 percent on less than $5.50 a day. In that same year, a year when extreme global poverty had fallen, there were still 689 million people living on less than $1.90 a day.[2] This number is expected to rise as the world deals with the aftermath of COVID-19. Living off of $1.90 a day equates to living off of less than $700 a year. At the time of this writing, roughly 10 percent of the global population is living in this extreme poverty.

Those statistics make it clear how economically abundant your life is, even if we might not be comparing apples to apples, since the standard of living in the U.S. may be higher as compared to other countries.

## Tip No. 5: Don't Fail at Things That Don't Require Skill

This method of managing your finances doesn't require technical skills. It's not like dunking a basketball or dribbling one. It only takes your time and your effort to get it up and running and then more time and effort in the form of maintaining the system. There is no reason for you to think that you can't do either of those things. As a general rule, I think it's silly to fail at things that don't require skill and only require effort. Effort is something you can control; you can even make it a habit. Skill takes a lifetime of practice, patience and time all multiplied by effort. Keeping your spending separate only requires some effort, something you are more than capable of.

## Get a Grip on Spending

□ Set up separate checking accounts for your Bills & Life and Fun & BS spending.

□ Choose an option for how you'll fund your accounts (automate it or do it your damn self).

□ Make sure your bill pay schedule works for your income schedule.

□ Make a plan to build a one-month buffer in your Bills & Life checking account.

□ Commit to practicing grateful flow or another type of gratitude practice regularly as an experiment. What does this practice cost you and how does it pay dividends in your life?

DO THE WORK

## CHAPTER 4

# What Are You Trying to Do With Your Life?

## Deconstructing Your Goals

One day in early January, I found myself taking a walk around my neighborhood with a friend of mine. As we trotted along, enjoying an uncharacteristically crisp day in Los Angeles, my friend asked me what my goals were for the year.

I responded by saying, "This year, my goal is to have no goals." It's not that I didn't have a desire to achieve things or to self-direct my life. On the contrary, what I had observed over the last few years of actually having had successes was that achieving a goal seemed to require a paradoxical approach. An approach where the goal is not an outcome with a distinct finish line. Instead, a goal could inform the process or system I'd need to commit to that would typically precede reaching my goal. So, instead of having the goal to save $10,000, I'd commit to saving 20 percent of every inflow ... indefinitely. And when I did this, I tended to exceed whatever my previous goal had been. I realized that instead of a goal being the ultimate end point, they should actually be the starting point. I feel like a cliché saying this, but I realized my approach had become less about arriving at a destination and more about loving the journey. And it's made making progress more fulfilling and sustainable.

I'm not discouraging the act of setting financial goals. I do discourage using this way of setting and trying to achieve goals as the only way to think about our financial futures. Goals in general are crude, blunt instruments that don't take into account the finer details of a dynamic life in a constantly changing modern world. Goals can be elusive and challenging for many reasons. At the core of achievement, goals require us to change our behavior, to act in the face of our fears and navigate circumstances outside of our control. Even if we succeed in changing the thing within our control— ourselves—we are still subject to outside circumstances, like a global pandemic or whatever the hell the stock market is doing.

It's easy to see why goals get all the glory. They're aspirational and sexy. Goals can give us hope, the feeling of progress, and they can provide the aimless a sense of direction. Reaching a goal is social media worthy. It's an opportunity for attention and recognition. In our current vernacular, it's widely acceptable to compliment people by just saying "goals."

But being too focused on an outcome in every situation is limiting and rigid. It's a one-dimensional perspective. It's inflexible; it kills the possibility of a different result. Deviating from the path or the goal might be considered a failure. And this is a big flaw in the goal-setting system. When you don't arrive at your intended destination, you've failed—a common experience we all have. Failure starts to feel like a feature of goals and not a bug. When thinking about goals like this, it forces us to ask if this is a good way to facilitate meaningful achievement in our lives.

I've fallen victim to the majority of the goals I've set. I stayed at a job that made me miserable and didn't pay me enough because I thought I needed to reach a goal in title and salary. I couldn't see another path. The goals I've had for my business have paralyzed me. When I held them in my mind, I couldn't take any action for months or sometimes years because I didn't want to head in the wrong direction of my goal. Now I see any direction would have been the right direction because I just needed to start. Sometimes you can't even know the eventual destination unless you start moving towards something, even if it's the wrong thing.

## GOALS ARE A GOOD STARTING POINT TO UNDERSTAND OUR DESIRES

Even if we choose to use a different framework for trying to influence an outcome, it doesn't mean the traditional way of setting goals is entirely useless. If you were building a bookcase and needed to remove a screw from a piece of the wood, but all you had was a hammer, you wouldn't throw out your hammer because it wasn't the right tool at that moment in the building process. You would just get a screwdriver and keep both tools because they're useful for different situations. The hammer will be useful at another time.

The same goes for financial goals. Financial goals are a hammer that can be useful. They're good to have in your toolbox, but they aren't going to be the only thing that helps you build your life. If you allow yourself to question your goals, you can discover your reason why your goal is important to you. It can reveal what you truly desire or fear. This kind of discovery can show you other ways to avoid those fears or have those desires met—perhaps a eudaemonic approach to well-being will reveal itself.

The irony is the only way to actually stay on track with trying to reach our goals is to let go of our attachment to them and learn how to appreciate and fall in love with the process of reaching them. And that piece is actually the only part of the equation we can control.

I've failed at achieving a lot of my financial goals. The first couple of years into my business, I had nebulous income goals. And I didn't reach them. I didn't save as much as I wanted to year after year. And for a while, I was really ambitious about how quickly I could get out of credit card debt.

The way that I was finally able to reach my goals was by letting go of the outcome and implementing processes and systems. In my business, I committed to using an accounting process described in the book *Profit First* by Mike Michalowicz, and after twelve months of using this system, I was able to increase my revenue by 136 percent. I decided to just save a portion of everything I earned and I saved the most I've ever saved by leaps and bounds. I separated my spending and suddenly I was able to spend a lot less than I thought possible.

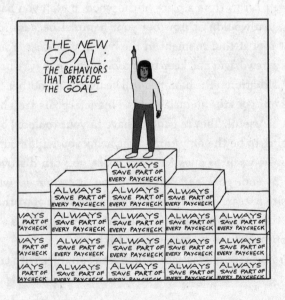

## DECONSTRUCT THE GOAL YOU ARE TRYING TO ACHIEVE INTO A BEHAVIOR THAT WOULD PRECEDE REACHING IT

Now, with nearly all things in my life, instead of having tunnel vision towards a singular goal, I use the goal to help me deconstruct the behaviors that precede a goal. And then I shift my focus to those behaviors and find ways to turn the behaviors into a process. When I do this, I get more out of the process, regardless of whether or not I achieve my goal. When I focus on my behaviors, there are fewer rules about the outcome. The fewer rules there are, the more ways there are to win. And when there are more ways to win, I can feel peace and joy in the present moment and avoid disappointment when I'm inevitably impacted by things outside of my control.

## WHEN THE SYSTEM FAILS, FIND WHERE THE SYSTEM BREAKS DOWN

Creating a system makes not reaching your goals feel so much less like a personal failure. Systems should do exactly what they are intended to do, but when they don't, it's important to take that as a sign that something within the system needs to be reexamined.

Let's say you're running the system of saving 25 percent of all your inflows, and over time you still feel you're really far away from having enough money in an emergency fund.

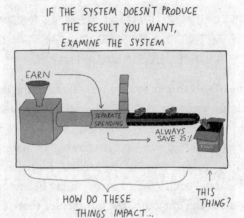

IF THE SYSTEM DOESN'T PRODUCE
THE RESULT YOU WANT,
EXAMINE THE SYSTEM

EARN

SEPARATE
SPENDING

ALWAYS
SAVE 25%

EMERGENCY
FUND

HOW DO THESE
THINGS IMPACT...

THIS
THING?

Instead of automatically feeling crappy for not reaching your goal, you can simply take a closer look at your system and start to ask some questions about what's going on. What things are impacting the outcome? Do you need to increase your savings percentage? Do you need to earn more? Do you need to do both? If you decide earning more would have the greatest impact on the process, what's a systematic way to approach this?

HOW TO REACH YOUR GOALS

AIM FOR
SUCCESS

MANAGE
FOR FAILURES

## REACHING GOALS BY WAY OF MANAGING FAILURES

Another way to think differently about goals is to focus on how you can fail instead of how you can achieve. When you think about ways you can fail, you can reverse-engineer solving for those failures. The system of separating your spending into different accounts in the previous two chapters is an example of using this strategy.

## THE POWER OF A PROCESS COMES FROM CONSISTENTLY RUNNING IT

Consistency is a really powerful force, but it's also underrated. We see its impact all around us all the time. A cliff by the sea is a cliff by the sea because waves consistently erode the rock. Dental health can be attributed to brushing and flossing consistently not intensely. For example, if I didn't brush or floss for years, I don't think brushing and flossing the entire day before going to the dentist could make up for the lack of consistency. And I can't even wrap my head around how many companies I patronized solely because I was consistently exposed to their marketing messages. Consistent behaviors impact our financial lives. Consistently underearning can result in debt, while consistently investing in the stock market is a reliable way to grow your money over time. Consistency is boring, but it often separates good from great.

Consistency creates momentum and over time the results compound. It can make up for a lack of skill. And processes that become habitual change how you self-identify. You're much more likely to identify as a saver if you consistently save, even if you only save a little. Compare that to saving a lot at one point in your life. You're less likely to identify as a saver. Identity further enforces your desire to remain consistent to keep your idea of yourself intact.

Despite whether or not you reach your goal, if you can create a process and run it consistently enough to turn it into a habit, you may find that the progress you're able to sustain is much more fulfilling than simply reaching a goal.

DO THE WORK

## Deconstruct Your Personal
## Financial Goals into Behaviors

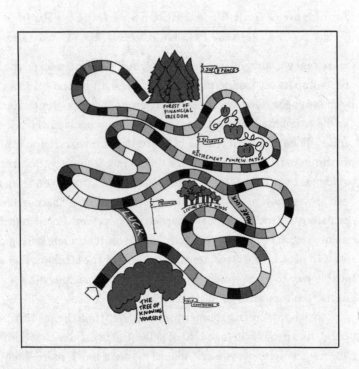

**You can use the following questions to help you better understand how to create behaviors that precede reaching your goal. Use these questions for as many goals as you have right now.**

- **What is your goal? (Pick one for now)**
- **Express this goal in terms of finances. How much does it cost and what is your time frame for achieving it?**
- **What are you trying to feel or avoid feeling by achieving this goal? In other words, what is your why?**
- **How do these feelings relate to what you value and how you identify yourself?**
- **What are the behaviors that support and would precede you reaching your goal?**
- **Which behaviors can you commit to now? How can you turn the behaviors into a process or a system? What are the details of this process?**
- **How do you think committing to those behaviors will make you feel? Are these feelings in line with how you'd like to spend and live your life? Are they in line with what you value and how you identify yourself?**
- **Go back and review your spending plan. Can you revise it to include this goal? If this doesn't fit into your current spending plan now, perhaps you can deconstruct what process would be required so that you can get closer to reaching it.**

# The Fundamentals of Finance

## Earning, Saving and Decision-making

Earning, saving and decision-making are fundamental blocks in your Pyramid of Financial Awesomeness. It's important to master these areas of your financial life because the higher levels of the pyramid literally build on these fundamental skills.

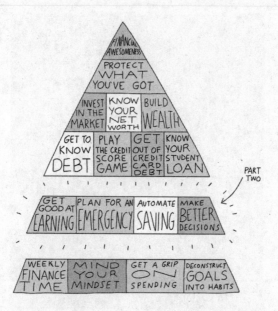

In Part 2, we'll discuss why we need to get good at earning money and different approaches to earning. We'll explore saving money: from struggles and shortcomings to solutions. Then, we'll dig into the importance of our financial decisions and learn techniques to improve them.

**CHAPTER 5**

# Get Good at Earning Money

I was a broke financial planner—a junior financial planner, to be fair, and broke is a relative term. But for someone who
was living in a major city and whose job was to advise wealthy people, it was weird that I had no wealth. I earned a base salary of
$36,000 a year to help people who earned at least ten times that
deal with turning all those earnings into wealth.

I started out as an assistant, which is one reason why I think
the company was able to pay me a salary that seemed low relative
to the industry standard. But I also never really gave income too
much thought or focus. I kind of assumed it would increase over
time and things would just work out—like it did for prior generations. I did not question the default. But neither did anyone I knew.
Income was just something that didn't get talked about when I was
growing up and with those I surrounded myself with.

It wasn't until I realized my income actually went down over
the years that I started to shift my focus. My wife, who was my girlfriend at the time, wanted to start her own interior and event

design company. In order to do that, she would need to forgo a steady income in the short term. Even with some savings, it was scary to figure out how we were going to live in a major city on one modest income.

To keep my costs down, I rode my bike to work almost every day. It was a nice 7.5-mile commute each way that helped me save $40 a week on gas and was just as important for my mental health as it was for my physical health—except for the fact that I was riding in rush-hour traffic in a city full of polluting cars. I started a garden to curb the cost of food. I replaced my store-bought shampoo with baking soda and water, and made sure to capitalize on every opportunity I had to consume free food at work. My hobbies were pretty cheap. Riding my bicycle and playing music didn't cost very much after I already acquired the equipment, which I could easily find lightly used off of craigslist. I was frugal, but it wasn't enough.

At first living like this was fine, but we couldn't save much money, since saving is a function of earning. This kind of existence felt precarious. If I would've gotten into a serious bike accident . . . well, that could've changed the course of my life. I know eventually, I would probably have earned enough money to feel more secure had I been patient and diligent. But before that time came, one fateful day, my perspective suddenly shifted and I lost my ability to tolerate earning so little money for so much of my time.

My boss had me doing the bookkeeping for his business; because of this I knew how much the business earned. I also knew how much he paid himself each month: $23,000. But on this day, even though I already knew the numbers, I was curious about something. I wanted to know how much he earned in a month relative to what I did in a year. So, I did the math. In a month he earned 64 percent of what I made in a year. In two months, he earned 127 percent of my annual salary. If we look at it another way, I earned around 13 cents for every dollar he did, which is crazy, but not uncommon.

According to the Economic Policy Institute, in 2019, the average CEO-to-worker pay ratio was 248 to 1.

In that moment, the stark contrast made me feel a lot of different things. I felt shame for feeling behind and stupid for feeling so grateful to be paid so little. I am not saying that I deserved to be paid as much as him. I was still very inexperienced and young. Plus, a lot of his compensation was from commissions, something I needed to build towards by signing my own clients. But the numbers staring back at me made me question all of my choices that led me to where I was. The numbers made me realize I wasn't saving *myself* $40 a week on gas by riding my bike, I was saving *him* $40 a week by not asking to be paid enough. I realized I was just accepting the damn default. Then my mind flooded with questions.

How could I help financial planning clients negotiate their pay but never negotiate my own? Was I afraid of being told I wasn't worth more because society actually thought I wasn't? Was I the kind of person that only knew her value through the lens of someone else's validation? Why was I accepting the default scenario where someone else determined how much I earned?

Questions only brought more questions: How much of what I learned from working with my clients could be applied to someone like me, someone in a much more precarious financial situation and with much less privilege? What role did I play in creating my own struggle? I know there is no such thing as fair, but what could I do to feel free in an unequal society?

Why was I feeling both grateful and resentful for my job? Why was this kind of employment the path so many of us choose to earn money? How could I have a finance and economics degree but have such terrible personal economics? What were my options? Where was my agency here?

This day sticks out in my mind because this was the day that I realized my obstacle was not my spending, it was my earning. I needed to earn more, not spend less. If I didn't figure this part out,

I'd struggle to progress up the Pyramid of Financial Awesomeness. Not only that, I also realized that nobody was going to save me or help me figure out how. No one would magically say, "You are suddenly a lot more valuable today than you were yesterday, you absurdly short, queer, brown woman." And since I was opting in to some of my circumstances by choosing to support my girlfriend and living in a city, I realized that I needed to figure this out on my own.

## YOU CAN'T OUT-FRUGAL UNDEREARNING AND YOU CAN'T OUT-EARN OVERSPENDING

The personal finance equation is frustratingly simple. Your income has to equal what you spend plus what you save (and invest). Or you can look at it like this: your savings has to equal the difference between what you earn and what you spend. Or what you spend has to equal the difference between what you earn and what you save. It's all the same equation.

I'm sure everyone can agree that balancing that equation is foundational for healthy financial well-being. Where opinions and beliefs diverge is how to go about balancing it. There is an overwhelming amount of advice and belief that people ought to focus most on spending.

THE PERSONAL FINANCE EQUATION

It makes sense to me why spending gets emphasized much more often than earning. Spending is something within your control that you can impact right this very instant by cancelling a subscription or choosing not to spend money today. The results are nearly instantaneous.

But there are fatal flaws in this thinking. There is always an expense floor, so you can only reduce your spending to that floor. When the price of things goes up, your income needs to track with increases. This is why regular pay raises are vital to keep this equation in balance.

When we emphasize ways to reduce spending over finding ways to expand income, we are choosing to think in terms of scarcity instead of abundance. This can result in locking your mind into believing that earnings are fixed; that it is determined by someone else and that you have no control over it. You must free your mind from this preconception so that you can begin to entertain the possibility that you can absolutely negotiate a pay raise, find a job that pays more or create your own employment.

Let me be very clear. Figuring out how to earn a sustainable living and balancing this equation as individuals on our own is definitely not the long-term solution to closing the growing inequality gap. In the long term, we will most likely need a combination of policy reforms that promote workers' collective power and a national conversation about economic inequality in its various forms, including disparities due to race and gender. We'll need strong worker collectives or unions that do a better job of building collective power so workers can bargain with their employers. We need to organize, but since this is something I know nothing about, I have no advice to give in this area. Beyond organizing, closing the income and wealth gap may require some kind of universal basic income. Of course, it's a worthy fight and we should fight it, but change at this level will take a while to be implemented and to see its progress. While we work on change at that level, we can also look within our circle of control to exercise agency over our earnings. In this chapter, we'll explore ideas and concepts to help you wrap your head around getting good at earning money.

## MAKING MONEY IS SIMPLE AS A CONCEPT, BUT CHALLENGING IN EXECUTION

As a concept, making money is all about understanding how what you do and create is valued by the people and organizations that benefit from what you do and create. In a perfect world, the creators of value (workers) and beneficiaries of value (customers and employers) agree on the price of the value. Of course, this doesn't always happen.

There are often lots of different people who get both measurable and nonmeasurable benefits from whatever it is you create or do for your job. This is obvious in a large organization where your work impacts the bosses above you, your co-workers, folks who you manage and the organization overall. You might implement new software that has a measurable benefit because it makes the team more efficient, which means the company makes more money by spending less. You might add nonmeasurable value by being pleasant, which boosts morale. Or you could have a high standard of excellence, which pushes everyone around you to try to meet that standard.

The value you create can also be seen through the perspective of the company's customers, clients or users. You might take customer input and implement it to improve the customer experience in measurable and nonmeasurable ways.

When you have a true understanding of the value you create for all these beneficiaries and from their various perspectives, you can begin to understand how this translates into how much you get paid to do what you do.

The other important aspect that needs to be considered is your ability to communicate and talk about the value you create. Can you explain why the value you create is worth the pay you are seeking? Companies do this in their sales pitches and employees can use this framework for negotiating their pay.

The challenge is when you believe your value is different from what your employers believe is your value. If there is a fundamental misalignment between the value you create and how much you think you should be paid for creating that value, you will have a conflict. Your conflict might be like mine, where you feel like crap because you think you should get paid more for all the value you're creating for the company and your boss.

The fifteen-million-dollar question is: How do you resolve the misalignment and get into alignment? The thing I didn't do while I was working at that financial planning firm, that I had to eventually do when I started working for myself, is to spend time unpacking simple concepts about value. How do I create value in the world? What skills do I have that other people value? Who are the people always asking me for help? What exactly are they asking for? Why is it valuable to them? Will people part with their money in exchange for my skills and creations? With what groups of people will my idea of my value line up with their idea of my value?

Sometimes the misalignment cannot be solved because of the nature of how a workplace is set up. If a workplace is set up where workers are exploited cogs and can actually only provide a limited amount of value by design, there is no room to give more and therefore get more. Think about assembly lines, places like an Amazon warehouse, where a worker's only job is to put items into bins. A worker can really only add value by working faster. Some workplaces aren't designed so that a worker can autonomously add value. In these environments, the definitions of value are rigid, and that's reflected in pay and in culture. This isn't true of all workplaces. Some places see workers as an investment. They understand the employer-employee relationship is a two-way street of mutual benefit and exchange.

## MAKING MONEY IS
## JUST A BUNCH OF PROCESSES

We all earn money because the company we work for sells a process (even if we work for ourselves). The moment I was able to view business through the lens of processes, it completely revolutionized how I viewed earning money and my relationship to work. It blew my mind, to put it lightly.

Whatever anyone sells, they ultimately sell a process. When we buy a product, we're buying the end result of that process. Coca-Cola has a repeatable process for creating soda. They also have a process for bottling, distributing and marketing.

When you pay for a ride from an Uber or Lyft driver, you're paying for their technological process that makes getting from one place to another in a random stranger's car so seamless that you don't need to take out your wallet.

A ceramicist, therapist and marketing agency all provide services that can be boiled down to a bunch of processes. A ceramicist has a process for making ceramics; all artists have a process for creating art. Whether you're buying a clay pot, therapy sessions, branding services or a bottle of Coke, you're buying the end result of a series of processes.

When you work for a company, you're a part of whatever process that company sells. And if you work for yourself as a freelancer, I encourage you to think about how your work is series of processes that are strung together and interwoven.

Thinking about earning money in this way blew my mind because it allowed me to create distance between myself and my work. Maybe you don't have this problem; maybe your identity is not wrapped up in your work. I think many of us have a complex relationship with what we do for work and how it's also the means for how we afford our lives.

Not everyone sees their job as merely a means to an end;

many also see it as a way to enforce our identity and our character, and to communicate status and class. We ask each other, "What do you do?" This is such an innocuous, normal question. But if it were posed as, "How do you afford your life?" we would be looked at as if we just asked a very odd question.

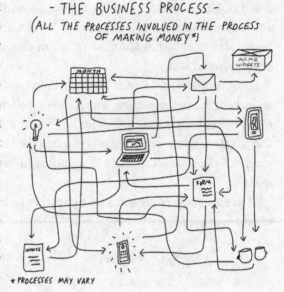

- THE BUSINESS PROCESS -
(ALL THE PROCESSES INVOLVED IN THE PROCESS
OF MAKING MONEY *)

\* PROCESSES MAY VARY

Our work can give us a sense of future security. We want to believe that our jobs and our livelihoods are secure, even though we know security is an illusion. It's scary to be a human on an insecure planet rocketing through time and space. If we recognize when this fear is at play, it might help us navigate our work life and employment decisions with a little bit more clarity. We might seek to find fulfillment outside of earning money and choose to look at earning money as a skill required for modern life or a bunch of processes or as experiments we can run.

## WHAT DO YOU BELIEVE ABOUT EARNING MONEY?

If I could give you a prescription that guaranteed you'd earn enough money to live your dreams, I wouldn't hold back. I'd bottle it up, sell it and laugh all the way to the bank. But, of course, I don't have the answer because there isn't one answer. We're all different, with different skills, and what you love to do all day might be someone else's personal hell.

I think one of the most important things you can do to get good at earning money is to first unpack your beliefs around earning money. Your beliefs create rules for how you think the world works. The solutions to your earning conundrums might be hiding because your rules have literally ruled them out. You have to believe it to see it.

Here are some really common beliefs I've heard and how believing them can limit you.

UNPACK YOUR BELIEFS ABOUT EARNING

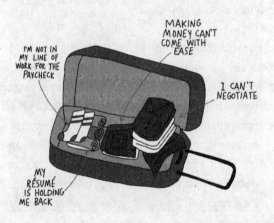

I'M NOT IN MY LINE OF WORK FOR THE PAYCHECK

MAKING MONEY CAN'T COME WITH EASE

I CAN'T NEGOTIATE

MY RÉSUMÉ IS HOLDING ME BACK

■ **"If I enjoy doing something, I shouldn't be paid for it."** If you have this rule, you are likely not allowing yourself to see job opportunities where earning money comes with ease because you don't mind the work. When you enjoy the work, you tend to naturally build a network of folks who also like the work and you tend to keep up in the industry because you enjoy it. These two factors alone can lead to opportunities you'd never know about unless you spent time doing work you enjoyed.

■ **"Only people who went to good schools get paid well."** If you believe this rule, you might never stretch and challenge yourself, which is rewarding on its own. You might pass on opportunities because you think you aren't the kind of person who does that.

■ **"The best way to make money is to be practical."** What is practical today is not guaranteed to be a sure thing in the future. If you believe in this rule, you create a false sense of security that might make you cling to a job in a dying industry. You might stay in a job that doesn't pay well because it's much more practical than making a change or taking a chance doing something non-traditional, like making money on the internet.

■ **"Making money is hard."** If you believe this rule, you won't see opportunities where you have the chance to let making money be easy. You might subconsciously create conflicts that cause you to struggle. It might hold you back from investing or working on a project that makes earning feel like a lot less effort than what you've been conditioned to believe.

This exercise of unearthing your earnings beliefs can be uncomfortable. I think subconsciously I didn't want to confront mine because I knew once I confronted them, I wouldn't be able to put back what I unearthed. This a necessary first step that might feel uncomfortable now but could have larger implications that go beyond you and your life. If more people spent time and energy unpacking their internalized beliefs about earnings, what larger impact could that have?

You might have discovered some of your beliefs about earning in the Do the Work section of Chapter 1. And you'll have the opportunity to explore your beliefs more at the end of this chapter. Before that though, there is one more idea I'd like to share about earning money.

## EARNING MONEY IS AN EXPERIMENT

Everyone's path to getting good at earning money might look different. Some people go the professional route, something not necessarily available to everyone. Other folks might learn a trade or cobble together freelance work.

I used to think getting a job was the only way to make money. Then I met start-up founders who raised millions of dollars using a pitch deck and some spreadsheets to sell the idea of a company. They created their own jobs out of thin air and convinced investors to give them money to hire themselves and create their own jobs. I've worked with clients who sell novelty clothing and products online and earn five figures a month. I've spent time with people who live in countries where the cost of living is significantly lower so their dollar-denominated salaries allow them to save money and work less.

I've become friends with people who get paid to observe and correct the way a performer moves their body on camera. I know artists, poets and musicians who get paid to express their human experience using their unique voice or perspective. I work with filmmakers who get hired by corporations to tell a story that sells more shoes, more hoodies, more whatever. Parents must be in disbelief when they realize that their children can get paid to play video games all day long or to unbox toys on YouTube. I personally pay thousands of dollars a year to be a part of online communities. Community was something I was sure could never be monetized, but once again, not only am I wrong, but I'm willingly opening my wallet.

Almost all of my close friends are entrepreneurs or artists who freelance their way through life—some more successful than others, all from different backgrounds. My day job is running a bookkeeping agency, but I also get paid to create and curate content about money. I didn't ever think this was a job I could do, let alone make money from. My entire career and the book you're holding in your hands right now is the result of running experiments over the years.

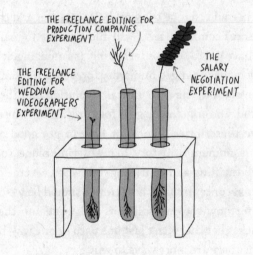

THE FREELANCE EDITING FOR PRODUCTION COMPANIES EXPERIMENT

THE SALARY NEGOTIATION EXPERIMENT

THE FREELANCE EDITING FOR WEDDING VIDEOGRAPHERS EXPERIMENT →

Thanks to the legacy of Edward Bernays, we live in a world where people don't just buy things because they actually need them. People also buy things because they want them. People buy to be in proximity to and for the privilege of association. For better or for worse, we can monetize community and get paid to curate the internet. Things that we previously thought couldn't be monetized, like attention or one-of-a-kind digital works of art, can be monetized. The mere fact that social media companies have tricked billions of users around the globe into using a "free" app, where the users work for the platform for free by posting content, is fucking crazy. This perspective is both frightening and amazing. But it's real—real money is being made. I'm not saying start a social media company or become an influencer. I'm saying that there are lots of ways to make money, ways we have yet to see or experience, but we first have to be open to that idea.

As technology advances, the options are only expanding. Our world is constantly changing, and technology that supports individual creators is just beginning to really shape how people earn a living. In the same way the electric guitar had to first exist before Jimi Hendrix could change the world, the internet and the technological advances coming after it will allow people to make a living in ways we have yet to see. It's terrifying. It's amazing. It's real.

Technology has changed humanity forever in the same way the cognitive revolution, the agricultural revolution and the scientific revolution did. The only way to go is forward. This is why it's impossible to give prescriptive advice for how to get good at earning money at this moment in history. In my lifetime alone, so much has changed. It's thrilling and confusing, but when we free our minds from outdated conceptions of how things should be we open up to see things for how they actually are and what's on the horizon. Maybe it sucks that there isn't just one path or one way, but I think it just means there are more ways to win.

I hope this helps you realize that getting good at earning money is like running an experiment. You observe data about value in the world and look at the money-making processes other people run. You try to see relationships between these things. You question your beliefs and assumptions and then you can hypothesize about what you think will work.

Negotiating your pay is an experiment. Starting a business is an experiment with lots of experiments within it. Running these is a lot like honing a new skill. Sometimes you try different temperatures or methods for preparing your roasted chicken. Maybe you learn a new way to stitch a button. Many paths lead to the same destination and only you can decide which path is right for you.

## USE THIS TOOL: THE WORK

This might be a tough chapter for a lot of reasons. Reflecting on how your value is represented by your wage can present negative thoughts and feelings, especially when your pay obviously illustrates that you're undervalued. As mentioned in previous chapters, there isn't anything inherently wrong with negative feelings. Not only are they a natural part of our human experience, but they can also be a help to us. Our negative thoughts can present opportunities to question and examine whether or not these thoughts are true. Doing this work, questioning what thoughts are true, can help us let go of the beliefs that other people have imposed onto us.

We can start to break down negative thoughts that have sneakily become beliefs. We can break down and examine beliefs like the ones I have struggled with. I used to think, "People like me will always struggle financially," "My status as a marginalized and oppressed person means I will never earn what I think I deserve," and the ubiquitous "I am not enough" and "I can't possibly earn more money."

I know it sounds real, real silly to double-click on these thoughts. But this tool is a way to unencumber yourself from the stories you've heard and retold to yourself. It's one tool to help you see things from a different perspective. It was this kind of perspective shift that helped me realize how the stories I heard were stories I continued to replay in my mind—and how I used these stories to fence myself into a way of thinking and being and acting. The most important thing I discovered was that I had agency to get myself out. I needed to imagine something new before I could take pragmatic, real actions.

Byron Katie is an author and speaker who developed a process of self-inquiry called The Work. It involves asking four simple questions about thoughts and beliefs that cause us pain. To do The Work you simply take a negative thought or belief and ask yourself the following four questions about it:

1. Is it true?

2. Can you absolutely know that it's true?

3. How do you react when you believe that thought?

4. Who would you be without the thought?

---

**DO THE WORK**

### Reflect on Your Earning Power

- **What do you believe about earning money? What is one story about work that you learned growing up?**

- **What do you wish you believed about earning money?**

- **What do you believe about working? What is one story about earning money that you learned growing up?**

- **What do you wish you believed about working?**

- **If you haven't already explored this, what do you believe about the relationship between work and earning money? What is one story about the relationship between earning money and working that you learned growing up?**

- **What do you want to believe about the value you create in the world and what you are paid in exchange for your work?**

- **What is your process for making money? Or how are you involved in a money-making process?**

- What other money-making processes could you run or get involved in?

- Does your current income level allow for healthy financial well-being? If not, what amount of money would you need to earn to feel like you earn enough? Is this number based on an aspirational spending plan? If not, what is it based on?

- What experiments could you conduct to explore how you can earn an amount of money that is enough?

## CHAPTER 6

## *In Case of Emergency, Save*

An emergency fund won't undo an emergency. It won't prevent you from losing your job or keep your dog from getting sick. It can't keep global pandemics at bay or change the outcomes of unfortunate loss. But at the very least, having an emergency fund won't make your situation more shitty. And at the very best, it'll prevent you from more financial hardship in the long run, like taking on debt you can't pay back. It'll give you some peace of mind in a stressful situation and insulate you from financial shocks.

A financial shock is often unexpected and sometimes expensive. These shocks can come in all shapes, forms and severities. Shocks can come in the form of global recessions, job loss, illness, root canals, freak accidents and even war. Experiencing a financial shock is not a matter of if; it's a matter of when and to what severity.

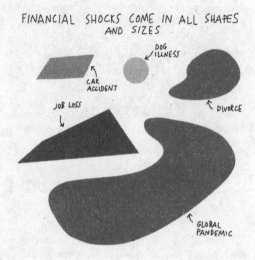

As a kid growing up in Southern California, my family would often take trips to the beach as a way to cool down on a sweltering hot summer Sunday. After a short drive, we'd stake out our spot and post up. I have fond memories of these days. My sister and I chased little sand crabs and went body surfing. Once, my cousin let us bury him in the sand. And, of course, I have a lot of memories of me and my sister digging giant holes and attempting to build sandcastles.

When you first start building a sandcastle, your inexperience allows you to underestimate some things. For one, you underestimate how hard it is to actually build a sandcastle. Sand is a delicate medium. The second thing you learn is that the afternoon tide will inevitably come in and threaten to wash away an entire day's work. You learn that you can't stop the waves from coming in, but you can always dig a trench or build a wall.

Your financial life is like a sandcastle. You spend time tending to it, building it and making decisions and choices that you hope will keep it from crumbling. You control what you can, but there are always things outside of your control—like whether or not you have the right tools or someone to help you build, when the tide will change and when the waves will start to move in. Financial shocks and emergencies are the waves threatening your sandcastle. The thing about the tides—and emergencies—is they will always come. Sometimes very suddenly as if out of the blue and sometimes gradually. When it does come in, hopefully you'll have dug that trench or built that wall.

In the same way a trench or wall is the best defense in weathering the shock of a changing tide, an emergency fund is the first line of defense against a financial shock. And this is why it's recommended that an emergency fund ought to be your first savings priority. It's the first line of defense. It's a world of comfort in a universe of uncertainty.

Despite the fact that most of us have a good rational understanding that emergencies and shocks will happen, many of us don't save enough or aren't saving at all. Beyond the simple math and mechanics of the personal finance equation, there are lots of reasons why humans struggle with saving money.

## THIS IS YOUR BRAIN ON DELAYED GRATIFICATION

In the 1960s and '70s, Stanford University researcher Walter Mischel conducted what is now famously referred to as the Stanford marshmallow experiment with children around the ages of four and five.

In this experiment, researchers would bring a child into a private room with a table and chair and place a marshmallow on a plate in front of them. Before leaving the room for fifteen minutes, the researcher told the child that if they did not eat the fluffy white confection that sat before them, when the researcher returned, they would bring the kid a second marshmallow.

Most kids tried not to eat the marshmallow; some were successful while others were not. Over the course of forty years, the researchers then followed up with the children from the experiment and kept track of each child's progress across various areas of their lives. The researchers found a correlation that the children who were able to delay gratification during the original experiment went on to have higher SAT scores, parental reports of better social skills, lower instances of obesity, were better able to deal with stress and had lower likelihoods of substance abuse than the kids who could not resist the marshmallow.[1]

Naturally, the researchers concluded that children who were able to delay gratification were more likely to be "successful" later in life. Logically this checks out. If someone chooses to focus on completing their work over screwing around online, they'll likely be more productive at work or complete homework assignments that impact grades. If someone consistently resists the urge to sink into their couch and instead runs a few miles, they'll likely be healthier than folks who give in to the instant gratification of vegging. Saving money is a form of delayed gratification because when we save, we forgo being able to spend money now in favor of having it to spend at some future date.

More studies with some variations have been conducted since the original findings that bring a granularity to the original conclusions. One particular study split the children into two groups.[2] The first group of children was exposed to a series of reliable experiences. The researchers first gave them used crayons, told them they would return with better crayons and they came back after two minutes with bigger, better art supplies. The second group was exposed to unreliable experiences. Instead of the researcher returning with bigger, better art supplies, they told the child that they had made a mistake and they didn't have other art supplies after all. Researchers did this with stickers too, promising and providing better stickers to the reliable group while not fulfilling the promise for better stickers to the unreliable group. After this priming, the marshmallow test followed.

As you can probably imagine, the children in the unreliable group didn't wait very long to eat the marshmallow. Why should they have waited? Considering their experience with the researcher, they had no reason to believe the researcher would return with another marshmallow. Fool me once, shame on you. Fool me twice, shame on me, right? Compare that to the kids from the reliable group; they were able to draw a positive link to delaying gratification and therefore were not only able to wait significantly longer than the other group, some successfully delayed gratification entirely and got the elusive second marshmallow.

What does this have to do with saving money? This study illustrates that an individual's ability to delay their gratification isn't a natural-born trait; our environment plays a role in our decision-making. We can extend that assumption to our upbringing, socioeconomic status and past experiences. All of these things impact our decision to delay gratification or not.

For example, if you were always given twenty bucks whenever you asked but spent it as soon as you got it, those two forms of instant gratification might lead you to believe that money goes as easily as it comes. Alternatively, if you grew up in an unstable environment where your family had money or food today but you couldn't be sure that you would have these things tomorrow or the day after, you may see little reason to delay gratification. It's actually more rational to consume the mallow right away or to spend the money you have now because what's reliable is what is happening in the current moment.

Another example of an unreliable environment is growing up with wildly different expectations of what you thought your life would be like when you grew up versus the reality of it. Many a millennial suffers from this mismatch of expectations and reality. Instead of researchers telling us that we'd get bigger stickers, parents, teachers and the general expectation from society was that we'd follow in the baby boomers' footsteps, getting stable jobs that will allow us to earn decent money in an ever-growing economy where the prices of homes would rise to no end, but we'd somehow be able to afford them. For many of us, those stable, well-paying jobs never materialized. Maybe this type of unreliability has made us more impulsive and susceptible to buying whatever an Instagram ad is selling because at least we know we'll get to enjoy our money now despite what that means for our futures.

Inequality exacerbates impulsivity over delaying gratification. For a person living in poverty, spending precious mental resources on a problem that is months away, or in the case of saving for an emergency fund, a problem that is technically imaginary, is a waste of energy and available resources. There are more pressing problems, like dealing with this month's bills. If that were not challenging enough, societal inequality encourages low-income families to spend on status items instead of saving, and as I mentioned in the first chapter, it can trap people in a loop of decisions that are financially harmful.

## THIS IS YOUR BRAIN ON
## INSTANT GRATIFICATION

Our modern consumer-driven culture places a high value on instant reward. We have one-click ordering, overnight shipping, same-day shipping, texts that are sent to their recipient instantly and the availability to stream or download more content than you could ever consume in your lifetime. The technologies that have made our world of instant gratification have outpaced our brains' ability to deal with all this instant gratification.

As adults in the modern world, we are constantly tempted to act impulsively with our money and indulge in instant gratification. We've gone from seeing a billboard on a highway to having our own personal little ad machines in our beds at night, spoon-feeding us marketing and advertising, getting us all hot and bothered for some bullshit we probably don't need to buy.

I know I already mentioned the role of the attention economy in an earlier chapter, but it's worth revisiting again in the context of delaying gratification. It's important to understand our reality. We live in an overwhelmingly capitalist world, where huge companies control our behavior. All-seeing, all-knowing algorithms and artificial intelligence work behind the scenes of our social media feeds. These companies hire psychologists and neurologists to help build technologies that groom us to consume and manipulate us over time. Technology companies sell your data to other companies and those companies now have the upper hand—they know you better than you know you. Whether or not you're saving your money is of no concern to them. You have to actively, consciously go out of your way to fight against this pull.

## THIS IS YOUR BRAIN ON TRYING TO IMAGINE AN ABSTRACT, IMAGINARY EMERGENCY

The challenge of saving money for an emergency fund is uniquely difficult. The potential of an imagined emergency sometime in the future is a very abstract concept that our minds have trouble grasping. This is especially true if you don't have a frame of reference because you've never experienced the kind of emergency where you've needed to rely on savings for a period of time. At the time of writing this, the world is eighteen months into the COVID-19 pandemic. It goes without saying that this experience will make the abstract concrete for the entire world.

## DESPITE CIRCUMSTANCES, FIND YOUR PERSONAL POWER

When we look at the circumstances that erode our ability to delay our gratification, we recognize that we're all born into circumstances that we did not choose. But remember that you coming into your power is a small, radical act within your circle of control. So are things like having a regular way to practice delayed gratification, accepting the unfairness of life as a gift to become resilient, leveraging technology to work for you to offset how it works against you and making a plan to save despite your circumstances. Since we've already acknowledged what might keep us from saving, let's look at how we can make a plan to save.

### How Much Do You Need to Save?

Before COVID-19, the textbook definition of an emergency fund was three to nine months of your fixed or essential expenses. Since the pandemic, a lot of financial experts have revised their advice and recommend that we all save one year's worth of our fixed and essential expenses. We can quibble about the number of months. The basic concept is that you want to have several months of cash available to afford all your bills and life expenses.

You might be wondering why the recommendation is to only save for essentials. The assumption is that in the event of a true emergency, you will most likely cut back on the nonessential spending. However, if you want to save enough to include fun and BS in your emergency fund savings as well, you absolutely can. The three-to-nine-month guideline is just a starting point.

One friend told me that she and her husband had a year's worth of expenses saved up in an emergency fund and wanted to know if I thought that was enough. I told her a year was plenty and at the time she asked me, the consensus among some financial experts was that a year might even be too much. She said anything less than that would make her feel incredibly anxious; it would keep her up at night. I've met folks who feel fine with the three months of essential expenses saved; they feel comfortable with that amount of risk.

I can't tell you what amount of cash saved is going to make you sleep better at night. I can only tell you what financial planners and experts typically recommend and their reasoning why. Ultimately, the amount of risk that you feel like you can tolerate is personal to you.

At the end of this chapter, you'll have a chance to create your emergency savings plan. Before then, let's look at an example. Meet Jamie, a woodworker who earns $50,000 a year after taxes and spends about $2,000 a month for their Bills & Life expenses. Based on these numbers, Jamie will need at least $6,000 (three months of Bills & Life expenses) or as much as $24,000 (twelve months) in their emergency fund.

There are some Jamies of the world that might already have an extra $6,000 or $24,000 laying around or in their checking account. Some Jamies of the world might already have saved close to $24,000 without really trying. These Jamies might find a lot of joy in inexpensive pursuits, they might have inherited a cool $50,000 from Mom and Pop. They might have also started the habit of saving very early on, or they might have the benefit of all three of these things, so setting aside money each month comes without much effort.

But there are some Jamies of the world who look at saving between $6,000 and $24,000 as an impossibility for a number of reasons. Some Jamies might have been diagnosed with a chronic illness that not only prevents them from working full time but also requires expensive treatments. Some Jamies might have student loans and credit card debt. They might have young children and aging parents to support. And the thought of having to save five figures while managing all of that might feel overwhelming. If you're one of those Jamies, don't panic. And don't get too focused on the big number. It's important to know that number because it will give you direction, but the work of saving comes from the consistent, small efforts that add up over time, so focus on that instead.

## Start Now and Save as Much as You Reasonably Can

Here's the most important thing to do: just start now, where you are. Start saving now. The habit is what is important. Once you have the habit in place, then you can amplify it, but don't worry so much about that right now. When you try to change too much, too drastically, there's a lot of room for frustration and feeling like you failed. When you start small, your progress is small, but when you start to see the balance in your savings go from two figures to three to four, that feeling of keeping a promise to yourself will reinforce your decisions and your savings habit. It might even encourage you to find different ways to increase your savings. At some point, you'll have that first financial emergency and the money will be there for you.

In the face of financial emergency, you'll be shown exactly how important the little things really are; in terms of money and life.

What's reasonable for one person is unreasonable for someone else. For someone who is in the middle of their career, earns a high income and lives in a town with a very low cost of living, saving 50 percent of their income might not be unreasonable. But for someone who is just starting out in their career, earning an entry-level salary and living in an expensive city, saving 50 percent is out of the question.

When you did your spending plan, I suggested to aim to save at least 10 percent of your take-home pay. Today, I might not find that amount to be unreasonable, but I have in the past. Even though I couldn't save 10 percent, I still saved as much as I could, and it was a little painful at first. If you can't save that much now, just start where you are. But realize, in any amount, for some of you, saving might be painful at first, but the regret and the consequences of not saving have the potential to be way more painful.

## Saving 20 Percent as a Rule of Thumb

General financial wisdom says that folks ought to be shooting for a savings rate of around 20 percent. This is especially true if you are entertaining the idea of retirement. I'll dive deeper into retirement in Part 5.

While 20 percent seems like a lot, I am a big proponent of saving at least 30 percent. This is a high savings rate, especially when you compare it to the actual savings rates in the U.S. Between January 1959 and October 2020: the average U.S. personal savings rate, which is the amount of savings in terms of percent of after-tax pay, was 8.9 percent and the median savings rate was 8.7 percent.[3]

I think it's obvious that a generous savings rate will help you fund your emergency savings in a reasonable (like less than five years) amount of time. The part that isn't obvious is *how* to increase your savings rate over time. If I had the true, universal answer to this question, I would be president or I'd at least have a staggering fortune for solving such a huge problem. Alas, I don't, but I can help you think through solutions that might apply to you.

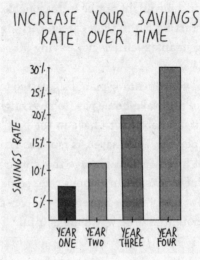

## INCREASE YOUR SAVINGS RATE OVER TIME

*Do It Gradually*

Remember the infuriatingly simple personal finance equation?

**Income = Savings – Expenses**

And remember how it can be expressed in various ways? For example:

**Savings = Income – Expenses**

This means we can increase savings by either adjusting income up, cutting expenses down—or a combination of the two. One way your expenses can gradually go down is when you eventually pay off debt. Once you pay off a debt, the payments you were putting towards your debt can now be subverted to your savings. This is a great strategy because you were already used to not spending that money, so psychologically, you won't feel the pain of saving it instead of spending it.

When we look at the income side I am going to make an assumption that as you continue to work your earnings will continue to increase. If that assumption is true, then saving as much of that increase as you reasonably can will get you closer to that high savings rate. I realize the challenge here lies in the fact that the cost of living may also be increasing along with your pay.

## Save Raises, Bonuses and Windfalls

If you are employed by a company generous enough to give you annual raises, saving as much as you reasonably can of your pay increase can be a way to bump up your savings without necessarily feeling the pain of saving. Remember the hedonic treadmill from Chapter 3? The concept that humans maintain relatively stable levels of happiness even in the face of both wonderful and terrible events. Well, the good news is we can leverage that funny little human quirk to our advantage. By knowing that a raise might make you happy at first, but that eventually you'll feel meh again in a few months if you increase your spending to match your increase in earnings, you can just cut your losses now and save your extra earnings.

I do realize that not everyone can count on annual pay raises. I also realize that sometimes a pay raise is only enough to keep up with inflation—the rising costs of things. While this strategy might be a slam dunk for some, it might not be possible for others. It was not possible for me either, which is a big reason why I left the workforce and began working for myself.

If you work for yourself, you have both a huge advantage and a unique risk. The huge advantage is your earnings are not simply determined by someone setting your wage. The unique risk is that your earnings are not determined by someone simply setting your wage. You have to figure out the earnings part for yourself. But when you do, it's not out of the realm of possibility to seriously jack up your earnings and your savings rate in a relatively short amount of time.

When I began working for myself, I had little in my emergency fund (I don't recommend starting a business without one) and debt to pay down (again, not recommended). By working for myself, I had much more agency over my earnings and I was able to pay down my debt while saving.

Not everyone in the financial world agrees that you should save money while in debt. Ultimately, it is a personal decision, but I think working on both concurrently helps insulate you from going further into debt.

## AN EMERGENCY FUND HELPS BREAK THE DEBT CYCLE

I'll dive deeper into dealing with debt in Part 5. For now, it's okay to focus on saving first because there is an important relationship between debt and an emergency fund. I know from experience that paying off debt and saving at the same time is not an easy thing to do. But having an emergency fund is even more vital when you are in debt because it can help you avoid sliding deeper into debt. Maybe you think, "I'll be fine without having savings for a few years while I tackle this debt." You could very well be right; you might be totally fine.

But you are taking a risk. The longer you're living without an emergency fund, the greater the chances are that you'll experience some sort of financial emergency. And if an emergency happens when you don't have cash to tap, you'll need to rely on debt, which perpetuates the debt cycle.

You might be familiar with the debt cycle if you've ever been trapped in it. Here's what it might look like: you've managed to pay down some of your debt only to accrue more because of an unexpected, expensive car repair or a last-minute flight home to see a sick family member. Taking one step forward only to take two steps back might leave you feeling deflated and defeated. It might be enough to make you feel like you want to give up. I wouldn't blame you for feeling this way.

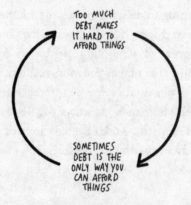

## THE DEBT CYCLE*

TOO MUCH DEBT MAKES IT HARD TO AFFORD THINGS

SOMETIMES DEBT IS THE ONLY WAY YOU CAN AFFORD THINGS

\* NOT PICTURED: LOW WAGE GROWTH, SYSTEMIC INEQUALITY AND RACISM.

But the risk of being trapped in this cycle is why it's crucial to work on building a savings while paying off debt. Although paying off debt might take a little bit longer or cost more in interest, the trade-off is worth it to me because it means you'll have the cash when you need it, which can prevent you from going further into debt. Plus, there can be a psychological benefit to having the cash on hand. It seems counterintuitive to have extra cash lying around when you can be using it on your debt, but having it might help you shift into a feeling of more abundance. This might sound silly, but by now we know how much our feelings about money impact our reality and the actions we do and don't take.

## DON'T FIXATE ON THE GOAL, APPRECIATE THE PROCESS

Just a friendly reminder not to get *too* fixated on the end goal. Focus on the habits that precede the goal and appreciate the process. Appreciating the process does not mean I think saving money will make you a better or more virtuous person. I don't think saving money has anything to do with virtue and I hope you'll be able to decouple these two things. If saving money happens to be a struggle for you, the process of struggling can be an opportunity to go through something that makes you more resilient on the other side. It can give you a personal frame of reference for understanding what it's like to be a human being who struggles. Having this understanding creates empathy. And if there is anything positive to gain from personal adversity, why not empathy?

THE SAVINGS STRUGGLE

Throughout our lives, we'll all face our own struggles. Specifically, with saving, you might reach your goal only to have an emergency set you back. Life might impose delays. There is a lot outside of our circle of control, but there will always be things within in it. And beyond what we actually control, there are even things we can influence. Stay focused on those things.

Getting good at saving money and embracing the process is something you'll use for a very long time, like a decade or four. I'm going to be like your super fit friend who annoys you because they say things like, "Being healthy is a lifestyle." Saving a portion of everything you earn and working towards increasing your savings rate is a lifestyle. It's not glamourous. But few things that are necessary are.

**DO THE WORK**

### Your Emergency Fund Savings Plan

- How many months' worth of expenses would you like to have saved in your emergency fund?
- How much do you have saved now?
- How much are you saving each month?
- What is your current savings rate?

**Here's the formula:**

(Monthly savings ÷ Monthly take-home pay) × 100 = savings rate

- How long will it take you to reach your emergency fund goal?
  - Your goal—your current savings balance = what you need
  - What you need / your monthly savings = the number of months it will take
- Is your savings timeline reasonable? If not, why and what is your detailed plan to make a reasonable savings goal?
- What will reaching your emergency fund goal allow in your life?
- What will reaching your emergency fund goal allow you to let go of in your life?
- Describe your emergency fund savings plan in detail. How much will you save? Will you set up automatic transfers? When do you plan on reaching your goal?

**CHAPTER 7**

# How to Be in Control
# When You're Not in Control

## Automate Your Savings

### THIS IS YOUR BRAIN ON HABITS:
### THE CASE FOR AUTOMATIC SAVINGS

Technology can work against us when it comes to getting us to spend our money, but it works for us when it comes to saving our money.

We cannot always be trusted to act in our own best interests because we are often not acting consciously to begin with. According to Duke University researchers David T. Neal, Wendy Wood and Jeffery M. Quinn, as much as 45 percent of our daily behaviors are habitual.[1] In other words, nearly half of the actions you take on a daily basis are based on your habits. Which means, nearly half the time we're all just walking around like zombies that aren't in charge of our behaviors.

You don't brush your teeth every morning because you actively remember or remind yourself to do it. You just do it automatically and without thinking because it's so ingrained that it's normal. If you have a daily commute you've surely had the experience of arriving home without the faintest idea of how you got there. That slightly off-putting feeling is part of why habits are amazing. They free up our brains so we can think about or do other things. Sometimes a habit is like having a shortcut. You can go on autopilot on your commute home and your brain is free to listen to a podcast, an audiobook or to think about a problem you're trying to solve.

Habits are cognitively amazing tools. In our brains we have neural pathways—connections between neurons—that are both created by and create our habits. These neural pathways get stronger with repetition. After we've performed a task enough times, we don't have to think about how it's done, the behavior is the new normal and a habit gets formed. It's just like establishing a weekly finance time habit. Not only does it become easier to do the more you do it, but the more you do it, the more your habits compound.

So, good habits that compound over time are worth more than the sum of their parts. Not only do they allow you to take action without having to make a decision, but over time you can get positive results with seemingly less effort. On the other hand, your bad habits reinforce bad behavior. These compound too. If you have the bad habit of not saving a portion of every paycheck, breaking it would normally require you to literally rewire your brain to build a new habit.

Here's more good news: if you receive a regular paycheck, you don't need to do the work to undo this bad habit. In order to create the good habit of saving you just need to override it by removing yourself from the equation entirely and leveraging technology. Even better news, as far as retirement goes, if you participate in an employer-sponsored retirement plan, like a 401(k), you'll notice that your contributions go in automatically from your paycheck.

Here's the semi-bad news: if you're a freelancer whose paycheck varies, you can still set up an automatic savings, but it will only be for a minimum amount; $50 a week as opposed to *exactly* 20 percent of your income. To save that exact percentage, you'll have to do it manually, making the transfer each time you are paid since your pay varies. Which is why I cannot encourage weekly finance time enough. To make sure you stay on task, make it one of the first things you do when you sit down for your weekly finance time.

In general, I think it's important to work on breaking bad habits and forming good habits. But I'm also a proponent of finding ways to make hard things easy to do. At this point in history technology has advanced to the point where we can leverage it to completely bypass having to rely on the mushy, ancient technology of our human brains. Brains that are a jumbled mess of processes—under the proper conditions our brains are capable of unparalleled abstract thought. What's also in our brains are old programs that drive us to devour cookies because we think potential nearby rivals may swoop in and eat them before we can. While we cannot—or maybe should not—try to outsource all of our good habits to technology, I think it's silly not to lean on technology to help us save more money.

Before we get into more of the mechanics and details of savings, I'd like to first address some common questions about savings that I've heard and collected over the years.

## WHERE SHOULD YOU PARK YOUR EMERGENCY FUND SAVINGS?

Before you set up your automatic savings, you'll have to decide where to park your emergency fund money.

### The Type of Account Matters

I recommend putting your money into a high-yield money market savings account. Most online banks offer these types of accounts.

To see which banks are offering the best rates, Bankrate.com publishes their top picks for money market savings accounts each month.[2] Yes, interest rates go up and down. Which is why sites like Bankrate.com publish these details regularly. I don't know of a good resource that aggregates this data for credit unions, unfortunately.

A high-yield money market savings account is remarkably similar to a regular savings account. Here are the subtle differences. Banks use funds from customers' regular savings accounts to lend to other customers for things like car loans, credit cards and lines of credit. Money market accounts pay a slightly higher interest rate than traditional savings accounts because banks use this cash to invest in short-term, highly liquid[3] low-risk assets.[4] Don't worry, high-yield money market savings funds are protected by the Federal Deposit Insurance Corporation (FDIC), just like the cash in your checking accounts. While there is always risk when you choose to believe in the value of money (because its value depends on our collective belief), the money you put into a high-yield money market account is considered riskless. In other words, don't worry, it's not being invested in risky things.

With a high-yield money market savings account, you can generally expect to earn a higher interest rate than a regular savings account. For example, a regular savings account might offer 0.5 percent, while a high-yield money market savings account is offering 1.75 percent. Just a reminder: the interest rates at the time of writing this might be different than what the interest rates are at the time you're reading this.

## YOU CAN'T SIT WITH US

YOUR BILLS ACCOUNT

YOUR FUN & BS ACCOUNT

YOUR BUSINESS ACCOUNT

YOUR EMERGENCY FUND

### The Bank Matters

I generally prefer having my emergency fund at a bank that is different from the bank where my Bills & Life and Fun & BS accounts are. I generally prefer online banks. The reason why I recommend this is because your emergency fund monies will be out of sight and hopefully out of mind, which will temper any temptation to spend it on nonemergencies.

This makes it inconvenient to make transfers, but that's a good thing. Waiting for three days to transfer your emergency monies means you'll have a three-day period to make certain you need the funds. It's another way to protect yourself against yourself.

I also like online banks because they tend to be cheaper. There aren't bank branches everywhere, which means the company doesn't have to pay those high commercial rents. This often means they can pass those savings on to the end user in the form of lower or no fees—of course, please verify with the bank you choose.

Alternatively, establishing your emergency fund at a credit union has benefits that go beyond the interest rate. Credit unions are member owned and tend to invest more in their community and their members than traditional banks—so they're arguably better than regular banks. When you become a member, you are establishing a relationship with the credit union. This can pay off when you want to apply for a car loan, line of credit or a mortgage since credit union rates tend to be among the best you can get.

## SHOULD YOU STILL SAVE FOR RETIREMENT IF YOU DON'T HAVE AN EMERGENCY FUND?

Since an emergency fund is the first step to having solid financial footing, it's a pretty common rule to prioritize it over other types of savings. However, you can still save for more than one thing while prioritizing your emergency fund. For example, if you are one of the lucky folks who has access to an employer-sponsored retirement plan like a 401(k), and your employer offers to match your contributions,[5] I would encourage you to take advantage of that match if you can afford it because it's free money from your employer. We'll explore retirement more in Part 4. First, it's time to get your emergency fund set up.

Remember, a retirement plan is designed to prevent you from using it like an emergency fund. There may be steep penalties for withdrawing money from it in an emergency.

If you can afford to, try to save at least as much as the employer match so you can take full advantage. Put the rest of your savings into your emergency fund. In other words, keep saving for retirement, just save less for now. The largest portion of your savings should go into your emergency fund because it's still the highest priority.

In the exercise from the last chapter, you calculated your emergency funding timeline, which is how long it will take you to fully fund your emergency savings. When you save for more than one thing, this shouldn't change your emergency funding timeline from reasonable to unreasonable.

## WHEN SHOULD YOU USE YOUR EMERGENCY FUND MONEY?

When an actual emergency happens, some folks are hesitant about using the money they've set aside for a rainy day. This hesitation might come from not wanting to deplete your savings after you've done all the hard work of saving it. It might come from not knowing what you define as an emergency.

If you have an unexpected expense that you absolutely have to pay for, like a medical emergency, this definitely constitutes the use of your emergency fund. You get laid off. Your dog eats lights off the Christmas tree. Your water heater breaks. You have to travel to visit your very sick grandmother. These are all valid emergencies.

Nonessential expenses, like a last-minute vacation, are probably not the most prudent reasons to tap your emergency fund. The hard part is realizing that not all decisions to use your emergency fund are black and white. There is a gray area that's different for everyone. You have to be the judge on whether or not to use your emergency fund for a gray-area emergency.

CAN I USE MY EMERGENCY FUND FOR THIS?

YEAH | MAYBE | NOPE

- NECESSARY + UNEXPECTED CAR REPAIRS
- IF YOU LOSE YOUR JOB AND NEED TO PAY RENT
- UNPLANNED MEDICAL COSTS

- YOUR CAR INSURANCE SHOT UP
- SOMEONE YOU CARE ABOUT NEEDS HELP
- YOU WANT TO START A BUSINESS

- TO GO ON VACATION
- TO UPGRADE YOUR WARDROBE
- TO TREAT YOURSELF

DO THE WORK

## Set Up Your Emergency Fund and Automate Your Savings

☐ **Decide on the bank or credit union you'll keep for your emergency fund**

☐ **Go through the steps to open up an account dedicated solely to your emergency fund monies.**

☐ **Go back to your emergency fund plan from the previous chapter (page 102) and review how much you'll save each month and with each paycheck.**

☐ **Decide on how you will automatically save:**

- **Directly from your paycheck to your savings account or**

- **An automated transfer from your Bills & Life checking**

☐ **Set up your automatic savings**

- **If you'd like to save directly from your paycheck, someone at your work's HR department can help you.**

- **If you decide on setting up the transfers with your bank, synchronize your transfers with your paydays.**

**If you're a freelancer whose income varies:**

☐ **Make sure your savings is on your weekly finance to-do list.**

☐ **You can use a simple spreadsheet that tracks what you've paid yourself and how much you should be saving based on your fixed savings rate.**

EMERGENCY FUND SAVINGS CHECKLIST

☐ SET UP A HIGH-YIELD MONEY-MARKET SAVINGS AT A DIFFERENT BANK THAN WHERE YOUR CHECKING ACCOUNTS ARE

☐ CALCULATE YOUR SAVINGS GOAL

☐ SET UP AN AUTOMATIC TRANSFER

## USE THIS TOOL: PRACTICE DELAYED GRATIFICATION BY BEGINNING A MINDFULNESS MEDITATION PRACTICE

I'm sorry for being from California and recommending that you meditate. I know that's so on brand and it's annoying when people tell you to meditate, but hear me out. Meditating is an excellent way to practice delayed gratification. When you sit down to meditate, especially when you first start, you immediately want to do something else—anything else. You want to scratch an itch, eat a cookie, pick up your cell phone. You want to check your email because that person said they were going to send a thing, or you want to check your email to make sure you sent that thing you said you'd send. You want to look at your calendar, plan your day or reply to a day-old text. Feeling this urge and then not indulging in it is a very low-stakes way to practice delaying gratification.

Having a regular meditation practice is a small, radical act. The simple practice helps you fortify your inner world. A mindfulness meditation practice not only helps you practice delayed gratification, so you do the things you don't really want to do and vice versa, but there are a whole host of other psychological and neurological benefits. Studies continuously examine and prove that a mindfulness meditation practice improves people's general well-being.[6] It helps improve stress and anxiety management. A practice enhances self-awareness and emotional coping. It improves our ability to pay attention and our state of mind.

There are lots of ways to meditate and lots of ways to learn how to meditate. I started meditating on my own sometime in 2012. I would just plop down on a cushion and focus on my breath. If I got distracted, I'd just begin again, refocusing my attention on my breath.

The Waking Up app by Sam Harris is a great tool to learn meditation and guide anyone, no matter where they are on the mindfulness journey. After having a solid practice I started using it to deepen mine. I wish it had been around when I first started meditating. The annual cost is minimal, but if you cannot afford it Sam Harris has generously allowed anyone who cannot afford it to email and ask for a free membership for a year.

To experience the real benefits of meditation, it has to become a relatively regular habit, so you'll need to figure out how to build it into your daily habits. I was able to stack this habit into my morning routine, but I know that doesn't work for everyone.

This traditional way of meditating isn't the only way you can develop a mindfulness practice. The people in my life who are dancers, athletes and bodyworkers who practice alternative medicine tend to have a practice that involves movement. Find what works for you. I hope you'll look at this exploration and commitment as a form of investing in yourself.

## Have a Mindfulness Practice

☐ **Choose how you'll learn.**

 • **Use a meditation app like Waking Up.**

 • **Work with a teacher in a group or one-on-one.**

☐ **If you choose to use an app, decide what time you'll practice daily. (Make it as easy as possible to build this habit. Try stacking it on a habit you already do daily, like after brushing your teeth in the morning or before you go to bed.)**

☐ **If you fall out of your routine, remember you can always begin again. You can also explore other mindfulness practices but remember, sometimes part of the journey is sitting with the resistance to practice.**

DO THE WORK

## CHAPTER 8

# How to Think About Financial Decisions

In 2010, I had the virtuous idea that I wanted to become a district attorney. The idea was borne out of two critical events in my life. The first was a recent layoff that forced me into an anxious state where I questioned what I was doing with my life and my career.

The second was because of a relationship I had built with a deputy district attorney a few years prior, around the time I was working at the bank. She represented the people in a sexual assault case against a man who posed as an officer for the Los Angeles Police Department in which I was the victim. Naturally I worked closely with the deputy district attorney. She won the case and he was convicted and sentenced to twenty years in prison.

This deputy DA helped me take a terrible experience and turn it into something meaningful by taking my power back and standing up for myself in court. It was such a meaningful experience that it made me think that I wanted to help people feel that same empowered feeling. And so, I decided I wanted to work as a lawyer in public service.

By the time I was ready to apply to law school, a process that took me a year to prepare for, I was working at a financial planning firm, getting a crash course in personal financial planning and learning how to think critically about debt. With our clients, I learned the importance of asking the right questions. Instead of simply asking, "How much would buying this house cost?" I learned to inquire about the emotional motivations for buying a house— like wanting to have a sense of security or putting down roots or having a project to occupy one's mind and time. As a financial planner, my job was to help our clients calculate the true motivations, costs and benefits of their financial decisions and to help them understand the fine balance between risk and reward.

So with those new skills in my arsenal and days before putting together my law school applications, I finally asked myself a critical question that unraveled a web of more questions. I wondered how much law school would cost.

I sat down and blasted out a spreadsheet. I did the math to project how much money I would need to borrow and arrived at what should have felt like a big, scary number. But instead, it was kind of meaningless because I couldn't understand what that huge number meant for my life.

In the same way I made my boss's salary relative to mine, I made this cost relative too. I put it into context and I figured out how much it would cost me each month to pay back what I borrowed. The number landed somewhere in the neighborhood of $1,000 a month. Which isn't too crazy if you earn a corporate attorney's salary. But I was planning on going into public service. So I did some research and found that as an entry-level deputy district attorney, I'd end up paying 34 percent of my take-home pay to student loans. That number made me uncomfortable.

I looked into income-based repayment plans and loan forgiveness, but it just led me to more questions. Was loan forgiveness a viable plan? Could I reliably predict that I could stay in a public service job for ten years? What if I didn't like it? If I then moved to the private sector, how big could my loan have grown by paying less than the regular payment? Was there a cap or could it grow to infinity? Would my career options be limited to practicing law to pay back the loan? Would that make me feel trapped? Was I trying to do something virtuous at the cost of shooting myself in the foot?

Then the questions got really real.

How would this debt impact a future marriage? What kind of lifestyle would it force me into? How would this amount of debt weigh on two women of color who would already be marrying their combined lack of privilege? Is this the kind of debt that could overstress a relationship and snuff it out? In my attempt to make things better for others, would I make things worse for me and my future potential family?

Was the debt the cost of doing meaningful work? Was it worth it?

I sat shocked and heartbroken when I realized going to law school would be a risky financial decision.

There's no way to know with absolute and total confidence the consequences of our decisions relative to an alternative choice. We can only do our best to make what we believe will be the best decision. And although we will sometimes make the wrong choice, by learning how to think about our decisions like this we can start to understand what our options will cost us.

You're going to be met with a lot of financial decisions over the course of your life. Most decisions won't really matter, but a few will be crucial. You might make one decision to solve one problem only to open up unintended consequences. So, learning how to make better decisions is a skill that can alter the course of your life.

## AVOIDING IRRATIONAL DECISIONS BY UNDERSTANDING THE WINDOW OF TOLERANCE

Before you make a financial decision, make sure that your nervous system is well regulated so that you are making decisions from cognition, not from an irrational, fight-or-flight response.

Daniel J. Siegel, MD, is a contemporary psychiatrist and writer who specializes in interpersonal neurobiology. He is credited with creating the concept of the window of tolerance. The window of tolerance is used to understand and describe normal brain/body reactions, especially following adversity or trauma. The concept states that we each have an optimal zone of arousal. When a person is within the window of tolerance, they can regulate their nervous system in order to deal with the natural ups and downs of being a human being on Earth. In the window of tolerance, one can reflect, think rationally and calmly make decisions without withdrawing or feeling overwhelmed.

When we're inside our window of tolerance, we can approach day-to-day life most effectively. We're able to handle emotions without losing control and we can make clearheaded decisions with rational thought. And even if we were to experience anxiety, pain, hurt or anger that can bring us close to the edges of the window of tolerance, we're generally able to use tools and strategies that can keep us in the window of tolerance.

### What Happens When You Move Outside the Window of Tolerance?

When a person experiences a circumstance that pushes them outside of the window of tolerance, they go into survival mode and the prefrontal cortex, the part of the brain that is involved in impulse control, decision-making, and regulating emotions, shuts down.

This means any financial decision you make outside of the window isn't really a decision, it's an action you're taking because you're trying to survive. It's why someone might take out payday loans at criminal interest rates.

When trauma and adversity disrupt our nervous systems we can experience hyper- or hypoarousal. Hyperarousal is the fight-or-flight adrenaline response that happens when you are pushed above the window of tolerance. When you're in this state, you might feel an increased heart rate, digestive issues, panic, anxiety, racing thoughts or hypervigilance with your surroundings. You may feel really intense panic, anger or anxiety. You may feel really overwhelmed and out of control.

Hypoarousal happens when you're pushed below the window and your level of arousal dips. This zone is characterized by a shutdown or freeze response. One may experience paralysis, numbness, emptiness, lack of motivation, exhaustion and disconnectedness from emotions.

If you've had experiences with trauma, which the great majority of humans have, you may react to stress and financial stress in extreme ways—from going into overdrive and feeling anxious, to feeling disconnected and going numb.

In my story at the beginning of this chapter, the stress of losing my job made me anxious. My initial law school decision was a fight response. It took me an entire year to really look at the cost and decide not to go. In order to make a rational decision using cognition, I needed to be in my window of tolerance.

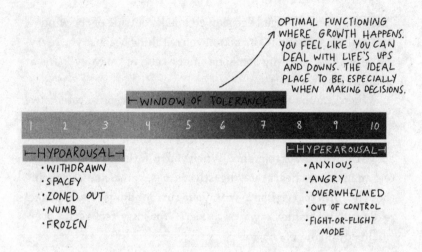

My years of not making enough money were traumatizing for me and, to make matters worse, I made bad financial decisions when I couldn't afford to. What surprised me when I finally started earning more was that I didn't magically make better financial decisions just because my income increased. In fact, I had to figure out why I was still making decisions that were not in my best interests. Why was I buying cheap furniture or cheap clothing that I'd have to replace sooner and end up paying more when I could afford to buy quality pieces that would last longer and end up costing less? Why was I still so impulsive sometimes? Eventually, I realized that my decision-making patterns were tied to old stories of what I used to believe about myself. I was only able to have the clarity and calmness of mind to address how I was making decisions by understanding the window of tolerance.

## Regulating Your Nervous System to Stay Within the Window of Tolerance

By staying within your window of tolerance, you increase the likelihood that your financial decisions will be made as a result of examining your emotions, digging into your motivations and making a rational decision despite any triggers, stressors and circumstances.

This is especially important because trauma in one area of our lives may show up in our financial lives. Someone with trauma related to authority may struggle with being able to communicate and interface with a banker, an accountant or a financial planner. Someone who feels shame and guilt about their student loan debt and trauma surrounding abandonment might struggle to communicate the reality of their situation to their partner or loved ones. If instability and uncertainty are both triggering for someone, like they were for me, they might make financial decisions that lead them to think they are in control but don't weigh the real risks. Someone who grew up in a household with a lot of conflicts might have used looking at clothes online as a way to self soothe. And after years of experiencing more trauma and a smaller window of tolerance, this person might find themselves using online shopping as a coping mechanism.

Getting into your window of tolerance is something you should know how to access in your daily life. There are lots of ways to regulate your nervous system so that when you feel pressed up against the edge of your window of tolerance, you can self soothe in a healthy, productive way. For example, when you sit down before weekly finance time, and before you have a negotiation or difficult financial conversation, you can get into your window of tolerance and regulate your nervous system with a simple tool. Here are some examples: Breathwork is a really amazing tool because you can do it anywhere, anytime. Strenuous exercise or other types of physical activity, like going for a walk, running or riding a bicycle. Listening to music, using a weighted blanket, taking a warm or cold bath, smelling something like essential oils or a flower. Dancing, humming or singing. Socializing, connecting with a loved one and laughing. Getting a massage, simply stretching your body and doing the grateful flow exercise are all ways to regulate your nervous system before approaching a financial decision. Try some of these activities and see how you respond.

In general, working with a licensed professional, like a therapist, is a great way to work through trauma that you think is impacting your ability to make financial decisions using cognition. I definitely think everyone should explore therapy because sometimes we don't even know how our adverse experiences from the past are reaching through space and time and controlling our behaviors today.

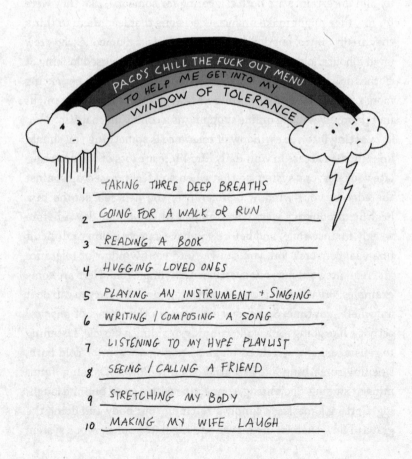

PACO'S CHILL THE FUCK OUT MENU TO HELP ME GET INTO MY WINDOW OF TOLERANCE

1  TAKING THREE DEEP BREATHS

2  GOING FOR A WALK OR RUN

3  READING A BOOK

4  HUGGING LOVED ONES

5  PLAYING AN INSTRUMENT + SINGING

6  WRITING / COMPOSING A SONG

7  LISTENING TO MY HYPE PLAYLIST

8  SEEING / CALLING A FRIEND

9  STRETCHING MY BODY

10  MAKING MY WIFE LAUGH

## AFTER YOU REGULATE YOUR NERVOUS SYSTEM, USE A THINKING TOOL TO EXPLORE A DECISION'S CONSEQUENCES

A really effective tool for examining the long-term consequences of our decisions is to use second-order thinking. Second-order thinking is looking at what will happen as a result of the first-order consequences. If consequences were dominos and our decisions set them off, second-order thinking is examining what happens beyond the first domino. In my law school decision, the first-order consequence was paying back the monthly debt. The second-order consequences were about how the debt could possibly impact my relationship and whether or not I'd have the freedom to work outside of law. I would also offer a third-order consequence: if the debt made me feel trapped, what would that stress do to my overall mental and physical health?

Your ability to think in second- and third-order consequences can help you understand the true cost of your financial decisions. It's a systematic way to improve your thinking and decision-making. By simply asking yourself, "And then what could happen?" you open up to possibilities, for better or worse.

Second-order thinking is a simple idea, but it's not always easy to execute. It forces you to find connections between things that on the surface seem unconnected. Over time, you can train your brain to think in this systematic, process-driven way. And once you think like this, you might be able to see second-order consequences that are extraordinary but require you to tolerate less-than-ideal first-order consequences.

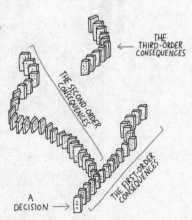

THE THIRD-ORDER CONSEQUENCES

THE SECOND-ORDER CONSEQUENCES

THE FIRST-ORDER CONSEQUENCES

A DECISION →

This process can help you navigate the kinds of financial decisions in the rest of this book, like debt and wealth, and the consequences that come along with them. I'm a firm believer that each person's ability to make decisions determines an overwhelming amount of what they are able to create in their lives. Since our decisions are some of the few things in the circle of control, our approach to decision-making matters.

When you make financial decisions, you can map out second- and third-order consequences, you can talk through them, you can write about them in a journal. What's important is giving yourself the space to explore your decisions only after you've set yourself to address them from a calm, rational space.

## Try This Method of Decision Making

☐ **Create your own menu of things you can do to get into your window of tolerance.**

YOUR CHILL THE FUCK OUT MENU TO HELP YOU GET INTO YOUR WINDOW OF TOLERANCE

1 _____
2 _____
3 _____
4 _____
5 _____
6 _____
7 _____
8 _____
9 _____
10 _____

☐ **The next time you need to make a financial decision, check in with your window of tolerance and use the menu** to regulate your nervous system. Then use the following template (or one like it) to explore first- second- and even third-order consequences.

# Dealing with Debt

The concept of debt precedes humanity's invention of it. We can see this in religious traditions, where concepts like original sin play out. If you were born into a secular household, you still might have been taught that you owe a debt to society or your parents. The idea of debt has been around before humans integrated it into our economics and finances.

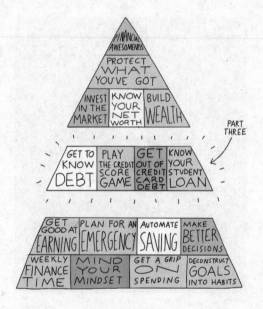

PART THREE

In Part 3, I'll explore humanity's relationship to debt and give you ways to reframe it so you direct your energy to paying it off or leveraging it to your advantage. I'll teach you how to play the game of credit scores and give some advice for dealing with credit card debt. We'll also navigate student loans and the decision to borrow money. By the end of this section, you'll have a greater understanding of this nuanced level of the Pyramid of Financial Awesomeness. Any time debt is involved there is always risk with the potential of reward, so the decision to take this path is always ultimately up to you.

## CHAPTER 9

# *Reframing Debt*

Some anthropologists believe that humanity has had debt longer than we've had money. Yet the unproven story that most often gets told leads us to believe that money preceded debt. We learn this unsupported story in school, literally because some white dude wrote it in a book. That white dude is Adam Smith. He is considered the father of modern economics and the book he published in 1776 is titled *The Wealth of Nations*. In that book he tells a story of the origins of money. While this narrative has become all too common, many anthropologists and economists argue this story is a work of fiction and there has been no evidence found to support Smith's story.

Here's the gist of the story. Smith describes some nondescript New England town market, a place where bartering was common. There's a blacksmith and a baker and they go to the market with their goods to trade. Bread for apples and horseshoes for cheese. Sounds like the original Burning Man, right? Smith then describes the classic dilemma with barter: the problem that arises when one merchant wants to trade with another merchant, but the desire to trade is not mutual.

Let's say you want to trade your eggs for some goat's milk, but the merchant who has goat's milk doesn't need your eggs. What are you to do? Maybe you ask the merchant what they want and you try to create a weird daisy chain of trading. Eggs for bonnets and bonnets for goat's milk? Adam Smith goes on to argue that this dilemma is at the heart of the origin of money. He argues that money was created to solve this barter problem.

The anthropologist David Graeber argues in his book titled *Debt: The First 5,000 Years* that this origin story of money has been retold in economics and history classes and it has been perpetuating the myth of bartering and the origin of money.

In his book Graeber cites the economist Alfred Mitchell-Innes, who disagreed with this origin story of money. Mitchell-Innes believed that barter was not only an uncommon way of exchanging goods, but that our idea that bartering led to the creation of money, which then led to the creation of credit (debt), is totally wrong and, in fact, backwards.

The evidence uncovered from transactions in ancient Mesopotamia during the Neolithic and Bronze Ages, around 8000 to 800 BC, supports this theory. Transactions during this period were credit based. While silver was used by temple bureaucrats it was often used as an accounting measurement of one's debts, not always as a form of repayment or for transactions. The repayment of these ancient debts could be settled with more or less anything one had around, like barley. For example, when a Babylonian went to a local alehouse in Mesopotamia, they ran up a tab that would be settled at harvest time.

This mind fuck is called the credit theory of money. As Graeber notes in his book:

> Credit theorists insisted that money is not a commodity
> but an accounting tool. In other words, it is not a "thing" at

all . . . [you] can no more touch a dollar or a deutschmark than you can touch an hour or a cubic centimeter. Units of currency are merely abstract units of measurement, and as the credit theorists correctly noted, historically, such abstract systems of accounting emerged long before the use of any particular token of exchange [money].

The obvious next question is: If money is just a yardstick, what then does it measure? The answer was simple: debt. A coin is, effectively, an IOU. Whereas conventional wisdom holds that a banknote is, or should be, a promise to pay a certain amount of "real money" (gold, silver, whatever that might be taken to mean), credit theorists argued that a banknote is simply the promise to pay *something* of the same value as an ounce of gold. But that's all that money ever is. . . . Conceptually, the idea that a piece of gold is really just an IOU is always rather difficult to wrap one's head around, but something like this must be true, because even when gold and silver coins were in use, they almost never circulated at their . . . value.

The creation of money, according to credit theorists, was not dependent on creating a better system than barter. Money is actually some kind of bastardized version of debt. It's kind of like those tickets you won at arcades from playing games when you were a kid. Those tickets are in theory IOUs from the arcade. You can redeem them at the prize store for pencils and plastic bullshit that will annoy your parents and then break as soon as you get home.

Let's say you are a web designer who designs a website for a client, Acme, Inc. Instead of paying you money, Acme, Inc. issues you an IOU. You can hold on to it until Acme, Inc. settles their debt and then you rip up the IOU. Or you can use that IOU to take the place of an IOU your company has. Maybe you have an outstanding invoice for legal work done by the legal firm called Cool Lawyers. You give them Acme, Inc.'s IOU and Cool Lawyers can then use that IOU to settle a debt they have with an accounting firm called Hell Yeah, Taxes. And now Acme, Inc. is on the hook to settle a debt with Hell Yeah, Taxes.

And if Acme, Inc. never pays their IOU, and it gets traded around because all these companies just trust that the IOU represents value, then the IOU is effectively money. Did you follow that bouncing ball?

You're maybe wondering why this is important to understand. Maybe it's only important so you can see that it's possible to reframe your understanding of debt. Maybe it's important to understand that debt is baked into our history as human beings. That without debt there would not have been money. And accepting that might help us collectively understand if it's even possible to move back towards a more human-centered approach to lending. I wish I had a clear answer for how to do this, but instead, what I have to offer is space to think about debt differently. In this chapter I simply want to explore ideas about debt and look at debt from various lenses.

## DEBT IS A DANGEROUS NECESSITY REQUIRED TO ENSURE OUR MODERN, CAPITALIST ECONOMY WILL KEEP GROWING

As long as our economy seeks growth, there will always be debt. Debt and money are both dangerous the way fire or vodka are. Fire is great. It gives us light, warmth and the ability to cook poultry to the internal temperature of 165 degrees. But unchecked, uncontrolled or, worse, combined with an accelerant, fire can be irreversibly destructive.

DEBT IS LIKE FERTILIZER FOR THE GARDEN OF YOUR FINANCIAL LIFE.

WEALTH

THE THINGS THAT STRANGLE YOUR WEALTH

THE TWO SIDES OF DEBT

DEBT CAN BE USED TO BUILD WEALTH AND FUEL ECONOMIC GROWTH.

DEBT CAN ALSO BE USED TO DESTROY WEALTH AND INHIBIT ECONOMIC GROWTH.

Debt allows businesses to make money they otherwise couldn't. Debt can allow families to live in homes that they otherwise couldn't afford to purchase right away. But, of course, unchecked, runaway or predatory lending practices and overspending can create an unnecessary burden of debt, as we saw with the 2008 housing crisis.

As long as humanity seeks growth and progress, as long as children want to be better off than their parents, as long as people stay on the hedonic treadmill and as long as we have a wealth gap, we're going to have debt because not everyone can afford to purchase an education or an asset like a house without borrowing. This is simply a fact.

# BEING IN DEBT IS NOT
# AN INTELLECTUAL OR MORAL FAILING,
# IT'S PART OF THE STORY OF HUMANITY

There is a pervasive idea throughout history across various religions and cultures that a debtor has a moral obligation to pay one's debts. And that failing to do so, regardless of why, is a reflection of one's own irresponsibility and immorality. I think paying your debt is like washing the dishes. We don't wash our dishes out of our moral obligation. We wash our dishes because we want to avoid the negative consequences. If we don't do the dishes, the roaches and rats will probably have a field day and it's generally gross. A not-so-great credit score and late fees are the roaches and rats that result in not paying back debt. And getting collection calls is generally gross.

Moral obligation has been a central theme throughout human history. Money is just one way to represent a theme that has been present all along. Ancient cultures and civilizations paid their debt to the gods with coins and by sacrificing animals and humans. Christianity's foundation has strong themes of debt. Adam and Eve ate the apple in the garden of Eden and humans were condemned and became forever indebted to God. Jesus's death was supposed to be the loophole to settle that debt, yet there is still the expectation to prove our worthiness to God.

This theme of debt became intertwined with morality and money in the sixteenth century when the Catholic church created the idea that one can effectively reduce their purgatorial debt by purchasing something called an indulgence.[1] It's kind of like today's version of carbon credits. When Protestants broke away from the Catholic church during the Reformation, the idea of debt and moral obligation didn't go away, it just showed up in a different form. A pastor and religious reformer named John Calvin argued that it was just for lenders to charge interest because borrowed money increased value for the borrower. And that, in fact, giving back some of that value to the lender through interest payments was the most just act.[2] Yeah, the most. So we've been dealing with the relationship between debt and moral obligation for centuries, thus kicking off generations of humans being weird and judgmental about debt.

Being in debt is not an intellectual or moral failure. I had a job straight out of college that I could only get myself to stay at for three weeks because that job was actually the crusty butthole of the finance industry. I'm serious. I only stayed long enough to complete the three-week training because I quickly realized the whole business was unethical. During the training, I could overhear my colleagues making phone calls, trying to sell old people bad financial products. These financial products were putrid mounds of dog crap that had been eaten by another dog and thrown up again. They were beyond trash and I'm embarrassed for not quitting that job the moment I realized what was going on. I think I was so shocked that it took me a while to process it all. I heard my co-workers try to convince little old ladies to refinance their credit card debt by taking out a loan out against the value of their paid-off nine-year-old car, or try to convince people who barely spoke English to take out home equity lines of credit for no reason other than they wanted a commission.

In between calls, the seasoned sales folks would complain about the company's new regulations that forced them to be honest on loan applications. They were angry that a borrower's pay stubs were now required to prove income and that the borrower could, I don't know, actually afford the damn loan. My co-workers candidly expressed to me how these new rules put a damper on loan approvals and their commission checks. They complained to me how easy money had gotten a lot less easy.

A lot of these people who I worked next to—because I will never claim that I worked *with* them—were, on average, not that smart.

It's the only explanation for their behavior that I can come up with—that they were not able to fully grasp some of the financial products they were selling. Nor did they fully comprehend the consequences of putting borrowers into these types of loans—from the borrower's perspective and from the industry-wide, global-impact perspective.

If intellectual failures are to blame for getting into debt, certainly the blame should be shared with the company and people who intentionally sell their fellow human beings terrible loans and flaming trash piles of regurgitated dog diarrhea disguised as financial products. Creating a system of incentives that drove people to behave in this way was certainly an intellectual, moral and creative failure. Responsibility can't just fall on an individual because the system did what it was designed to do.

## YOUR DEBT (OR AVOIDANCE OF IT) COULD BE THE RESULT OF UNHEALED TRAUMA

Living with trauma is like walking around with a small rock in your shoe. The most effective way of getting rid of any pain the rock is causing is to obviously take off your shoe and remove the rock. From a psychological perspective, removing the rock of trauma can take time through counseling, therapy and learning how to be mindful of what triggers your trauma.

If you don't remove the rock, you might change how you walk in order to avoid the pain. Maybe you limp or limit the weight of your foot on one side or compensate in some other uncomfortable way. If you did this long term, there would probably be some consequences, maybe a blister or callus on your foot. Or maybe you develop an issue with your knee or hip because of how you changed your gait.

Trauma is powerful in this way. If we don't put in the time to face it, work through it and excise it, it can dictate how we behave and that behavior can manifest itself in all sorts of weird ways. Life's traumas can reveal themselves in a person's proclivity for debt. Someone who has suffered abuse might feel worthless. But owning expensive things that can only be afforded by charging them to a credit card could be a way to prove their value and worth. Someone who is in a constant state of stress might overspend in order to avoid negative feelings. If the outside world feels unsafe, buying stuff might feel like you're protecting yourself from the potential of outside harm.

In Chapter 1, we explored how trauma informs our beliefs and our behaviors with money. Let's return to that lens again. If you've had cycles of being in and out of debt, could trauma be the root cause? If that resonates with you, I encourage you to explore and find an avenue for healing that feels right for you. For folks who feel like they are trapped and repeating old patterns, healing trauma can be the first step to making real progress.

## THE BEHAVIORS, IDEAS AND ATTITUDES THAT GOT YOU INTO DEBT ARE NOT GOING TO BE THE BEHAVIORS, IDEAS AND ATTITUDES THAT GET YOU OUT OF DEBT

This idea is worth revisiting again. For folks whose debt has been more a result of choices over circumstances, getting out of debt can require you to absorb new ideas, attitudes and behaviors. Sometimes that means you have to let go of old ideas, attitudes and behaviors to create space for new ones. Other times it means adding in new beliefs. Someone who may have previously only seen themselves as a victim to their debt might begin to see themselves as a victim who also has the capacity to take responsibility for the position they're in. Taking responsibly allows one to automatically take some of their power back. This new attitude can create significant change where there was once only a little movement.

If your behaviors got you into debt, as opposed to circumstances, like a catastrophic illness, then the behaviors that will get you out of debt will need to change. If you've never asked for a raise or negotiated your pay, things I rarely did, you might want to consider changing that behavior.

Your attitudes towards things like consumption might have to change. Instead of constantly consuming things, what if you constantly created things? Art, music, meals, peaceful, easy feelings vibrating into the universe forever?

Maybe your attitude will change from, "I'll figure this debt out," to, "Maybe I should talk to some professionals about figuring out this debt."

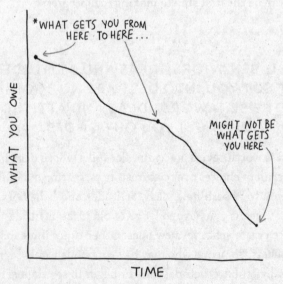

* WHAT GETS YOU FROM HERE TO HERE ...

MIGHT NOT BE WHAT GETS YOU HERE

WHAT YOU OWE

TIME

* THOUGHTS, BEHAVIORS, IDEAS, BELIEFS, ETC.

## LOOK AT YOUR DEBT FROM A RADICALLY DIFFERENT PERSPECTIVE

We don't deserve to have bad things happen to us, but when they inevitably do, they can be a gift. They can transform us, teach us a lesson or create meaning in our lives. Even if you feel like your debt is a messed-up thing that happened to you as opposed to a decision you made, I'd like to invite you to look at your debt from a radically different perspective. Where can you find the gift? I'm sure you'll think I'm positive to a fault, but when I'm faced with a difficult moment, I ask myself to find the gift and it helps me remember that one perspective is not the only perspective. While it's easy to see the gift in positive situations like when a puppy smiles at you or we are unharmed in an accident, it's much harder to see the gift in tough situations like when someone we love becomes ill or when we realize how crushing our debt it. But this is the duality of everyday life. Sweet is only sweet because it's contrasted against salty or bitter or some other flavor.

For those who have been able to find the gift in their experience with debt, they may view it as a part of the journey that got them to where they are today. It helped them and was there for them when they didn't have the money. It was a lesson they needed to learn. It forced them to deal with a deeper issue and that improved their life overall. It was something they overcame to prove what they are capable of. They looked within their circle of control and choose a story to tell themselves that shifted their perspective.

Sometimes we need the space of time before we can appreciate the gift of bad circumstances. If you're feeling that way about debt today, you can't see the gift, I understand. Perhaps today it's just good to keep in mind this idea of finding the gift. And over time you may be able to have that moment of realization. Until you can find the gift in your debt, practice grateful flow to appreciate all the other gifts you've been given.

Remember that gratitude helps you feel less stressed about the human experience you're having. It allows you to have some power over how you're feeling. Finding the gift doesn't mean you aren't rationally aware of the perils and injustices of the inequality baked into our economic systems. But it can help you deal with the adversity you're facing. It can help you build a better relationship with debt and money. It can give you respite so you have the energy to deal with it in a productive way. It allows you to assign more value to the things you have, not the things you don't have. Gratitude is like a light switch. It allows you to see what was there all along.

## DEBT AS A TOOL FOR BUILDING WEALTH AND NOT AS A WAY TO AFFORD LIVING EXPENSES

Debt is inherently risky for both the person lending and the person borrowing. Remember ancient Mesopotamia and the alehouses? Farmers would run up their tabs and settle their debts after the harvest. When harvests were good, debts were settled. Simple enough, right? The trouble with this debt system is when harvests were bad. Peasants might default and become hopelessly indebted to the rich. Many would need to surrender their farms, and sometimes family members, into debt bondage. In this instance, the way debt was used to finance daily consumption and the uncertainty of harvests was a recipe for disaster and social unrest.

Many people today still use debt in this way—to afford everyday life. I don't have a blanket solution for this problem because there are so many huge, systemic factors at play. Sure, there are some people who are living outside of their means and their solution is straightforward: earn more, spend less or both. But there are also large swaths of people who are not paid enough and who are living the reality of what centuries of classism, racism and slavery have unleashed. Until we address the real issue, this root issue, we'll continue to have people who need to use debt in this way because they have no other choice. If you've been lucky enough to personally evade or solve the systemic issue of underearning, then you're also lucky enough to use debt as leverage instead of out of desperation.

In perfect circumstances, people use money, not credit, to purchase things they need on a regular basis, instead of using debt and hoping the harvest will cover what's owed. This approach allows us to consciously and strategically use debt as a more effective tool. When debt is used to finance something that will increase in value in the future, debt is being used as a tool. Let's call this smart debt.

Some examples of using smart debt are taking out a business loan to grow your business revenues, a mortgage to buy a home and student loans to get an education. You hope your business will grow and become more valuable with funding. You hope that in thirty years, your home will have increased in value. And you hope access to education will improve your employment prospects.

## HOW DEBT IS COMMONLY CATEGORIZED

Some forms of debt are considered better than others. But since the nature of debt is paying what is owed, deciding which category of debt is better than another is like having to choose between the following:

- being punched in the face in exchange for a cupcake you already bought and ate four weeks ago;
- being kicked in the crotch in exchange for being able to drive a car to work; or
- being thrown down a flight of stairs each month, but you own the flight of stairs and the house attached to it.

# THE DEBT MATRIX

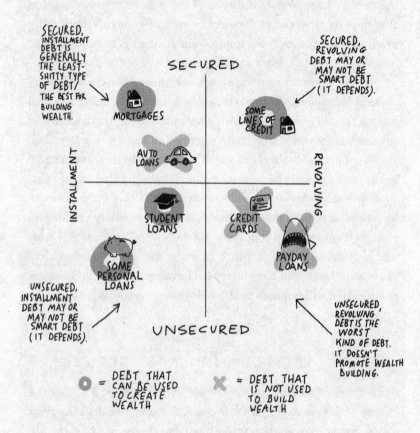

SECURED, INSTALLMENT DEBT IS GENERALLY THE LEAST-SHITTY TYPE OF DEBT/ THE BEST FOR BUILDING WEALTH.

SECURED, REVOLVING DEBT MAY OR MAY NOT BE SMART DEBT (IT DEPENDS).

SECURED

INSTALLMENT

REVOLVING

MORTGAGES

SOME LINES OF CREDIT

AUTO LOANS

STUDENT LOANS

CREDIT CARDS

SOME PERSONAL LOANS

PAYDAY LOANS

UNSECURED

UNSECURED, INSTALLMENT DEBT MAY OR MAY NOT BE SMART DEBT (IT DEPENDS).

UNSECURED, REVOLVING DEBT IS THE WORST KIND OF DEBT. IT DOESN'T PROMOTE WEALTH BUILDING.

⊙ = DEBT THAT CAN BE USED TO CREATE WEALTH

✖ = DEBT THAT IS NOT USED TO BUILD WEALTH

## Secured or Unsecured Debt

Secured debt is any debt backed by an asset (something of value) as collateral. Collateral makes lending less risky for the lender and often results in a lower interest rate. If the person who borrows money cannot pay it back, the lender can seize the collateral, sell it and use those proceeds to pay back the debt. A car loan is a good example of secured debt. Unsecured debt has no collateral. Student loans and medical debt are examples of unsecured debt because they can't seize your education or the medical procedures you've had.

## Revolving or Installment Debt

When you borrow money classified as revolving debt, you usually have a maximum amount that you are allowed to borrow, but you are not obligated to borrow it. A credit card is a common example of revolving debt. The interest rate, like the monthly payment, may fluctuate depending on how much you've borrowed and paid back. There is not a set number of payments that must be made to pay off the debt. With credit cards, you can be in debt forever. Credit card debt that you can't keep up with has the potential to be the Hotel California of debts: you can never leave. Non-revolving loans are installment loans. Installment loans allow you to borrow a fixed amount of money and pay it back in installments over time.

## Would You Rather Be Punched in the Face or Kicked in the Crotch?

In general, here are the types of debt ranked from the least-worst to the criminal.

■ **Secured, installment debt is the least-worst kind of debt.** Mortgages fall into this category. They're the best of the worst because your payments go towards "building equity"—increasing the value of your home you actually own. As a borrower you can still get screwed, but the collateral is available if you can't make your payments. A car loan is usually secured, installment debt, but the value of your car goes down over time, technically making it a bad investment. See how the category of loan matters, yet it's not the only thing that matters when considering borrowing money?

■ **Unsecured, installment debt is the second worst (tied with secured, revolving).** Medical debt is typically unsecured, installment debt. Student loans fall into this category and we've seen over the last many years how some people took out this kind of loan in an attempt to ensure their job prospects in the marketplace. We've also seen how that investment hasn't paid off for a lot of folks the way they imagined it would. Which demonstrates that the cost of the loan and the return on its investments are things to consider when borrowing money.

■ **Secured, revolving is tied for second worst.** A good example of this type of loan is a home equity line of credit that allows you to borrow any amount up to a maximum amount. And the value of your home is collateral for the line of credit.

■ **Unsecured, revolving is the worst.** Credit cards are unsecured, revolving debt. Credit cards are great if you use them and pay off your balance each month. When you can't pay off what you've borrowed each month, unsecured, revolving debt can become a slippery slope precisely because the debt is both unsecured and revolving. Since its revolving, the limit of how much you can borrow can change, making it easy to borrow more than you can afford. Since its unsecured, you'll have a higher interest rate, which makes borrowing more expensive. When you aren't borrowing against an asset, all you have is the liability.

■ **Payday loans are in a category all their own: trash can fire in hell.** Payday loans are a deal with the devil. You borrow money that you must pay back in full in a very short amount of time—like a few weeks—and you borrow the money at a very high interest rate. Payday lenders are legal loan sharks who prey on people who are desperate and oftentimes unable to access other forms of credit.

They are criminal and designed to trap people in debt. Knowing that this kind of lending was created to be a Band-Aid for larger systemic issues makes me cringe for being part of a humanity that would necessitate this invention in first place.

Looking at debt categorically can help you understand the mechanics of how borrowing works. This is especially important when you are considering the decision to borrow money. The decision to borrow money considers the type of debt, whether the debt is something one can afford, and the cost of the debt compared to the potential wealth it can help you build. We'll explore these things more in depth in the following chapters.

## KNOW THE EMOTIONAL TOLL OF DEBT

Dealing with debt can cause you to have mental health issues or exacerbate preexisting mental health problems. Dealing with debt may also make you feel better. But before you feel better, the act of dealing with your debt might first make you feel worse. If you're predisposed to mental health issues or anxiety, you should consider how your debt may impact or is impacting your mental health and well-being. It might seem counterintuitive to spend money on therapy and counseling if you're in debt, but there are affordable options, like a clinic that charges on a sliding-scale or working with almost-licensed professionals who are finishing their last year of school.

### Reframe Debt

- What's an early memory you have of debt?
- What story or rules did you create because of that memory?
- Write a different story about that memory.
- If you are or have ever been in debt and have felt shame and guilt because of it, write a letter to your debt. Express your feelings; you'll see that they are complex. Consider thanking your debt for what it's allowed you to do. Check out Deardebt.com for some examples and inspiration.
- Is your debt impacting your mental health? If so, what are some things you can do or places to find support?

**CHAPTER 10**

# How Credit Scores Work and How to Play the Game

I'm fascinated and weirded out by credit scores. These three-digit numbers help lenders judge the likelihood that they'll get paid back. Our scores determine our creditworthiness. Yes, a system of scoring that we can't really opt out of if we ever want to borrow money, rent an apartment or, in some instances, get a job will determine whether or not we are worthy of credit.

The modern system of credit scoring we know and begrudgingly participate in today originated in 1956 with the company Fair Isaac. The company was founded by Bill Fair and Earl Isaac. These two white dudes came up with a systematic way to predict lending outcomes and to grade credit risk by giving it a FICO score. FICO is short for Fair Isaac Company. The company developed and still tightly controls the algorithm that weighs different factors and determines your credit score.

If you follow the logic of why we use credit scores, they seem to make sense: lenders need to trust that we'll pay them back. But the system encourages the use of debt, which presents a conflict of interest for the agencies that regulate them. The trick with credit scores is that we as individuals are not the customers. Yes, kids, just like with social media, we are the product. Surprise!

The lenders and creditors that let individuals borrow money are the customers. The credit bureaus, also called credit reporting agencies, sell our information for a fee to lenders and creditors. Then these lenders and creditors use this data to determine whether or not they will lend to us and at what cost. From the credit bureau perspective, what better way to ensure a revenue stream than to ensure that a high credit score relies upon having multiple lines of credit? We have to pay to play. And the more lines of credit you apply for, the more your score is reviewed, and more fees go to Fair Isaac and other credit reporting agencies.

Credit scores could be viewed as a tool to level the playing field by making creditworthiness a math problem. The algorithm might make computing risk easier but it doesn't take into account circumstances outside of our control. It's very black and white. A missed payment is a missed payment is a missed payment. It doesn't matter if you got too sick to work or used the money for your loan payment to play one hand of blackjack. Regardless of what caused a misstep, redemption from a misstep can take a long time. If someone loses their job and can't make their payments, they are punished with a lower credit score and those defaults remain on their report for seven years.

This way of credit scoring can create a system where people in poverty who most need access to credit get penalized for being in poverty. Folks in poverty rely on credit, but the financial precarity of poverty means you're also likely to default or to apply for new credit more often. Both of these things negatively impact credit scores, which make it harder to access the credit these people need access to.

When it comes to economic and racial inequities, this system of credit scoring highlights an existing, upriver problem. It shows how a legacy of racist policies that made it hard for brown and black folks to access credit created a cascade of other issues, like having to turn to predatory lenders.

Reforming the credit scoring system is an upriver problem that involves fixing both the incentives that drive credit agencies and the fact that so many people need access to credit for daily living. I know it seems like a lot when you get a 50,000-foot critical view of all the flaws within a system. Sometimes the best thing we can do is understand that being critical is a great first step in the journey of addressing these big systemic issues. What's also true is that until that happens, we still have some agency to impact our credit. There are still things within the circle of control.

## DON'T GET TOO CAUGHT UP

Before we get into the details of keeping a healthy credit score, I think it's important to remember not to obsess over it. A number that you can use to compare yourself to others is easy to fixate on. If you haven't given your score a lot of care in the past, the road to redemption might be long, but there is a road. Try to find the balance between realizing your agency to impact your score and understanding that the overall system has mismatched incentives and could stand to be improved.

I can understand why folks fixate on credit scores: it's like a grade in school. But remember, while a score is tangible, it's not as valuable as other immeasurable things. Things like how awesome your creative pursuits are or how much your spouse loves you. If you start to get too weirdly obsessed, remember that it's just a tool for our silly modern world that two random dudes made up a long time ago and it matters, but so do other things in our lives. What helps me feel less attached is looking at my credit like playing a game.

## PLAYING THE CREDIT GAME

Learning how to play the credit game is important because it impacts to what degree you'll be able to do the following:

- Rent an apartment or house
- Have the water and power on turned at your apartment or house
- Get a cell phone
- Buy a car
- Buy a house
- Borrow money to finance a large purchase or start a business

## WHAT IS A CREDIT REPORT VERSUS A CREDIT SCORE?

Your credit report is a history of all the instances that you used credit or borrowed money. Your credit score is a three-digit grade based on an algorithm that measures your credit risk and credit worthiness based on the information in your credit report.

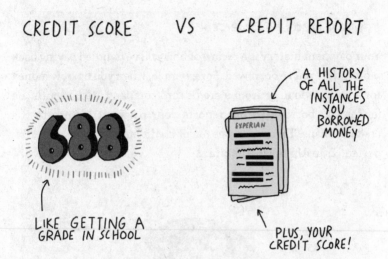

CREDIT SCORE VS CREDIT REPORT

A HISTORY OF ALL THE INSTANCES YOU BORROWED MONEY

EXPERIAN

LIKE GETTING A GRADE IN SCHOOL

PLUS, YOUR CREDIT SCORE!

## HOW IS YOUR CREDIT SCORE CALCULATED? IT'S MOSTLY A SECRET.

Figuring out how it's calculated is like trying to crack Coca-Cola's secret recipe. The elusiveness lies in the fact that the actual calculation is not public information and can and has changed over time. What we do know is that the calculation consists of five different elements, and the weight or level of impact each element has. While the calculation does change every now and then, these five elements have consistently and historically been the most important factors in determining one's credit score. So with that half-disclaimer, you can always see if and how these factors have changed by visiting MyFico.com.

At the time of writing this, the categories and their weighted impact are payment history (35 percent), credit utilization (30 percent), length of credit history (15 percent), new credit (10 percent) and type of credit used (10 percent).

## Payment History—35 percent

Your payment history is a record of how you've handled paying back money that you've borrowed. For example, when you borrow money for a student loan or from a credit card company, each month the lender you borrowed from reports your payment history to the credit bureaus. There are three major credit bureaus in the U.S.: Experian, TransUnion and Equifax.

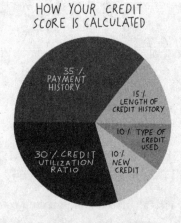

HOW YOUR CREDIT SCORE IS CALCULATED

35% PAYMENT HISTORY

15% LENGTH OF CREDIT HISTORY

10% TYPE OF CREDIT USED

30% CREDIT UTILIZATION RATIO

10% NEW CREDIT

### Quick History:
### Why Are There Three National Credit Bureaus?

In the U.S., three big national credit bureau companies have the most clout. Back in the day, there were many smaller companies. The smaller companies were regional, each one only serving their respective markets in the West, Midwest, South and East. Over time the big three began to scoop up and acquire smaller credit reporting agencies, eventually covering enough territories that they became national.

Even though the big three are the major players, dozens of smaller, specialty credit reporting agencies still exist for different markets.

The big three report differently because some lenders may report credit activity to only one bureau. Some companies may report to all three, but the data could appear different simply due to the fact that the data is compiled at different times.

At the time of this writing, the Biden administration has expressed the possibility of reforming credit reporting by creating a public reporting agency. We won't know the details until reforms become law, but even with changes, it will still be important for each of us to understand how scoring works and impacts our lives.

Since approximately 35 percent of your credit score is made up of your payment history, missing even one payment can have a huge impact. The impact is also long lasting. Missing or late payments stay on your credit history for up to seven years.[1] But the upside is, once you start making your minimum payments regularly, over time that late payment impacts your score less and less.

## When Does a Late Payment Get Reported?

Usually the company you are borrowing money from reports your credit payment history every thirty days and they generally only report payments that are late by at least thirty days. That means if you're two days late on a credit card payment, it's more than likely that you'll get a late fee, but your credit score will not be negatively impacted until you're at least thirty days late on the payment. If you miss your payment two months in a row or for sixty days, you'll get reported twice: once for being thirty days late and then again for being sixty days late.

### Credit Utilization Ratio—30 percent

Your utilization ratio is how much of your total available revolving credit you're using compared to how much revolving credit you have available. One important thing to note is that your credit utilization rates are solely based on revolving credit. Revolving credit are credit cards or lines of credit. Installment loans like a mortgage or student loans are not included in your utilization ratio. Sometimes the credit utilization ratio gets called debt utilization ratio. They're the same thing and here's how you calculate it:

**The total credit balance ÷ Your total available credit =
Your credit utilization ratio**

When you multiply that ratio by 100, you'll get it expressed as a percentage.

CREDIT UTILIZATION IS LIKE THE
AMOUNT OF GAS IN THE TANK
RELATIVE TO THE TANK'S CAPACITY.

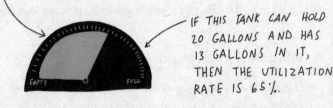

IF THIS TANK CAN HOLD
20 GALLONS AND HAS
13 GALLONS IN IT,
THEN THE UTILIZATION
RATE IS 65%.

$(13 \div 20) \times 100 = 65\%$

Let's imagine your credit card limit is $1,000 and your balance is $300. Your credit utilization ratio is 0.3 or 30 percent. In general, the lower the ratio, the better your credit score will be. A good rule of thumb is to keep a credit utilization ratio below 30 percent.

You want to make sure your utilization rates are below 30

percent for each card and for all your credit cards combined. For example, if you have a total of two credit cards that have a combined balance of $2,500 and a combined available credit of $25,000, then in that moment, your credit utilization ratio is 10 percent. ($2,500 ÷ $25,000) x 100 = 10 percent.

Since credit bureaus are in the business of grading you based on your behavior with credit, it makes sense that the amount of credit you have has an impact on your score. If you max out your credit cards or regularly maintain a high utilization ratio, it could be the symptom of a larger problem: your income is not able to keep up with your debt payments. If you can't afford your current debt, from a lender perspective, this makes you less desirable to keep lending money to. This lack of creditworthiness translates as a lower credit score.

One thing you can do right now to increase your credit score is to ask your credit card companies for a higher limit. But, of course, with a greater limit comes greater responsibility. If having a higher limit is not something you can trust yourself with right now, you might want to only increase the limit on credit cards that you can put a spending cap on, wait until you feel like you can trust yourself a bit more or make sure you are keeping your balances below 30 percent each month.

## Length of Credit History—15 percent

The longer you have a good credit history, the better. Two people who have never been late on a payment aren't comparable if you don't consider the length of time. Someone who has never been late over the course of twenty or thirty years seems like a safer bet than someone who has never been late for only one year. Consistency is key.

If you have been credit card averse for many years, you can incorporate using a card for some of your regular spending. Start off really simple and try using a credit card for your utilities and groceries. This shouldn't disrupt your spending plan too much, but it will require you to do the admin work of setting up bill pay for your new credit card.

I always recommend applying for a credit card with a bank you already have a relationship with. Especially if you don't have credit history and you're just starting to build your credit and learn how to use credit cards.

## New Credit—10 percent

When you apply for new credit, it does bring down your score temporarily. I can understand the behavior that the credit agencies are trying to encourage by doing this. They don't want people applying for new credit all the time because with access to too much credit, there is the risk of borrowing too much. Just because I understand the incentives doesn't mean it's less weird though.

Financial constraints can cause people to apply for credit more often than those who aren't as strapped for cash. Each time one applies for credit, each inquiry results in one's score getting dinged a bit. If this sounds like people in poverty get penalized for being in poverty, it's because that is 100 percent true, unfortunately. Even if the intention wasn't to penalize folks in poverty, the result actually does.

But if you're shopping around for a mortgage or car loan, don't sweat the inquiries that much. The credit rating agencies will be able to piece together the narrative and see what's happening and your score should recover once the shopping process is complete and you've locked in a loan. The window to do this rate shopping in order to impact your credit as minimally as possible is anecdotally reported as fourteen to forty-five days. Again, all this credit report stuff is very cloak and dagger, so if you'd like to err on the side of being conservative, use the fourteen-day window. What this means is if you'd like to see what two or three different lenders will offer you for an auto loan, apply for them all within the same fourteen-day window to minimize how much it will impact your credit score. And within this same fourteen-day window, abstain from applying for other types of credit if you can.

If you are a regular person, as opposed to the kind of person who spends hours gaming the credit card points system, you probably don't need to be applying for new credit. Stick to your credit cards for years at a time. If you stop using your cards, don't close them, but keep an eye on the activity by running your credit report every quarter and reviewing it. Sometimes enough time passes and the credit card company eventually closes them.

## Type of Credit Used—10 percent

In terms of your credit score, debts that have fixed terms—a fixed payment, over a fixed period, at a fixed rate for a fixed amount—are considered better forms of debt than a credit card. These kinds of fixed debts are usually loans. Loans typically have a lower interest rate than credit cards and if you make all your payments on time, you'll pay it off. There is a path to payoff, which is why it's considered better, as opposed to credit card debt, which is something you can carry for years, or decades even.

## WHAT'S NOT IN YOUR CREDIT REPORT

Your credit report will only have information on your debts. And the lenders have to choose to report to the bureaus, which most do. But I mention this because if you've had a loan from the Bank of Grandma or some other family member, those things won't be on your credit report. Checking accounts, savings accounts and your investments are not things that get reported to the bureaus.

## WHAT'S A GOOD SCORE?

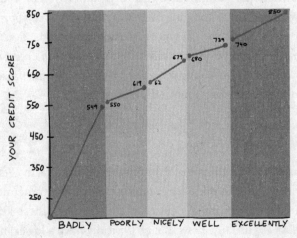

Your credit score is both a carrot and a stick. An average to above-average score is rewarded with lower interest rates and better credit and debt options. And below-average scores are punished with high interest rates and crappy credit and debt options. Your score can end up costing you or saving you thousands of dollars.

For example, take two different people who want to borrow $200,000 in the form of a thirty-year fixed mortgage. Let's say that Jaime has a credit score in the highest range, between 760 and 850, and they qualify for a mortgage at 3.307 percent. Charlie, with a credit score in the lower range, 620 and 639, qualifies for a rate of 4.869. At these rates, each month Jaime pays $184 less than Charlie for their mortgage payment. Over the life of the loan, Charlie ends up paying $66,343 more than Jaime.

Rebuilding your credit can take a while, especially if you have some missteps that are currently keeping it out of the excellent range. Don't sweat it too much. Time heals all wounds; it can also do wonders for your credit score.

## Know Your Credit Score

☐ **Review your credit report to make sure it's accurate.**
**By law, you are entitled to one free copy of your credit report per calendar year. Order online from annualcreditreport.com, the only Federal Trade Commission (FTC) authorized website for free credit reports, or call 1-877-322-8228.**

**Alternatively, some banks like Capital One offer free credit score monitoring. See if your bank offers free monitoring.**

☐ **Review your credit report at minimum every three months. You want to review your credit report to make sure you aren't a victim of fraud. As much of our lives exist online, and data breaches become a normal part of life, keeping an eye on your credit report can ensure that you get errors fixed as soon as possible. The last thing you want is a surprise when you're applying for credit!**

- **Set up a recurring event in your calendar or enter future review dates into your analog planner.**

- **When you review your credit report, make sure you recognize all of the loans and credit cards on your report.**

- **If you do have an error, the FTC website has the steps you can take to correct an error.[2]**

*DO THE WORK*

**CHAPTER 11**

# How to Get Out of
# Credit Card Debt

In the U.S., having credit card debt is seen as pretty normal. This is unfortunate for many reasons. First, it's a financial stressor. It's like what smoking does to your body. Smoking alone can harm you, but it can also make other things worse because it's a stressor. With a credit card, even if you do your best to keep up with payments, when a financial or economic shock happens—and it will—the credit card debt is an added stress. Second, credit card debt is risky. High interest rates and minimum payments mean that the debt can grow indefinitely. This means you can literally be in credit card debt forever.

## HOW DID WE GET HERE?

Credit cards are a relatively new technology that have allowed humans to do what they were already doing, but on a scale that's faster, larger and more anonymous. It's like how email helps us do more of what we were already doing: we were already communicating, but email helped us do it faster, somewhat anonymously and at a larger scale. Social media did this too. We've been comparing ourselves to one another for ages. Remember, this adaptive evolutionary trait in humans is a feature, not a bug. But now we can compare ourselves on a faster, larger and somewhat anonymous scale.

Credit today looks very different from the alehouses in Mesopotamia thousands of years ago. Before credit cards, people borrowed and lent to one another. It was person-to-person transactions. Today when we use our credit cards, we're borrowing from a giant, faceless corporation. It's a very efficient system, but the question is, should it be so damn efficient to borrow money?

Before credit cards, using credit was done more out of necessity.

For example, farmers would receive seeds on credit. They'd turn those seeds into a harvest and use it to pay back what they borrowed, plus interest. Today, we still have purposeful borrowing like this. Small business loans and student loans operate on a similar premise. But unlike purposeful loans, credit cards were meant to encourage consumption of goods beyond what was necessary. Some of the early cards were coinlike tokens and paper cards that were issued by a store. Think of it like a frequent buyer card, but instead of getting your tenth frozen yogurt free, you used it like a credit card specifically for that store. This encouraged customer loyalty and consumption.

Of course, culture played a role too. The use and demand for credit cards grew with the mass production of consumer goods. Banks started to issue credit cards that could be used at stores within a few blocks of one another. But it wasn't until Bank of America's efforts to promote widespread credit card adoption that it became widely acceptable and normal to use in our society.

In September 1958, Bank of America decided to conduct an experiment in the town of Fresno, California. They sent out 60,000 already activated, unsolicited credit cards to consumers. These cards had a $500 limit, which may or may not seem like much today, but in 1958, a daily newspaper would only set you back about seven cents.[1]

This stunt became known as the Fresno Drop, and as you can imagine, pre-activated cards in the mail meant this was like Christmas morning for fraudsters. Despite its hiccups, the stunt worked. Ten months later, Bank of America had mailed out over a million credit cards all across California. Eventually, legislation caught up that made it illegal to send unsolicited, already activated credit cards to consumers. The Bank of America credit card, called Bank-Americard, became Visa. And the rest is, as they say, history.

You already know the story of how Edward Bernays invented modern marketing and advertising and how that has fueled our desire to endlessly accumulate things. Fast forward to 2019 and more than 70 percent of Americans adults have at least one credit card and the U.S. as a whole has about $900 billion in credit card debt.[2] Are we simply spending more and using our credit cards because the credit and the consumer goods are available? Kind of.

Since the 1970s, several studies have supported the anecdotal suspicion that credit cards encourage spending. In 1979, Elizabeth Hirschman, a prominent theorist in marketing and economics, conducted surveys of customers shopping in several branches of a department store and found that folks who had a store-issued credit card spent more than folks who used cash, and the folks who possessed the most credit cards spent the most.[3] Multiple studies have shown that restaurant tips are larger when patrons pay with card instead of cash.[4] These studies also reveal that credit cards don't just encourage us to purchase more things. When we pay with a credit card, we are also willing to pay a higher price for any given item. It's a double whammy for consumers and a double win for consumerism.

## TRANSACTIONAL DECOUPLING

One simple reason that explains why credit cards make us liberal spenders is because there is no immediate pain associated with using a credit card. Your checking or savings account balance doesn't go down when you swipe. And whatever cash you have in your wallet remains in your wallet. Credit is an anesthetic that numbs the pain of spending.

Our human brains are bad at valuing future things. Tomorrow's pain of having to pay is hard to compare to the pleasure of today's purchase. Just like credit scores, credit cards are not inherently bad. But what they do is highlight and exacerbate existing inequalities on both an individual and societal level.

## CREDIT GIVES US A DELUSIONAL
## SENSE OF SATISFACTION

Individuals can use credit as a balm to feel better off than they really are. When you can still buy necessities or luxuries, albeit using debt, you still feel satisfied without actually earning the income to support your purchases. You can fake it until you make it. As long as you're feeling content, regardless of your progress, you may not feel the need to change anything in your life, like your job or how you're spending.

THE DEBT DELUSION CYCLE*

YOU USE DEBT TO BUY THINGS YOU CAN'T AFFORD

IT FEELS LIKE YOU CAN AFFORD THINGS YOU CAN'T

\* NOT PICTURED : WAGE STAGNATION, UNDER EMPLOYMENT, UNEMPLOYMENT AND MORE!

As long as consumers rely on debt to buy things, companies don't have to change their behavior either. Owners and shareholders can continue to keep workers' pay down while benefiting from their labor. It's a double win for companies because they can get away with unsustainable wages, yet they can still sell their products and services to the very people who can't afford them so long as they have credit. It's really an incredible bubble of denial that we have constructed. This contributes to why it's become normal to be underpaid and overleveraged. It's never just one cause—remember how everything is connected and interwoven.

So, if you are in credit card debt, you already know that it's important to get out of it. You already know that it's expensive, it's stressful and that paying interest is keeping you in a bad situation or making it worse. The energy that goes towards debt management is energy that can't go towards your relationships, your creativity, and your joy. I'm not mentioning all of this to make you feel bad about your debt. What I want you to feel is a sense of urgency.

How would you react to a small trash can fire in your room? You'd probably not be able to ignore it, because it can get out of control real fast. And you'd probably act urgently and swiftly to minimize the damage. And most importantly, once it's snuffed out, to the best of your ability, you'd probably make sure the circumstances that caused it can't cause it again.

Credit card debt is this small trash can fire in the corner of your room. Let's deal with it swiftly and urgently before it gets out of control. Let's make a plan to get the hell out of credit card debt. Before we tackle the practical steps, let's consider some nonpractical aspects of this process that will impact the actions you decide to take and the ones you're afraid to.

## BE WILLING TO BE UNCOMFORTABLE AND DO THINGS YOU'VE NEVER DONE BEFORE

Getting out of credit card debt will require change. Circumstances can change; you can earn more or consolidate your debt. If we assume circumstances might remain fixed, then the things that you can change are your ideas, attitudes and behaviors. Changing any one of these things will require you to be uncomfortable at times.

Bending who you are, what you believe and how you act so that it can work within the constraints of a system is an uncomfortable thing to do. Going from being the person who only pays the minimum payment each month to being the person who pays two or three times that amount requires you to first make that decision and then to figure out what needs to change to support that decision. Continuing to choose that decision consistently might also be challenging and uncomfortable. Remember: the path of progress is one where each new level is met with a new devil. And getting past it means constantly revising how you think, what you believe and how you act.

## ACCEPT RESPONSIBILITY FOR THE POSITION YOU'RE IN

One of the first uncomfortable things you might consider doing is deciding to take responsibility for the position you're in, regardless of how you got into that position. Accepting responsibility for your debt does not mean that you are accepting fault. When you take responsibility, you get to choose how you'll feel, you get to find where and how you have agency in the situation. These are all ways to take your power back and to act within your circle of control.

Throughout our lives, we'll continue to find ourselves in situations where we are not at fault, but we have to take responsibility. People will misunderstand the intentions behind our words, but in order to come to an agreement both parties must take responsibility. Your kid might bite another kid at school. Even if the other kid started it, it's not just your kid who has to take responsibility; as a parent, you do too. This is life. Even when we are victims, taking responsibility for our feelings can be the first step to transforming them.

SOMETIMES DEALING WITH DEBT REQUIRES US TO TAKE RESPONSIBLITY FOR THE POSITION WE'RE IN ...

EVEN IF THE CIRCUMSTANCE OR SITUATION IS NOT ENTIRELY OUR FAULT

Consider looking at your credit card debt like a position you are in or a circumstance you're experiencing. Shit happened; conditions may have backed you into a corner, but to get out of that corner, you have to first accept responsibility for the position you're in.

## 1. Find Your Why and Stay Connected to It

There are a lot of forces at work that would prefer you overconsume and stay in debt. Fighting against this is hard. Doing hard things requires us to face challenges, make sacrifices and change ourselves because we cannot change our circumstances. Not everyone wants to do this, and I understand that choice. Since you're still reading, my guess is you're up for the challenge.

Find a reason why doing this hard thing matters. And throughout this process, stay aligned with the reason why you want to get out of debt. Remembering why can help you stay focused on it.

Write about your why, think about your why, print out your why on a little card and put it in your wallet. Whatever you do, stay connected with your why.

## 2. Stop the Digging: Consider Taking a Break from Using Your Credit Cards

I'm not suggesting you never use them again. But for now, how can you ensure that your attempt at getting out of credit card debt will be long-lasting? Does using your credit card create the right environment for what you're trying to accomplish? Or is it wise that you and your credit have a cooling-off period so you can take the time to focus on paying off what you owe?

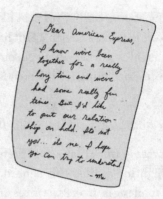

After you're feeling like you're more in control of your debt, then you can decide if you are able to be in a relationship with credit cards that works for you. If you started using credit cards without really thinking about it, like I did at eighteen, you might not have really made an informed decision to use credit cards because you were still so young and trying to figure out what's best for you. Now you can give yourself the opportunity to reflect on your experiences, take into account what's best for you and truly decide.

### 3. Know What You Owe: Make a List

Making a list helps you understand what the hell you're dealing with. It gives you the lay of the land so you can wrap your head around the situation. It's the first piece of putting together a plan.

Here's what should be on your list:

- Name of the lender (who you owe the money to)
- Total amount you owe (principal)
- Interest rate you are paying (APR, or annual percentage rate, stated as a percentage)

- Minimum monthly payment. Look at the total number here too because you might need to pay more than if you have high-interest credit card debt.

- Type of debt (credit card, student loan, personal loan). Even though this plan is geared towards credit card debt, you can also include your other debts so you can see it in context and relative to all your debt.

- Reference your credit report to double-check your list.

## 4. Explore Your Payment Plan Options

Even if you only have one credit card to pay off, I think it's still important to create a game plan for how you'll eliminate the debt. How much will you need to pay each month and for how many months? You are in essence creating a payment schedule like an installment loan.

To map out a payment schedule, you'll want to use a tool to do the calculations for you. My favorite is a free, web-based tool called Unbury.me. It is pretty simple and straightforward to use. Here's how:

- First, load the debt details from the list you just made into Unbury.me to begin analyzing what repayment options you have.

- Use this sliding lever at the bottom of the payment plan section to choose how much you are paying each month towards all your debt. The tool will give you payment plan options based on whether you want to pay back the highest interest first or lowest balance first.

- You can use similar tools too, like a spreadsheet or app that does these kinds of calculations. The underlying math is all the same! Cool, huh?

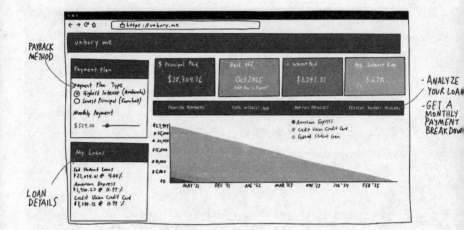

## Paying Down the Highest Balance or Higher Interest Rate First?

Paying back the highest interest rate first will probably save you the most money in interest, so that seems like the "smartest" and most rational option. But paying the lowest balance first, despite the interest, has psychological benefits. Seeing that debt disappear may boost your confidence, motivate you to keep going and show you what you're capable of accomplishing. When you completely pay down a balance to zero, it's like watching the basketball go through the hoop; you feel a sense of accomplishment. Even if it costs more to prioritize paying off the lowest balance over the highest interest rate, the confidence you build to keep you going might end up being more valuable in the end.

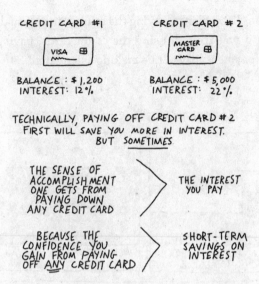

CREDIT CARD #1

VISA

BALANCE : $1,200
INTEREST: 12%

CREDIT CARD #2

MASTER CARD

BALANCE : $5,000
INTEREST: 22%

TECHNICALLY, PAYING OFF CREDIT CARD #2
FIRST WILL SAVE YOU MORE IN INTEREST.
BUT SOMETIMES

THE SENSE OF
ACCOMPLISHMENT
ONE GETS FROM
PAYING DOWN
ANY CREDIT CARD

> THE INTEREST
YOU PAY

BECAUSE THE
CONFIDENCE YOU
GAIN FROM PAYING
OFF ANY CREDIT CARD

> SHORT-TERM
SAVINGS ON
INTEREST

## The Minimum Payment Is a Trick

While using the Unbury.me tool, you'll quickly learn that if you want to shorten the time it takes to get out of credit card debt, you must pay more than the minimum monthly payment. If you can, always pay more than the minimum. No matter what strategy you choose to make credit card debt disappear, you must pay more than the balance due.

The minimum payment was supposedly created with good intentions. It offers consumers flexibility when they need it by allowing them to pay only a minimum amount. However—the minimum payment is a trick. Only paying the minimum is like falling down a trapdoor only to emerge owing more than you ever planned to borrow. Different credit card companies use different formulas for calculating what your minimum monthly payment is. In most cases, you can expect the monthly payment to be between 1 and 3 percent of the total balance. So if you're accruing double-digit interest on a four- or five-digit balance, paying the minimum only makes a small dent. And if you are still using the credit cards, paying only the minimum payment may not be making a dent at all.

HERE'S HOW A CREDIT CARD'S MINIMUM PAYMENT IS A TRICK

TOTAL BALANCE

THE WATER IN THE PITCHER IS YOUR TOTAL CC BALANCE.

WHEN YOU MAKE A PAYMENT, YOU POUR OUT SOME WATER.

BUT WHEN YOU DON'T PAY THE BALANCE YOU'RE CHARGED INTEREST.

THAT'S MORE WATER ADDED TO THE PITCHER.

FRESH INTEREST

ONLY PAYING THE MINIMUM PAYMENT KEEPS YOU IN DEBT LONGER AND RACKS UP INTEREST.

THAT'S THE TRICK!

## 5. Make Sure Your Plan Is Reasonable

Use the tool to explore your options. Given how much you are currently paying, how long will it take you to get out of debt? Is that a reasonable time frame for you? If it is, then it sounds like you just need to choose a payment plan and stick with it.

What would make your pay-off plan unreasonable? The time frame might be much longer than you are willing to accept because you need to get out of debt faster. The monthly payments you are making aren't sustainable because it leaves you with too little to spend, to save and to breathe. The interest that you'll end up paying by the end is something you are not willing to accept as the cost for getting out of debt.

Whatever reasons make your payback plan unreasonable, here are some other payback options: You can cut your expenses or increase your income and redirect that money to pay down your credit card debt. You can negotiate a lower interest rate with your credit companies. And you can look into consolidating or refinancing your credit card debt. Let's double-click on these options.

## Cut Expenses

If you think you still have ways you can reduce or optimize your spending, revisit your spending plan. If you haven't made the grab for low-hanging fruit, maybe now you could. Call your cell phone company to see if there is a cheaper plan you could be on or set up a meal train with some friends where each night one person cooks for everyone.

Cutting expenses and using that money to pay down credit cards is often the quickest way to start attacking your debt because you're diverting funds you already have. This only works if you are being paid a wage that supports your living expenses, including your debt. And it continues to illustrate why I am such a proponent of focusing on the other side of the financial equation: income, the other lever you can pull.

## Seriously Increase Your Income

In the same way that cutting your expenses is within your circle of control, so is increasing your income—even if it might be hard to believe, there are definitely things you can do to impact your income. Some things, like negotiating pay, are relatively easier to do than other things, like starting a business. As I mentioned in Chapter 5, getting good at earning requires your willingness to experiment with ideas or within different environments.

In fifth grade, I had a really awesome science teacher. He taught us the scientific method for pursuing knowledge: first, make an observation, then ask a question, do research, come up with a hypothesis, test it, gather the data, analyze the data and arrive at a conclusion. I view earning money and running a business through the lens of the scientific method. One awesome benefit of this kind of thinking is that it creates distance between my personal feelings about my worth and my pay. It forces me to think about my self-worth in a context divorced from my pay. For example, when a client doesn't want to pay our bookkeeping rates, I can observe the outcome and analyze the data and conclude that being rejected is not a reflection of my worth. Sometimes it's simply a misalignment of values or that the company is not the right size, so it doesn't economically make sense for them to engage us.

If you would like to accelerate getting out of debt by increasing your income, what kinds of income-increasing experiments can you run? If you're within the environment of traditional employment, can you run a negotiating-pay experiment? If that's a question you'd like to form a hypothesis around, the first step would be to do some research on negotiating. You can find a MasterClass that offers general negotiation techniques from a professional negotiator who worked for the FBI. You can also find coaches that specifically help women of color negotiate higher pay or specifically help engineers in the tech industry. As you craft your hypothesis and begin to run your negotiating-pay experiment, your research will help you understand the different variables you need to consider.

We each have to find our own paths in this uncertain world, but we can look at what other people have done to inform, educate and inspire our own experiments. It might feel frustrating that there aren't exact steps you can take to increase your income, but when there is more than one path, then there is more than one way to win. For some folks, increasing their income happens naturally as their career progresses over time. Other folks, like myself, might try their hand at hacking their own path. Whichever method you choose, whatever experiments you run, I hope you'll find a way to appreciate the process.

## Negotiate a Lower Interest Rate on Your Existing Credit Card Debt

It is possible to call your credit card company, ask them for a lower interest rate (APR) and have that request granted. The real question is, is it probable? There is only one way to find out and that's by asking. Even if you can afford your debt, you should do this anyway.

Here are some tips for getting on the phone and doing this.

- **Don't be a dick.** I've worked in a call center for a bank. And when customers called in and they were dicks right off that bat, I didn't want to help them. Maybe you already know how to be a pleasant person in society, maybe you already know that it's easier to catch flies with honey than with vinegar. Maybe you already know that there is a human being on the other end of that line who deserves to be treated like a human being. Maybe you know all this but your frustration with your debt makes you act unsavory. I get it. But take a beat, get into your window of tolerance, do a grateful flow or whatever you need to do to compose yourself and don't be a dick to the person who can help you.

- **Use what little leverage you have by making it seem like the competition can win your business.** Know that the employees' job is not to give you a lower interest rate. You can't simply ask for a lower rate. You have to set the stage for your ask.

When you go into the call, start by mentioning that you have been a customer for however many years and that you want to remain a customer. But a competing card company has offered you a much better interest rate, you can even say a 0 percent balance transfer option for twelve months. And you're seriously consider taking the offer.

Sometimes the person on the other end of the line will help you and try to lower your rate and sometimes they won't. It's still worth asking. If the first person doesn't grant your request, you can always call back to see if you can persuade a different representative. And you can do it the same day or a week later. You might get better the more you try. And the more you try, the likelier you are to succeed.

I've done this style of negotiating with cell phone companies and cable companies. It's worked with credit card companies for many people. When I was getting out of credit card debt, I didn't negotiate lower interest rates because I refinanced my credit card debt into a loan so that I could pay much less in interest. This is a great option, but the challenge with refinancing or consolidating is that you often need good credit to be approved.

## Explore and Understand Your Refinancing and Consolidating Options

Refinancing your credit card debt is in essence having another lender pay off your debt, then paying back this new lender for paying off your debt. It does sound a little bit like robbing Peter to pay Paul, but if you do it correctly, it's effective. Consolidation is when you take more than one debt and combine them into one single loan.

Consolidation and refinancing usually only make sense if you can accomplish one of two things. You either lower the amount of total interest you'd pay or lower the monthly payment amount. Accomplishing one of those things will usually allow you to go from "Wow, this debt is totally unmanageable" to "Yeah, this sucks, but there is a light at the end of the tunnel."

When it comes to your consolidation and refinancing options, you can consider a family, friend or even employer loan. You can apply for a personal loan. And the last resort option, which opens you up to a lot of risk, is playing the balance transfer game.

### Option 1: Refinance with Someone You Know

If you're privileged enough to have a family member like a parent or a rich Uncle Paul or even an employer that would be willing to refinance your credit card debt, then I would seriously explore that option.

Financing with someone you know is typically the lowest cost of all loan options. There is no loan origination fee, you can ask for a lower rate or flexibility in making payments, there are no applications and no credit score required. But beware of the psychic tax, the emotional cost or how this will impact your relationship. If the person you borrow from is not the person you want to owe money to because they'll hang it over your head in messed-up ways, like making passive-aggressive comments about buying something new, then it might not be worth it.

Tips for navigating this gracefully:

- Offer the person you're borrowing money from an interest rate. Look at what high-yield savings accounts are currently offering. Consider offering an interest rate slightly above this as a way to make your offer attractive. The assumption here is that if they keep the money in savings as opposed to lending it to you, they make less money because of a lower interest rate.

- Give them loan terms and make a contract. It doesn't have to be super formal, just something in writing. Lay out the amount you'll borrow, the number of payments, the interest rate and the monthly payment. Hint: Unbury.me can help you create the payment plan.

- Set up an automatic payment to make sure you keep up with the payments.

- Before you borrow the money, ask or determine what the process should be if you need the flexibility of skipping a payment.

### Option 2: Refinance or Consolidate with a Personal Loan

Your relationship with your family or their financial circumstances might make a loan from them a non-option. You may consider a personal loan through your bank or credit union. This is a great option if you have a solid credit score and if you're committed to being out of credit card debt.

With a personal loan, you turn your unsecured, revolving credit card debt into unsecured, installment debt. There is a clear path to paying it off. Unlike a credit card, you can't keep borrowing more than what you've borrowed for the loan. However, it means your credit card will have a zero balance and the opportunity to rack up more debt. The option to get a personal loan can be a lifeline. It can be a second chance and a fresh start. It's a form of privilege and luck. And you need to be committed to overhauling your relationship with your money and your credit card in order to reap the long-term benefits.

There are other lenders that specialize in personal loans and refinancing credit card debt. All lenders will have different fees, rates and terms, so you'll need to do your due diligence to understand what your options are. Knowing how to look at these kinds of loans is something we'll cover in the next chapter.

There have been newer companies popping up that specialize in refinancing credit card debt, like Payoff.[5] SoFi is a company that originally came on the scene to help refinance student loan debt, but now they offer personal loans.[6] For people who have trouble with traditional lenders, there are also peer-to-peer lending options like Lending Tree and Prosper.[7]

More often than not, personal loans carry fees of 1 percent to 6 percent, called origination fees. So you might end up paying less by simply tackling your existing debts in a systematic way, rather than consolidating.

### (Not a Great) Option 3: Balance Transfers

A balance transfer is when you transfer your credit card balance to another credit card with a low promotional rate, usually 0 percent. Balance transfers can work well for people who are really disciplined, but it's also a slippery slope because you end up with more credit cards. This could be tempting, and you may end up in more debt if you don't actually address the underlying circumstances and behaviors that got you into debt. A balance transfer can be a good stepping-stone. You can take advantage of a promotional period of 0 percent interest to pay down your debt entirely or it can set you up to get a personal loan to manage the rest.

There is almost always a balance transfer fee. The balance transfer fee is a percentage of the balance you're transferring. For example, if you want to transfer $8,000 and there is a 3 percent balance transfer fee, that fee is $240 ($8,000 x 3 percent = $240).

## 6. Know When to Seek Professional Help

If going through these options makes you come to realize that you cannot afford your debt or will not be able to in the foreseeable future, you might want to seek professional help to deal with your credit card debt. Here are some dos and don'ts about seeking professional help:

### Dos[8]

- Seek assistance from debt management nonprofit organizations.
- Make sure the organization's credit counselors are certified.
- Check to see if the company you want to work with is certified with the National Foundation for Credit Counseling.[9]
- Make sure the fees are reasonable and get quotes from comparable organizations.
- Find out if the company is bonded and licensed to do business in your state.

### Don'ts/Avoid

- A for-profit private company's goal is to make a profit. That is not a great goal for a company that is supposedly trying to help you get out of debt. For-profit private companies make money off of their customers. Nonprofits often get funding from the government, foundations and donors.

## SOME CLOSING THOUGHTS ON CREDIT CARD DEBT

*Take the Time to Understand What Circumstances Led You into Debt*

Did you start a business? Did you lose your job? Did you buy a bunch of junk you shouldn't have? Did you just not care? Have you been underearning for too long and the debt was a way to make ends meet? Everyone's circumstances are different, so each person must understand theirs. If you have credit card debt, how did you get there? Why did it get there?

Knowing the circumstances that got you to where you are now is important because if you are going to try to change them, you have to know what they are first. Once we can identify these things, we can begin to understand the choices we made.

If there are circumstances that have been outside of your control, maybe the solution is to ask a different question. Come at the problem from a different angle. Remember the ways of thinking and circumstances that got you into debt will probably not be the same ways of thinking and circumstances that will get you out of debt.

For some, it's asking for help from people who can afford to help. For others, it's finding ways to get around the circumstance that has been standing in their way.

If you don't think your debt is a result of your choices but instead of your circumstances, it might be hard for you to come up with a plan to pay it off because you don't feel like it's within your control. But in order to get out of debt, you do have to look for what's within your circle of control and choose to have agency over those things. If you want to change your situation, you might have to do things you've never done before.

Addressing your credit card debt allows you the opportunity to call attention to the underlying issues—to get to the root of the problem and solve it there. Because using credit cards to bridge the gap to afford anything—whether it's essentials like food or shiny objects that you don't need—is a symptom of a larger issue. It might reveal things that are unfair, individually and societally, but only then can our work begin.

## Commit to Being Consistent

Working through your debt is an opportunity to build your mental fortitude. It's a chance to commit to something and show up for yourself. Life will have its struggles. Some folks with lots of good fortune might be able to keep the struggle at bay for a long time, but eventually something will happen, and they will struggle. We'll all experience loss and pain and the whole spectrum of not-great feelings. Some folks may experience struggle early on and, oftentimes, they're then better equipped to deal with stress later on. It's not a contest about who struggles more or worse. It's just a given that we'll all struggle.

It might seem crazy, but it's possible to embrace opportunities to struggle. It will teach you things about yourself. It'll make you face yourself. It'll challenge you. It will help you build the mental fortitude for another situation where you'll have to struggle.

You will not get out of debt if you don't commit to the actions that will get you there. You might have to forgo dinners out with friends or have frank conversations about splitting the bill. You might have to make hard decisions about where you live and who you live with. Facing your debt might make you blow up other areas of your life. Part of why I avoided facing my underearning was because I knew the truth meant I had to change things I would rather avoid than face. Changing things is scary. It's so much easier dealing with the devil you know.

But being in that kind of denial is unsustainable. Once you start to face these hard things, it does get easier to face hard things. This is how folks build resiliency. And resiliency is an essential quality for coping with the uncertainty of being a human on Earth navigating the modern economy.

**To stay the course, know what works for you.** Maybe listening to podcasts about eliminating debt will keep you on track. You could join a community of other people who are trying to get out of credit card debt. You could print out your payment schedule and hang it in your room. It could be staring at your cute baby's face for ten minutes a day to keep you inspired. Find what works for you to keep you going.

**Know your debt-free date.** Once you're committed to a pay-off plan, you'll have the date of the final payment. Commit this date to memory, put in on a calendar and use it to help you stay the course.

## Make a Plan to Get Out of Credit Card Debt

DO THE WORK

☐ **Spend some time unearthing your why. Why is it important for you to get out of credit card debt?**

☐ **Stop digging yourself into debt: seriously consider taking a break from using your credit cards. It sounds super silly to write a letter to your credit cards telling them you need to take a break, but if silly leads to getting out of debt, then who cares?**

☐ **List out your debts**

☐ **Explore payback plans**

- Sign up for Unbury.me (or a comparable app)

- Enter your debt details, including your payment information

- Decide on a payment plan for your debt

  - Highest interest first

  - Lowest balance first

  - Some other strategy

☐ Reflect on whether or not this plan is reasonable. Will you get out of debt in a reasonable amount of time? Is the total interest you'll end up paying a reasonable amount of interest? Is the total amount you pay in monthly payments sustainable?

☐ If your plan is unreasonable, don't worry, you have options: take a moment to journal, come up with ideas, express yourself, etc.

- Review your spending plan and find ways to divert spending from your Bills & Life or Fun & BS towards paying down debt. Have you explored all the low-hanging fruit?

- Can you dedicate energy to increasing your income?

- Call your credit card company to negotiate a lower interest rate.

☐ Explore your options for consolidating or refinancing your debt. Research your options and compare what's available.

- Can you get a friends, family or employer loan? What are the non-financial costs that come with this?

- **Can you apply for a personal loan from a bank, credit union or similar lender?**

- **Is the risk of playing the balance transfer game worth the potential payoff?**

Once you've decided on your path and plan to getting out of credit card debt, write it out in detail. What is the date you'll be credit-card-debt free?

**CHAPTER 12**

# To Borrow Money or Not to Borrow Money?

## How to Think About the Debt Decision

*The essence of finance is time travel. Saving is about moving resources from the present into the future. Financing [through borrowing money] is about moving resources from the future to the present.*

—Matt Levine[1]

Thinking about debt as an incredible, time-traveling tool not only makes the world of finance seem much cooler than it actually is; it can help us understand the reality of borrowing money. Whenever we borrow money today, we're taking money out of the pocket of our future selves.

THE TIME-TRAVELING MAGIC OF BORROWING MONEY

Under the right circumstances, the trade-off is worth it. This is the idea behind "smart" debt. The hard part is being able to determine if the trade-off will be worth it. Conceptualizing the impact of taking on debt is like thinking about your money in another dimension—a future dimension with unknown variables. Without perfect information about the future, like what job you'll have or if you'll have to support family members, it makes this decision challenging.

I've seen my fair share of ways that borrowing money didn't pay off as expected. I've met people with a quarter million dollars in student loan debt with no viable strategy to get out of it except to aim for the fences and hope for the best. I've sat across the table from clients who bought a home at the peak of the housing bubble only to make the tough decision to walk away from it in the years following the 2008 crash. I've listened to immigrant parents that borrowed money from their retirement accounts to help their children afford a college education at reputable institutions, only to not be able to afford to pay themselves back. For almost all of these people, they did what they "were supposed to do," but still ended up more financially screwed than they could've imagined. They banked on the best-case scenario without considering the worst possible outcome.

So how do you plan for the worst while expecting the best? Without seeing into the future, there is no way to truly ever know if we are making the absolute best decision given the circumstances we are forced to exist in. The next best thing is to have a systematic way of making the decision to go into debt. We can do that by looking at debt through four filters: what you can afford, how debt may impact your future wealth, how much a lender can screw you (the terms of borrowing) and knowing if the true cost of paying back the debt is worth it to you. The big assumption about using this framework is that you are making the decision to go into "smart" debt in order to build future wealth and not to consume things in the present.

## CAN YOU AFFORD TO PAY BACK WHAT YOU BORROWED?

The first filter in deciding if you should take on debt is whether or not you can afford to pay it back each month. When you're trying to figure out how much debt you can afford, do not blindly trust the companies that are trying to lend you the money to tell you what you can afford.

I don't think people who make a living selling borrowed money to other people are bad people. I just know that it's their job and for many, there is a commission involved. So there is an incentive to get you to borrow money. That's how the system works. Not just in theory, but in reality. Remember my crappy telemarketing job? It gave me a front seat to sales folks making false assumptions about what a potential borrower could afford.

Knowing how much you can afford is like wiping your butt. For the majority of your able-bodied life, it is your job to wipe your own butt. It's not a fun job, and while folks whose job it is to sell you a loan will try to do this job for you, they're not going to do as good of a job as you will, because it's your butt that's on the line, not theirs. Ultimately, it's your responsibility to determine for yourself how much you can afford in monthly debt payments.

When you decide you'd like to borrow money in the form of a mortgage or student loan, the first thing to determine is how much you'll need to borrow and how much you'll need to pay back each month. It doesn't matter how valuable the thing you are borrowing might be in the future if you can't afford to pay for it in the present.

First, do research to find what you think the total cost of what you're financing is and how much of that cost will need to be borrowed. A simple online loan calculator can help you understand what your monthly payment will be for your loan. Bankrate.com has a simple loan calculator and specific calculators for different kinds of loans.[2] You can also download a premade spreadsheet if you want to build out different borrowing scenarios and compare payments and terms.

Once you have a general idea of what your monthly payment will be to pay back what you've borrowed, revisit your spending plan to determine how affordable that payment is. What does that additional payment do to your personal economics? Does it mean you have to find where to divert spending to make your personal finance equation balance? Once again, the need to balance this personal finance equation points to either diverting how you spend money or increasing your earnings. Time and again, it becomes hard to ignore that having some control over being able to increase your income is a way to have agency over what you can afford to borrow. It's a different approach to solving the problem of affording debt, and while it might not be right for everyone, I wouldn't be doing my job if I didn't highlight it.

If you're considering a student loan and you aren't sure what you'll be earning once you graduate, you'll have to do some research to find out what entry-level salaries for your chosen field and job are. Then you can create an imaginary spending plan based on where you think you'd live and all the associated costs with that living scenario. Why this exercise isn't a mandatory one for high schoolers baffles me. Another way to determine how much your monthly loan will cost you and if it's affordable is by looking at your debt-to-income ratio.

## USE THE DEBT-TO-INCOME RATIO (DTI) AS A RULE OF THUMB

When lenders want to lend you money, they don't ask to see your spending plan to make sure you can afford it—although I wish they would. They use a ratio called the debt-to-income ratio as a rule of thumb for how much a person can afford in monthly debt payments relative to their income. The debt-to-income ratio is meant to reveal how much of your monthly income, expressed as a percentage, goes to paying your debts.

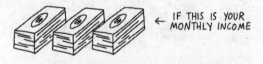

THE DEBT-TO-INCOME RATIO IS A WAY TO UNDERSTAND HOW MUCH OF YOUR INCOME GOES TO PAYING YOUR DEBT

← IF THIS IS YOUR MONTHLY INCOME

← AND THIS IS HOW MUCH OF YOUR INCOME GOES TOWARDS PAYING BACK YOUR DEBT,

THE DEBT-TO-INCOME RATIO IS A WAY TO COMMUNICATE THAT USING A RATIO, WHICH IS JUST ANOTHER WORD FOR PERCENTAGE.

Here's how you calculate your current DTI ratio:

1. Add up your monthly debt payments including credit cards, loans, and mortgage.

2. Divide your total monthly debt payment amount by your monthly gross (before taxes) income.

3. The result will be a decimal, so multiply it by 100 to solve for your DTI percentage.

4. After you know your current DTI, you can go back through steps 1 through 3, but add in the additional monthly payment for the cost of the loan you are considering taking on.

HOW A LENDER VIEWS YOUR
DEBT-TO-INCOME (DTI) RATIO

| 0% | 15% | 40% | 100% |

YOU'RE A GREAT PERSON TO LEND TO. A SAFE BET.

YOU'RE A GOOD PERSON TO LEND TO. A GOOD BET.

IT MIGHT BE RISKY TO LEND TO YOU. LENDERS ASSOCIATE A HIGHER DTI WITH A HIGHER RISK OF PAYING LATE OR NOT PAYING AT ALL.

Here's how to understand what this ratio means. A debt-to-income ratio of up to 15 percent is considered a healthy amount of debt because it assumes that a person using 15 percent of their monthly income to repay debts won't struggle to make payments.

CAN YOU AFFORD TO BORROW MONEY?
THE THREE LENSES OF AFFORDABILITY

Lenders generally prefer that borrowers have debt-to-income ratios lower than 36 percent. However, there are some cases where mortgage lenders will still lend money to people with DTIs as high as 43 percent.[3] Every lender is different and every borrower has their unique circumstances. These rules of thumb might skew a little depending on different factors. But as a general rule, the lower the DTI, the better your chances of getting approved for a loan.

If your DTI is too high, you might consider seeing how borrowing less money, if that's an option, impacts your DTI. Try recalculating your loan payment with your loan calculator.

I just want to reiterate a few of things about DTI. Remember that it's a tool for lenders, the ratio is based on your income before taxes instead of after taxes and even if a lender approves your loan, it's not a guarantee of affordability. This is why it's important to look at your spending plan to make the personal decision about what you think you can afford each month.

## DEBT-TO-ASSETS RATIO: HOW YOUR WEALTH IS IMPACTED BY BORROWING MONEY

Another ratio that lenders use to determine how much debt you can afford is called your debt-to-assets ratio. Assets are cash, investments or other valuable things that can be turned into cash. The debt-to-assets ratio measures how much of your assets were financed with debt.

Here's how you can calculate your debt-to-assets ratio:

1. Add up the total dollar amount of all your debts. (These are things like the entire balance of what is owed on any loans and credit cards.)

2. Add up the total dollar amount of all your assets. (Assets are all the money in your checking and savings accounts, the value of your investments, including retirement, any real estate you own or other valuable things that can be sold for cash.)

3. Divide the total from number 1 by the total of number 2. (Dollar amount of debt you owe ÷ Dollar amount of assets you own = Debt to asset ratio.)

4. The result will be a decimal, so multiply it by 100 to solve for your debt-to-assets percentage.

5. After you know your current debt-to-assets ratio, you can go back through steps 1 to 4, but add in the additional debt for the loan you are considering taking on.

A ratio of 10 percent or less is a very healthy debt-to-assets ratio. A good rule of thumb is to keep it under 30 percent. A ratio over 50 percent is considered high and risky. A higher debt-to-assets ratio means that you owe a lot relative to what you have. The higher your ratio, the more at risk you are of not being able to afford to pay back your debt if your financial situation changes.

If the amount of money you'd like to borrow would put your debt-to-asset ratio above 50 percent, consider the risks of borrowing. Manipulating the ratio to make it healthier comes from either having less debt (borrowing less or paying down debt) or having more assets on hand (increasing the value of your cash balances, savings or investments balances).

Once you have determined that you can afford the monthly loan amount and you understand how taking on debt impacts your wealth, you'll probably start looking at lenders and loans.

## HOW DO LOANS WORK? WHAT'S IN A LOAN?

When you use smart debt, you'll borrow money in the form of a loan, not credit cards. With all loans, there are always these factors that are also the details of your loan:

- The amount you borrow (principal)
- The cost of borrowing (the interest rate or APR)
- The length of the time you'll pay the loan back (the loan term)
- And the monthly payment

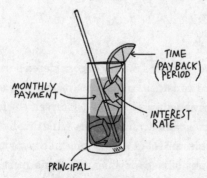

A LOAN IS LIKE A COCKTAIL

TIME (PAY BACK PERIOD)

MONTHLY PAYMENT

INTEREST RATE

PRINCIPAL

MANIPULATING ONE ELEMENT IMPACTS THE OTHERS

All of these factors impact one another. Think of it as a cocktail. There's the ice, the liquor, the mixer and the garnish. Changing one element of a cocktail will change the drink; it's just a matter of how material each change is. Once again, there are plenty of loan calculators that you can find online, like apps for your phone or spreadsheets you can download to help you play around with how these various factors impact one another.

When you shop for a loan, refinance debt or choose a repayment schedule for student loans, these calculators are very helpful so you can understand the trade-offs you're making. For example, if you stretch out a repayment plan, you might end up paying more interest while lowering the monthly payment.

And yes, you should shop for loans, the same way you shop for a new camera or car or whatever thing you geek out over. Shopping around with various lenders and banks could save you hundreds or even tens of thousands of dollars over the life of a loan. Don't just go with the first lender that wants to lend you money. Find out who else is willing to lend you money and compare their offers. You might even be able to pit these lenders against one another so that you can get the best deal possible.

### Keep an Eye Out for Lenders Trying to Get Cute with Your Loan

Whenever I have borrowed money or considered borrowing money, especially what I consider large sums for things like education or for expanding my business, I always ask myself the following question: How can the bank screw me over with this loan? That might sound cynical, but for folks who belong to groups that have been oppressed or marginalized for generations this question is a healthy way to think critically about the reality of borrowing money. As much as it is an opportunity for you to borrow money, it's also an opportunity for the bank to make money off of you. When you take out a loan, knowing how much you can afford is a good first step. The next thing you want to be aware of is knowing when the bank is trying to get cute with your loan.

In general, the best kind of loan is a boring one. One that lays out exactly what you need to pay each month for a fixed number of months so that at the end of those months, you owe nothing. This is installment debt, where each payment is a fixed amount. Each payment pays down a portion of what you borrowed (principal) and the cost of borrowing (interest). And your last payment is not a huge sum (unless you can afford to pay a huge sum). Examples of loans like this are the plain-vanilla, classic thirty-year fully amortized mortgage or a five-year fully amortized auto loan.

## LOAN PAYBACK SCHEDULE

| ANNUAL INTEREST | 7% |
| LOAN TERM (YEARS) | 2 |
| PAYMENTS PER YEAR | 12 |
| LOAN AMOUNT | $50,000 |

| PERIOD | PAYMENT | PORTION OF THE PAYMENT THAT GOES TOWARDS INTEREST | PORTION OF THE PAYMENT THAT GOES TOWARDS PRINCIPAL | BALANCE |
|---|---|---|---|---|
| 1 | $2,238.63 | $291.67 | $1,946.96 | $48,053.04 |
| 2 | $2,238.63 | $280.31 | $1,958.32 | $46,094.72 |
| 3 | $2,238.63 | $268.89 | $1,969.74 | $44,124.98 |
| 4 | $2,238.63 | $257.40 | $1,981.23 | $42,143.74 |
| 5 | $2,238.63 | $245.84 | $1,992.79 | $40,150.95 |
| 6 | $2,238.63 | $234.21 | $2,004.42 | $38,146.54 |
| 7 | $2,238.63 | $222.52 | $2,016.11 | $36,130.43 |
| 8 | $2,238.63 | $210.76 | $2,027.87 | $34,102.56 |
| 9 | $2,238.63 | $198.93 | $2,039.70 | $32,062.86 |
| 10 | $2,238.63 | $187.03 | $2,051.60 | $30,011.27 |
| 11 | $2,238.63 | $175.07 | $2,063.56 | $27,947.70 |
| 12 | $2,238.63 | $163.03 | $2,075.60 | $25,872.10 |
| 13 | $2,238.63 | $150.92 | $2,087.71 | $23,784.40 |
| 14 | $2,238.63 | $138.74 | $2,099.89 | $21,684.51 |
| 15 | $2,238.63 | $126.49 | $2,112.14 | $19,572.37 |
| 16 | $2,238.63 | $114.17 | $2,124.46 | $17,447.92 |
| 17 | $2,238.63 | $101.78 | $2,136.85 | $15,311.07 |
| 18 | $2,238.63 | $89.31 | $2,149.31 | $13,161.75 |
| 19 | $2,238.63 | $76.78 | $2,161.85 | $10,999.90 |
| 20 | $2,238.63 | $64.17 | $2,174.46 | $8,825.44 |
| 21 | $2,238.63 | $51.48 | $2,187.15 | $6,638.29 |
| 22 | $2,238.63 | $38.72 | $2,199.91 | $4,438.38 |
| 23 | $2,238.63 | $25.89 | $2,212.74 | $2,225.65 |
| 24 | $2,238.63 | $12.98 | $2,225.65 | $0.00 |

A fully amortized loan that you can afford and that will help you build future wealth is an example of smart debt. It's a loan that has a payment schedule where both the principal and the interest get paid down over the life of the loan. As long as you pay all those payments, you will pay off your loan. The word *amortization* has the word *amort* in it, which is derived from Vulgar Latin *admortire*, meaning *to kill*. With a fully amortized loan, you are in essence killing the debt over time.

Fully amortized loans tend to have the least amount of potential to screw people over. I say least because you could still get screwed with a high interest rate, with loan fees or with unfavorable terms—for example, a huge penalty if you can't make one or miss payments.

Two types of cute loans are interest-only or adjustable-rate loans. These kinds of loans can be useful for people or businesses who can afford a lot of risk. An interest-only loan is a loan where you only pay the interest for a fixed period of time and then at the end of the loan or for another fixed period, you will have to pay back what you borrowed plus interest. Why does this even exist? It's a cheap loan for people who might buy and sell houses—think people who flip homes. They have a short window to pay only interest and they sell the house before they have to pay back what they borrowed. These kinds of cute loans might be appropriate for you once you understand how they work and fit into your personal financial situation. Until then, think of them as an advanced tool. You first want to master the basics of loans and master your own understanding of your personal financial situation before you use these advanced tools.

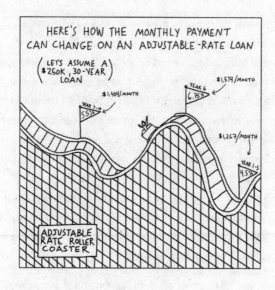

An adjustable-rate loan is a loan whose interest rate can fluctuate based on the market. Adjustable-rate mortgages (ARMs) seem attractive when interest rates are low because a low interest rate impacts the monthly payment. However, if interest rates go up, so will your payment. Rates might go so high that you can't afford your payment each month. This is what happened to a lot of people leading up to the 2008 housing crisis. They were sold subprime loans, which are a type of high-cost loan with an adjustable rate. But when interest rates went up, many of those folks couldn't afford the payments at the new interest rate.

Subprime loans have been disproportionately sold to minorities and low-income communities. Lenders and banks see minorities and low-income communities as higher-risk borrowers, meaning they are worried about getting paid back. So they charge higher interest or they create lending products that are designed to make a profit regardless of whether or not the product is designed to fail. This is fucked up and ends up being expensive for all of society.

This is why you must be vigilant. You need to be able to spot when a lender or bank is trying to steer you into a type of loan that is not appropriate for your financial situation, or when lending practices are predatory and racist. Unfortunately, when we cannot always rely on government oversight to protect us as consumers, the next best thing we can do to arm ourselves against falling victim to these lending practices is learning how to examine our lending options.

Here's a set of questions to ask yourself when you are offered money to borrow or refinance your current loan.

1. Is the thing I'm going to buy with my borrowed money likely to be worth more than what I'll pay for borrowing it? Is this smart debt or debt for consuming things that will be worthless after I've consumed them?

2. What are the terms of my loan (amount borrowed, interest rate, payment amount, term, down payment)?

3. What is my repayment schedule that shows what I need to pay each month to pay back this money and owe zero dollars at the end? Can I afford this repayment schedule?

4. Will I pay interest and principal with each payment? (Is it fully amortized?)

5. Do I pay interest on just what I borrow or do I pay interest on the interest too? (Is the interest simple or compounded?)

6. If I make all my scheduled payments, will I owe any additional payments at the end of my loan?

7. If I don't make all my scheduled payments, will I owe any additional payments at the end of my loan? What is the maximum amount that I would owe as a balloon payment? IS IT INFINITY DOLLARS? If the answer is yes, you might owe infinity dollars, strongly reconsider how much of a risk you're taking. Can you find another angle?

**8.** What happens if I can't repay this money? What options would I have?

I know this seems like a lot of work, but this is the type of education privileged folks get just by having parents and grandparents who randomly drop this knowledge on them during a road trip to a vacation house. This is how they are taught to think about borrowing money so they don't get screwed by the system, but instead leverage it to create more wealth. This is how they make something from nothing, literally.

## HOW DO YOU FEEL ABOUT DEBT?

| IT'S AN AWESOME TOOL | IT CAN BE A GREAT OPPORTUNITY | IT HAS ITS MERITS | IT'S RARELY THE BEST OPTION | I'M SCARED TO USE IT |

## IS BORROWING MONEY RIGHT FOR YOU?

Doing the math to decide whether or not you want to borrow money is actually the easy part. The hard part is when the math stares back at you and you need to decide if it's something you want to do. This is a very personal decision. When deciding whether or not debt is right for you, remember to use second-order thinking to explore the consequences beyond the first domino.

## Borrowing Money Costs Life Energy

Borrowing money costs money, but making money requires your life energy. When you go into debt, it's important to know how much paying back borrowed money will cost you in life energy and if it's worth it. One way to know whether or not borrowing is worth it is to know yourself really well. What do you want for your life? How will debt impact that?

The person who wants to surf all day and work a catering or bartending job in the evenings will probably not feel any need to take on any debt whatsoever. Comparatively, the person who doesn't care so much about what their day to day is like as long as they get to party their face off in Las Vegas every month will probably feel fine about having student loans as long as they can afford their Vegas lifestyle. In fact, they might require student loans to ensure a salary that can afford bottle service. The person who wants to have a family and own a nice home in the suburbs and drive the carpool on Tuesdays will probably feel really content that they are using smart debt to create wealth and a life for their family.

Using debt to build wealth is like drinking red wine for your health. Mind the guidelines and recommendations. Proceed with caution.


## Use This Tool: Body Compass

In recent years, scientists have begun seriously studying how our bodies can *think* and the link between the body and the brain.[4] Our emotions might get labeled as residing in our brains, but to a large extent we feel our emotions in our body. Being able to read these signals in our body can help us co-regulate in stressful situations and they can even help us work together to feel calm or to heal. Have you ever just needed a hug or needed to give someone a hug?

Our bodies contain a lot more knowing and wisdom than our modern culture and society has previously acknowledged.

So how can knowing this about your body help you navigate financial decisions? You can tap into what your body is feeling to help you understand what you truly desire. In other words, connecting with your body allows you to listen to your intuition so you can find answers to hard questions like, "Should I change careers?," "Do I really want to go to law school?," "Am I resistant to buying this nice mattress because I think I don't deserve the things required to take care of myself?," and so on and so forth.

This tool, coupled with second-order thinking, will give you a holistic, pragmatic approach to making financial decisions.

Another one of my coaches taught me the body compass exercise, which was originally created by Martha Beck. The exercise consists of two separate exercises where you bring up old memories, one at a time.

1. First, bring up a negative memory. Get into the memory and get into the feelings that come up. Then take the time to scan your body from head to toe and name the sensations you're feeling. You might feel your shoulders tense. You might feel your palms sweat, heat on your face and chest, your heart race, energy in your belly and a constricted throat. You might feel heavy. You might feel weighed down. You might feel full of tension. Just name these feelings and notice them.

2. Then do the same thing but with a positive memory. Recall it. Get into the feelings and scan your body. You might feel a sense of calm, you might feel your belly breathing deeply, maybe you feel butterflies. You might feel yourself smiling and feel generally airy, light, peaceful and full of an energy that feels good. Once again, name and notice these sensations.

One benefit of this exercise is that you can show yourself you are able to control how you feel by just conjuring up a memory and tapping into those sensations.

The other way to use this information is when you need to make decisions. Ask yourself a question, imagine the various outcomes one at a time and sit with the feelings of those outcomes. Feel those sensations and name them. Try it with small things, like what you should have for dinner, and with bigger questions, like is this project something you truly desire. I understand that sometimes we have to make decisions based on needs and not wants. But knowing our wants in the face of needs can help us strategize how to bridge the gap.

## The True Cost of Debt

- What's your debt-to-income ratio?
- What is your debt-to-assets ratio?
- Besides the interest you pay, what does having this debt cost you?
- Are there things you would like to use your life energy on instead?
- What does being able to use debt allow you in your life? If you don't have any smart debt, reflect on what it would allow in your life.
- How does your smart debt allow you to use your life energy in ways that you value? If you don't have any smart debt, reflect on what it would allow you to use your life energy on.
- If you are planning to use smart debt to create future wealth, map out the details.

DO THE WORK

## CHAPTER 13

# Spend a Long Weekend with Your Student Loans

*In many ways, student debt is the new herpes. Almost everybody has it. It stays with you your whole life. And eventually, you're gonna have to tell your fiancé about it.*

—Trevor Noah

The first time one of my clients needed help navigating their student loans, I had already worked a handful of different financial services jobs. I was pretty used to navigating financial websites and internal platforms, and had a degree in finance, but when I logged in to see all the loans, it took me a while to understand what I was staring at.

I am lucky and privileged to have avoided the grisly fate of having student loan debt. Strangely, what helped me avoid massive debt was my complete naivete in navigating college applications and, frankly, my lack of ambition. But there were two things that really helped me: old-fashioned good luck and my parents. They paid for the first year that I attended a state university in California and the next couple of years after I dropped my major and went to community college while I figured out what the hell I was supposed to do with the rest of my life.

After two years at a relatively affordable community college, where my parents paid for my classes at the cost of $18 per unit, I transferred to Cal State, where the costs were 90 percent more expensive than community college. But I once again avoided bad luck and stumbled into a fortunate situation. When I transferred, I also started working at a huge bank that you may have heard of called Bank of America. The bank had all sorts of employee benefits, from paid vacation and sick days for part-time workers to a program called tuition reimbursement.

Here's how the program worked. The bank would reimburse their employees for the cost of their tuition, up to a certain amount, if the classes we took were at what they deemed to be a qualified school and for what they deemed to be qualified courses. We also had to earn at least a B or higher to get reimbursed. Since I was at a state school and all my classes were in business, finance and economics, I qualified for the program. I just needed to get B's and my state college tuition would mostly be paid for.

When it was time to enroll in my first semester at the state college, I charged the few thousand in tuition costs on my credit card. This decision was both risky and stupid, but this highlights a few important points. First, that twenty-year-olds making decisions to borrow thousands of dollars might not go all too well. Like so many young people, my college decisions were ill-informed and not necessarily financial. Instead, the decision to take on long-term student loan debt is often impacted by things like the normalization of debt, familial expectations, societal pressure and the very real need to get an education because of how much it impacts what an employer is willing to pay you.

The second point it illustrates is that dumb luck played an important role in my financial future—as it still does. Of course, it doesn't mean that I didn't have to be responsible, earn my B's and stay employed. Luck and skill both matter.

As I write this, President-elect Joe Biden has yet to take office and therefore his plan to address the dumpster fire that is the student loan crisis has not been implemented. I know it's naive to dream that this chapter on student loans will be irrelevant in the near future. Even with the potential of unconditional loan forgiveness up to a certain amount, reforms to make the loan forgiveness program actually work and the prospect of free college education for folks who cannot afford it, there will still be debt associated with going to school.

Not everyone's family will be able to pay for a college student's living expenses like mine did. Not every student will have been like me, gainfully employed by a generous employer while working towards my degree. A lot of students may also be supporting family while simultaneously earning a degree. Hopefully in coming years, legislation will be enacted to help ease the burden and drastically reduce the amount of money students borrow to go to college. While a lot can potentially change for future borrowers, there is still the matter of everyone who already borrowed the money.

If you're navigating student loan debt, the best thing you can do, like so many things in the world of personal finance, is arm yourself with knowledge. Get to know your student loans the way you'd get to know someone you're dating—very intimately.

For instance, nothing puts a relationship under a microscope like a long weekend trip or a vacation. When you are forced to constantly be in close quarters and to troubleshoot stressful situations with a person for the first time, you get to know that person more than you otherwise would in normal life.

You get an uninterrupted, front-row seat to their neuroses and idiosyncrasies. You'll observe their scheduling perspectives, how they respond to adversity and emergencies, how they adapt to change, what their priorities are, how they budget and how they see the world. When you learn all of these things, it might solidify your desire to be with this person or it might reveal that your values and differences create a divide too big to cross together.

You have to get to know your student loans in this very intimate way. You need to know how your loan terms will impact your big life events, like what options you have if you're unemployed or underemployed for a period of time. You need to know when refinancing is something you should consider or if it's totally not right for you. Your student loans are a part of your life until they aren't, so getting to know how they work can help you navigate them as you reach your life's milestones.

GET TO KNOW YOUR STUDENT LOANS THE WAY YOU
GET TO KNOW YOUR PARTNER ON A TRIP

WHAT ARE YOUR OPTIONS IF OR WHEN YOU CAN'T MAKE PAYMENTS?

WHO IS YOUR LOAN SERVICER?

KNOW THE TYPE OF LOAN YOU HAVE. FEDERAL, PRIVATE, FIXED RATE OR VARIABLE.

Spend the time learning about your loans now. It's a preemptive move, so you'll know what your options are if and when you need to explore them. Options give you a feeling like you have a choice in the matter, which makes you feel like you have some freedom.

Lots of people feel as if student loans are something that just happened to them, like they signed some paperwork not really knowing what they were committing to. Sadly, that's normal. While getting into debt may have felt like a non-choice, now is your opportunity to actively choose to be educated and engaged with your debt. It's a way to take responsibility for the position you're in, regardless of how you got into that position.

## KNOW WHAT KIND OF LOANS YOU HAVE

Before you can look closely at what your options are, you first have to know what kind of loans you've got.

Do you have federal loans or private loans? Federal loans are issued by the government or a bank or financial institution on the government's behalf. They generally have lower, fixed-interest rates and eligibility for federal programs like income-based repayment plans (IBR) and loan forgiveness. What kind of federal loan do you have? There are direct subsidized loans, direct unsubsidized loans, direct PLUS loans and federal Perkins loans, to name a few. Different types of loans will have different eligibility requirements for federal relief. Knowing what requirements your loan programs are subject to starts with first knowing exactly what kind of loans you have.

To add another layer of complication, it's possible to have more than one type of loan. Making sense of the type of loans you have now can eliminate surprises later. For example, if you know when and why one of your loans would be treated differently than another although the circumstances are the same, you can try to plan for that contingency during a recession or an inevitable financial shock.

Private loans are issued by financial institutions, which means their terms and rates can vary compared to federal loans. With private loans you might have to start paying them back back sooner than federal loans, like when you're still in school. Private loans aren't regulated by the Department of Education the way federal loans are.

## KNOW WHO YOUR LOAN SERVICER IS

While you determine the kind of loan you have, you'll also likely uncover who your loan servicer is. If you haven't, that's next. The lender that you originally borrowed money from might not be your loan servicer. Although the federal student loans are issued through the government, the actual servicing of the loans is sometimes contracted out and handled by a loan servicer. Servicers handle the banking and administrative functions on behalf of the government and it's possible that your servicer changes throughout the life of your loan.

If you don't know where to start, try the National Student Loan Data System (NSLDS) to see who your loan servicer is. If you have private loans but you aren't sure who your loan servicer is, a good place to start is your credit report.

## KNOW HOW MUCH YOU OWE, WHAT YOUR RATE IS AND WHAT YOUR MONTHLY PAYMENT IS

Now it's time to understand your loan's terms. It's important to find out exactly what you owe. When I was working as a financial planner, the first time I logged into a client's student loan account I was shocked to see how confusing everything was. There were multiple loans and multiple loan servicers, which meant there were different interest rates and payment amounts too. How much you owe, how many loans you have and what your interest rates are are the details you need to truly understand what you owe.

Use a tool that you like to help you keep track of your balances, interest rates and payment amounts. My favorite web tools for tracking debt are Personal Capital for having a big-picture overview and Unbury.me or Tiller HQ for figuring out and tracking a monthly payment plan.[1]

## THE CASE FOR MAKING PAYMENTS AUTOMATIC

When you log into your loan servicer's website, you'll be able to see when your payments for each loan are due, but if you've been making your payments, chances are you already know when your payment is due.

If you don't have your payments being made automatically from your Bills & Life account, consider if automatic payments would be helpful for you. For some people they are. For those people, paying them manually means setting up unnecessary calendar alerts for due dates. A calendar alert for paying a bill might be needlessly disruptive to them because getting an alert over dinner with friends would be more annoying and more of a bummer than motivating. For other people, logging in and paying their bill during weekly finance time might make them feel engaged because they can see the balance change each month. Part of dealing with your student loans is finding a system for repaying them that works for you. When you have a structure or system in place that takes into account your emotions, you can find ways to support what you want to feel.

## KNOW THE EXACT DATE YOU'LL BE STUDENT-LOAN-DEBT FREE

It's good to know that there is a light at the end of the tunnel. Just like with credit card debt, know the day that you'll make your last student loan payment. You can find out your debt-free date by using a loan calculator like Unbury.me. Commit it to memory or write it down somewhere that you'll see it. Use it to help you realize that you won't be in debt forever.

## KNOW HOW EXTRA PAYMENTS WILL IMPACT HOW QUICKLY YOU'LL GET OUT OF DEBT

Play around with repayment tools like Unbury.me to see how much an extra $50 a month will impact when you'll get out of debt. If that works for your monthly cash flow, you might consider making those additional payments to get out of debt faster.

You can also consider breaking up your monthly payment into two. Paying half of your payment every two weeks allows you to sneak in an extra payment for the year.

Here's a bonus: find out if you can apply extra payments towards your principal so you can lower the principal faster and reduce the amount of interest you end up paying. Oftentimes you need to request to apply extra payments in this way. It shouldn't be a shock that lenders don't automatically apply extra payments to the principal; remember they make money from interest.

In the next chapter, I'll get deeper into interest and how it can compound, but here's a simple way to understand why principal-only payments help you pay less in overall interest and help you pay off your loan sooner. The amount of interest charged is based on the principal you owe. When you make a principal-only payment, you're shrinking the principal. Even though the interest rate stays the same, that interest amount is a function of a smaller principal. If those words were too boring to understand, here's an analogy. Think of interest as whipped cream and a piece of cake as the principal. A smaller piece of cake limits the amount of surface area there is to put whipped cream on.

PRINCIPAL-ONLY PAYMENTS    REDUCE TOTAL INTEREST
(BECAUSE INTEREST IS A FUNCTION OF PRINCIPAL)

## UNDERSTAND HOW INCOME-BASED REPAYMENT PLANS AND LOAN FORGIVENESS IMPACT YOUR LOAN

In 2017, when some of the first applicants of the loan forgiveness program submitted their applications, some loans were not forgiven because borrowers did not consolidate into qualified repayment programs. Other times, borrowers did not have an employment certification form completed every year. That means that for ten years, people made their student loan payments thinking they would be forgiven, only to submit their application and get denied. *Forbes* reported in 2019 that 98 percent of borrowers who applied for student loan forgiveness were denied.[2] We heard similar stories of this happening to borrowers during the Great Recession: borrowers were working with someone at the bank to restructure their loan in hopes that they'd keep their home only to have it foreclosed on.

At the time of this writing and based on proposals the Biden administration has released, I feel hopeful that new reforms to student loan laws will make the repayment process less harmful to borrowers. According to these proposals, things like income-based repayment plans and loan forgiveness will be programs borrowers must opt out of instead of into. This has the potential to benefit many. But just like the marshmallow experiment in Chapter 6, we've been told before that loans would be forgiven, and they weren't, so it's not easy to forget how expectations were set and not met.

## STAY INFORMED SO YOU KNOW HOW CHANGES IMPACT YOU

To keep things interesting, the student loan laws can change. As long as you have debt, you'll want to make sure you're staying up to date and informed with how the changes impact you and your loan.

When I want to stay informed on a subject, I find an email newsletter that will continuously educate me and keep the subject at the front of my mind by constantly pinging me with emails. I imagine there are some people who would hate this strategy, but for those who don't, I recommend sign-ing up for an email newsletter from a company like Student Loan Hero that specializes in helping people with their stu-dent loans. Heather Jarvis, a student loan expert and advo-cate, also publishes updates via her blog and newsletter.[3] Other folks might find an online com-munity to help them stay up-dated.

Find a method for staying informed that works for you. Just realize that part of taking responsibility for your debt is keeping up with what's going on in the student loan world for as long as you have student loans. Think of following along and staying on top of your student loan like the debt is your city's baseball team and you are the type of person who likes baseball.

## KNOW HOW TO THINK ABOUT REFINANCING AND CONSOLIDATION OPTIONS

Student loan consolidation and refinancing are terms that often get interchanged, but they are two different options.

When you consolidate your loans, you merge all of your federal loans into one bill and your interest rate is a weighted average cost of your original loans. Your repayment terms don't change, and you pay exactly what you would pay if your loans weren't consolidated. Consolidation is all about convenience, not saving money. Consolidating your federal student loans is free; all you have to do is apply for it at StudentLoans.gov.[4]

Refinancing, on the other hand, is combining all your loans regardless of whether they are federal or private or both into a single payment. The process is different because you are taking out a new loan to pay off the original loans. Refinancing is typically offered through private lenders, not the federal government, and you'll get offered one single new interest rate.

Refinancing isn't right for everyone. Particularly, refinancing federal loans into private loans means that you'd be giving up a lot of federal benefits. In almost all cases, this trade-off isn't worth it. Here's an example to consider: During the COVID-19 pandemic, federal student loans were given the benefit of emergency relief. By contrast private student loan lenders weren't required to offer the same help to borrowers. When you refinance federal loans into private loans, you no longer have these baked-in federal benefits and for the most part, whatever you'd save in interest might not be worth what you forgo in potential benefits. Another way to think about this is that you're paying for the federal benefits of an income-based repayment plan or loan forgiveness.

With that warning, if you're still considering whether refinancing is right for you, ask yourself the following questions:

- Are you having trouble making your monthly payments?
- Are you benefiting from an income-based repayment plan or will you benefit from loan forgiveness? If you are, refinancing might make you ineligible for receiving these benefits. This is a huge benefit to give up.
- Are you looking to remove the cosigner on the loans? Refinancing is a way to accomplish that.
- If you have a private loan, with an interest rate that is variable or high, will refinancing allow you to lock in a lower and/or fixed rate?

### A Quick Note About Interest Rates and Refinancing

Interest rates are like hairstyles—sometimes they change. In the 1980s, the average mortgage interest rate was 16.63 percent. At the time of this writing, it's 3.052 percent. That's quite a difference. When you hear folks talking about refinancing because interest rates are so low, what they are saying is that when they originally borrowed money at a fixed rate, that fixed rate was higher than what's available as a fixed rate in today's market.

While refinancing can potentially save on interest over the life of the loan, there are other factors to consider if it's right for you. Particularly with student loans, and I can't stress this enough, refinancing with a private lender means your loans aren't eligible for federal benefits. With other forms of refinancing, remember that when you refinance, you're taking out a new loan. Look out for loan fees and factor those in so you know the true cost of refinancing. Consider how a new loan might extend how long it takes you to repay the loan.

## KNOW WHAT OPTIONS YOU'D HAVE IF YOU HAD A FINANCIAL HARDSHIP

It seems weird to find out about what hardship programs are available before you need to use them, but it can make going through a financial hardship a little less stressful when you know what to expect. Find out what kind of deferment or forbearance options you have with your student loans.

Deferment allows you to postpone payments on your student loans. Most federal loans are automatically deferred for six months after graduation. If you have a subsidized loan, interest doesn't accrue during deferment. If you have an unsubsidized loan, interest does accrue.

Forbearance is like a deferment in that it allows you to postpone making payments. The main difference with forbearance is that interest will accrue, so your balance will increase. When interest accrues, this is how debt grows—something we'll discuss in the next chapter.

Deferment and forbearance are not long-term solutions for dealing with your student loans, but they can be helpful relief options if you are dealing with a significant financial hardship.

## KNOW THE CONSEQUENCES OF IGNORING YOUR DEBT

I'm sure you know that there are consequences for ignoring your debt. Let's get specific about what they are. There are late fees if you don't make your payment before the grace period ends. If you're thirty, sixty, ninety, or one hundred and twenty days past due, these delinquencies will be documented in your credit report and your score will go down each time you reach one of these delinquency milestones. Yup, it's like being kicked when you're already down.

If you keep ignoring your debt, you may go into default. When you go into default, you might have a judgment against you that results in your wages or tax returns being garnished. That means money gets taken out of your paycheck to go towards your loans; you don't see that money. If you have federal loans, going into default might risk your eligibility for relief options and programs.

Ignoring your student loan debt doesn't make it go away. In

fact, even filing for bankruptcy may not discharge your student loans. I sincerely hope this changes soon.

## KNOW THAT YOU ARE NOT YOUR STUDENT LOAN DEBT

Debt is a situation, not a state of being. You are not your debt. You are a human being in the modern world that sometimes has to deal with situations and circumstances that are not ideal. Shit happens. It's what you do when shit happens that defines how your life can go from that point forward. You can be a person who takes responsibility for the position you've found yourself in by working on paying your debt. You can also be a person who fights for economic justice because you don't want others to find themselves in debt like you. You can do both of those things at the same time and still your debt will not define who you are.

DEBT IS A
SITUATION,
NOT AN
IDENTITY

# IF YOU'RE CONSIDERING STUDENT LOANS, BE REALISTIC ABOUT THE RETURN ON YOUR INVESTMENT

If you don't have student loans but you're considering applying for some to go to school, it would behoove you to realistically evaluate how much student loans will cost you relative to what you'll be able to earn. Remember, debt is a useful tool if you can leverage it for buying an asset and if you can afford the debt payments. The asset in the case of student loans is your potential future earnings.

I met a woman who once told me that her student loan debt had grown to around $250,000. She had undergraduate loans and then took on more when she went to graduate school to earn an MFA in film. Her strategy to pay back her loans was to establish herself as a commercial director. The irony is that she needed to make commercials in order to afford her fine art degree. Thankfully, she was living in Los Angeles, where that plan is possible. However, I doubt that her motivations for getting a graduate degree was to create commercials to sell processed food and luxury cars. She wanted to make films, which is something that is totally possible to do without a graduate degree. From an investment perspective, unfortunately I'm not sure her degree will generate a return. From a life satisfaction perspective, maybe it has.

When it comes to taking on student loan debt, understand the trade-offs you'll be making. Research salary expectations. Understand the true cost of your debt. What will you be giving up when you decide to pick from the pocket of your future self? Make sure that feels worth it to you.

# Spend a Weekend,
## or at the Very Least an Afternoon or Two,
### Getting to Know Your Student Loans

Use the following prompts to help you get to know your student loans.

- What kind of loans do you have?

- How much do you owe, what is your rate and what is your monthly payment?

- Who is your loan servicer? What is their customer service number and website?

- What is the exact date you'll be student-loan-debt free? (Use Unbury.me or another loan calculator.)

- If you can afford to make extra payments, how much will your extra be? How will this impact how much interest you pay and how long it will take you to pay back your loans? (Unbury.me will illustrate this for you.)

- Which loans are eligible for income-based repayment plans?

- Does your work make you eligible for loan forgiveness? If so, which loans are eligible for student loan forgiveness? Are you 100 percent sure that you're doing everything right to make sure your student loans will be forgiven? ARE YOU REALLY SURE?

- Are your loans eligible for consolidation? Should you consider consolidation?

- Is refinancing your loans something you need to consider? Refer to the questions on page 218 to help you understand if that's a good move for you.

- What options do you have if you have a financial hardship? Are your loans eligible for forbearance or deferment? What is the process to apply for forbearance? What is the process to apply for deferment?
- Do you know the consequences of not repaying your debt?
- Do you know that you are not your student loans? You are more than your stupid student loans. You're a human person. And you matter because you are a human person. You know that, right?

## PART 4

# Treat Yo (Future) Self:

## Investing and Retirement

Now that we've gone through the dredges of dealing with our debt, it's time to build the next level of your Pyramid of Financial Awesomeness: investing and building wealth. In so many ways, this level is a magical, mysterious mind-fuck because it's all about using money to create more money. This is the bedrock of the finance industry and the concept of retirement rests upon the assumption that one can amass wealth through the wizardry of compounding.

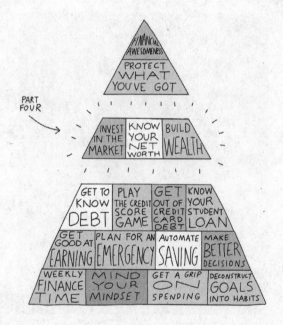

We'll explore the foundations for investing, how to think about it and why participating in investing is for everyone and not reserved for those who are already wealthy. We'll also explore some of the underlying mechanisms that make the stock market "work," and I'll teach you how to think about hiring professional help.

**CHAPTER 14**

# How to Think About Investing

How many times have you thrown a penny away? Like you saw a penny on your desk, or you got it as change, and instead of putting it in your pocket to use later, you threw it in the actual garbage? Okay, maybe you don't even use cash anymore, but you've definitely seen pennies laying around on sidewalks and on the grass in parks, discarded and uncounted as valuable. I'm not trying to judge you or the lack of respect you have for pennies; I'm just trying to illustrate how the penny has undoubtedly lost its value over time.

The penny used to be worth something. In 1909, you could buy a copy of the *New York Tribune* for one cent. In 1932, you could travel a mile in the Southern Railway system.[1] And maybe you've even heard a grandparent or great-aunt speak of buying candy at a local five-and-dime for a cent.

How does a penny go from getting you an entire newspaper to being so invaluable and annoying that you'd rather throw it away than carry it around?

When money becomes less valuable over time, it's usually due to the invisible force of inflation. Inflation is when the price of things goes up over time, which in turn makes the value of money go down over time. It's like when an ice cube slowly melts and adds water to a glass of whiskey. You might not notice the difference at first, but the more the ice cube melts, the weaker the whiskey becomes because it gets diluted. In this analogy, the whiskey is your money's purchasing power (what your money can buy) and the ice cube melting into it is inflation. The analogy doesn't fully explain *how* inflation works, but it does a good job of illustrating the *results* of inflation.

Inflation can feel like a sinister force because as it increases, it means your money is less valuable.

For example, if the price of burritos goes from $5.00 in 2018 to $5.50 in 2019, that's a 10 percent increase in price. Inflation or the rate of inflation is expressed as a percentage.

While inflation may cause the same amount of burrito to cost more year over year, most economic experts will agree that a little bit of inflation is good for economic growth.

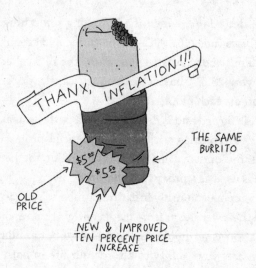

THANX, INFLATION!!!

THE SAME
BURRITO

OLD
PRICE

$5⁰⁰

$5⁵⁰

NEW & IMPROVED
TEN PERCENT PRICE
INCREASE

Deflation occurs when the prices of goods and services begin to fall. Usually, this happens after an economic downturn. Too much deflation can push the economy into a deeper and more severe crisis. For example, the hourly wage for a certain position might fall from $25 per hour to $20 per hour. Long-term deflation can cause stagnation, which could cause more significant problems. It's easy to see that decreasing wages are not exactly a recipe for a bustling economy.

Seeing and feeling the impact of inflation is a lot easier than understanding why it's happening. When it comes to inflation, it's complicated. There can be a lot of different factors that push up the prices of things. An increase in the money supply and lower interest rates could stimulate demand and create inflation. A shock in the supply chain could be the culprit of increasing prices.

## HOW IS INFLATION MEASURED?

As hilarious as it would be only to measure inflation in the cost of burritos, that's not exactly how it works. In the U.S., periods of inflation or deflation are identified by using something called the Consumer Price Index (CPI). CPI is measured and calculated by the U.S. Bureau of Labor Statistics (the BLS). The BLS collects its data from surveying 23,000 businesses and records the prices of 80,000 consumer items each month.[2]

The CPI is flawed and is definitely not a perfect measure for inflation; it is oftentimes criticized by financial professionals and economists for underestimating inflation. But for better or for worse, CPI is used as a proxy for inflation.

The BLS reports monthly inflation numbers. You can find them directly on their website or from media outlets that report financial data.[3] Inflation is an important measure to be familiar with because it impacts your ability to afford your life in both the short-term and the long term.

## DEALING WITH INFLATION IN THE LONG TERM: INVEST YOUR MONEY

Investing your money is a way to fight inflation in the long term. It's not enough to just save your money for the long term, you have to invest it or else you'll guarantee it will lose its value over time because of inflation.

Let's say you save $10,000 in cash today, and you keep it in a high-yield money market savings for thirty years. Let's say you get a 2 percent return each year. You'll probably get a few hundred bucks every year, and after thirty years, you'll have about $18,114. Awesome! Until you compare that with investing. Let's say you invest $10,000 today and you get a 5 percent return each year. In thirty years, you'll have about $43,219. And, of course, if you just kept that $10,000 under a mattress, in thirty years you'd still have $10,000, but after three decades of inflation, it wouldn't go as far; it would be "worth" a lot less.

# WHAT HAPPENS TO $10,000 IN THIRTY YEARS...

UNDER A MATTRESS

IN A SAVINGS ACCOUNT THAT EARNS 2%.

IN AN INVESTMENT ACCOUNT THAT EARNS 5%.

YOU STILL HAVE $10K BUT IT BUYS YOU LESS.

YOU'LL HAVE $18,114

YOU'LL HAVE $43,219

If this is your first real introduction to the world of investing and you feel like this world is not for you, I completely understand. When I worked as a financial planner I was the only woman on the financial planning team. Of course, I wasn't just promoted to financial planner; I had to first create the position of junior financial planner as a stepping-stone, even though I already had the responsibilities before the title.

At the end of the year the firm had a guys' night out for the financial planning team, which I was on. But the event was only for our male clients and employees. I was excluded. I literally did not belong there; I was still on the outside while I was on the inside, and no one at the company even questioned if they should change the event to include me.

Not feeling like you belong has its perks. It naturally fosters an open mind because it forces you to always think about other people's perspectives. It makes being uncomfortable comfortable. And it often means I never feel like I need permission to try new things or to be in new spaces because the feeling that I don't belong anywhere is just normal. It lets me explore whatever I want to explore, be wherever I want to be.

Even though I never felt like I belonged in the investment world, that never stopped me from trying to gain access to it. My whole life has been about finding ways to get access to places, people and things that historically haven't been given easily to people like me. What I'm trying to say is, don't let this industry full of old white dudes in ill-fitting suits make you feel like Julia Roberts in *Pretty Woman* when the shop clerks think she can't afford the dresses in their store. Don't let them make you think you don't belong. Don't let other people's bullshit about trying to keep you down create barriers in your own mind. Those are their limitations about you, not your limitations about you. They're just hoping that you'll believe the same bullshit that they do: that access and power should be limited. Fuck. That.

Investing is for everyone. Especially now. You don't need to go to the bank and look a certain way or know the right guy—or be a guy—to be able to invest. You can start your account from the comfort of your own home, in your underwear, with *Gilmore Girls* streaming in the background.

If you've had resistance to investing before, the rest of this chapter is a way for you to face the ideas that may have created that resistance. The resistance is like a tightness in your body. If you don't address it and work on loosening what needs to be loosened, strengthening what needs to be strengthened and releasing what needs to be released, you'll find ways to overcompensate for the tightness. And overcompensation creates new issues that can distract you from the real issue.

So let's dig into the real issues so we can move through them and feel less weird about investing.

## "ONLY RICH PEOPLE INVEST."

Is it that people who are successful tend to be the kind of people who wake up early or is it that you must wake up early in order to become a successful person? The question is about causation versus correlation. This is a common flaw in logic that we see in all areas of our life.

A lot of people think only wealthy people can invest, when in fact most people become wealthy people by investing. Here's the big fat secret: you don't need to make a bunch of money to invest. You can invest right now, with a little bit of money, and over time, your investments will grow.

## "I DON'T HAVE A LOT OF MONEY TO INVEST."

You don't need to have $15,000 lying around in order to start investing. You can start with investing $25 to $50 a month. The way you get started with investing is the way you get started with literally anything else in life. You just start where you are. And you keep showing up and after a little bit of time, you can look back on your progress. And my hope is that after a year, you look at the free money that your investments made you and you feel a sense of accomplishment for sticking with investing and it motivates you to keep going and to shift your priorities.

## "I DON'T WANT TO LOSE MONEY."

In the long run, you are guaranteeing that you will lose money by not investing because of the wonderful invisible force of inflation. Just ask anyone in a generation before you how much a carton of milk or a loaf of bread used to cost and you'll see exactly how inflation makes cash less valuable over time. So if you really don't want to lose money, then you'll understand that you must invest your money.

## "NOW IS NOT A GOOD TIME TO INVEST."

This is the mother of all cop-outs and believing it will hold you back from doing anything and everything throughout your life. For the most part, there is never a perfect time to do anything. Changing jobs, getting married, falling in love, getting divorced, moving to a new place or starting a business. Don't stop yourself from starting because you think the time is not right. In the long run, you'll realize that you should have started sooner because the longer you invest, the greater your chances are of feeling financially secure and creating wealth.

## "BUT I STILL HAVE A LOT OF TIME, SO I CAN START LATER."

Even if you do, you will wish you'd started sooner. I wish that I'd started way sooner. A little bit early on goes a long way. It often goes a lot longer than a lot in a shorter period. Even if you start small by saving some birthday or graduation money, start as soon as you can. Remember, compounding interest requires time to pay off. Don't take my word for it; the math speaks for itself.

CASE #1                          CASE #2

BETHANY INVESTS                  CHARLIE INVESTS
$5,500/YEAR STARTING             $5,500/YEAR STARTING
AT AGE 25 UNTIL AGE 35.          AT AGE 35 UNTIL AGE 45.

ASSUMING AN ANNUAL RETURN OF 6% AT AGE 65...

BETHANY                          CHARLIE
HAS                              HAS
$416,370.79                      $232,499.27

## "BUT ISN'T INVESTING UNETHICAL?"

It sure is. Historically wealth was built through violence, colonial-
ization, war and oppression. The main motivator for colonizing the
New World was the opportunity to make money. And investing and
building wealth are intertwined with colonialism and patriarchy.
Before Wall Street became the financial center where stocks and
bonds are bought and sold, it was originally a site where human beings were bought and sold into slavery. And yes, we can invest in socially responsible companies, but the mechanism for investing is
inherently exploitative and extractive. I have no prescription for
how to reconcile this reality. But every day, the products that we use
are in some fashion exploitative. There is no perfect solution or perfect blueprint for trying to be a more ethical investor. We're all
watching it take shape in real time. Ten years ago, I would get
laughed out of the room when I mentioned socially responsible investing to other financial planners, but now it's taken very seriously.

Being a human being on planet Earth means that we have to
constantly make concessions and compromises. We have to weigh
the cost of doing something that has a benefit. We have to use
second-order thinking and listen to our intuition. When it comes to
investing, I think being a conscientious objector would do more
harm than good for many average people. The second-order consequences of not investing would be needlessly harmful to folks who
need to harness the power of compounding. The motivation for investing is to keep up with inflation and the cost of living so we can
live. I suspect most folks are not trying to become insanely wealthy
and then planning on using that wealth for nefarious purposes. I
don't think fighting inequality and contributing to a retirement account need to be mutually exclusive acts. And I hope that as more
people become aware of the realities and histories of our modern
systems, that policies will be implemented to pay for injustice, that
reparations will be paid, and that redemption is possible. Until

then, we have to accept the reality of the world we live in and do our best not to cut off our nose to spite our face.

## "I DON'T KNOW ENOUGH ABOUT INVESTING TO FEEL COMFORTABLE INVESTING."

You probably didn't know enough about how Instagram worked before you decided to download the app, start an account and give away all your personal data, but chances are you did it anyway. And you probably did that with Facebook too. Whatever hobby you're into, whether it's ceramics or gardening or woodworking, there was a time you didn't know anything about that subject. And whatever your expertise is, like knowing how the publishing world works because you've been in it for ten years, you definitely weren't born with that knowledge. Even if you were born with your knowledge because you're an oracle or something, you still had to spend time honing your craft and learning more about how it works.

It's okay if you don't know enough about investing to feel comfortable investing at this very moment. But acknowledging that and choosing to remain ignorant is not okay. It's an excuse to hide from something you don't want to face. And if that's true, why don't you want to face it? I don't know the answer; only you know. Think about it. Are you afraid of who you'll become after you learn about investing? Do you think your friends won't be your friends or your loved ones won't love you? Are you afraid of feeling stupid or bored to tears? Are you worried that you'll have to confront past mistakes and financial neglect? Are you anxious about facing the math of retirement? Do you just want to play it safe and stay feeling comfortable?

Whatever your answer is, investing now is a chance to prevent financial insecurity for your future self. It's the opposite of debt. Your current self is putting money into the pocket of your older self. So if you care about your cute, old, wrinkly, future self, then your young, brave, current self has to step up. Protect that old cutie.

---

### Investing in Your Future Self

**Draw a picture of your cute older self. Write a letter to them promising that you'll spend time studying the following chapters so you can understand investing and start investing for their sake.**

- **What beliefs and rules do you have about investing?**
- **What beliefs and rules do you want your cute older self to have about investing?**
- **What beliefs and rules do you have about retirement?**
- **What beliefs and rules do you want your cute older self to have about retirement?**

DRAW A PICTURE
OF YOUR CUTE, OLD SELF

**CHAPTER 15**

# How to Stock Market

One of the fun things about marriage is seeing the things that shaped the person you love. My wife and my upbringings weren't terribly different, but there were certain things my parents didn't spend money on or have money for that my wife's family did. For example, my family almost always brought our own food to theme parks so we wouldn't have to pay those high theme park food prices. My wife's family didn't do this; the theme park food was part of the experience for them. But my parents sent me to summer day camp while my wife and her siblings spent summers at home with grandparents, or even alone.

On a trip with my wife and her family to Las Vegas, I realized how my trips with my family while growing up were also different. When my family would go to Vegas, it was me and like ten of my cousins in a Circus Circus hotel room fending for ourselves. We were living the dream of eating pizza and drinking soda morning, noon and night, while all our parents took shifts gambling and watching us. On trips with just my immediate family, we never paid for entertainment. We would entertain ourselves for free by walking around the strip and observing the sights, the lights and the people.

But my wife's family spent money on entertainment and experiences; they went to shows and spas and did a lot of shopping. I had never been to a Las Vegas show before my wife's family took me. So I was surprised on this particular trip that one night we would be going to see one. For a reason that is unclear to me, the show we went to see was Criss Angel's *Mindfreak*.

Criss Angel, if you're unfamiliar with him, is the bad boy of magic. He has long, black hair with side-swept bangs à la emo bands in the early aughts. Sometimes he wears eyeliner and leather pants. I had definitely heard of him but that was the extent of my familiarity with his work. Why was this the show all of us were going to see? I'll never know, but I was not disappointed. It was very entertaining, and it has clearly stuck with me.

This is where I learned a couple of things. I learned that Las Vegas shows have incredible production quality. Even if the content is something you don't expect to enjoy, like the bad boy of magic, it's still wildly entertaining and impressive. The other thing I learned was that Criss Angel's magic was so good it was scary. I was flabbergasted by his illusions. I should be embarrassed to admit this, but it seemed so real. In fact, at some point I thought, "This guy really is an angel or a demon or at least some kind of sorcerer who was on Earth and decided one day that he was going to be his regular angel/demon/sorcerer self here. And to get away with it, he could just become a famous magician."

I thought about some of the crazy illusions from his show for days. How he went from the stage to the middle of the audience in one poof of smoke. Even if there was a trapdoor, how could he travel so fast? There's no way it could have been a body double either. Clearly, I'm still in awe.

Magic is not and has never been cool, but I've always been fascinated by it. It was never something I really got into myself, but whenever it was around, it felt exciting. I love that magic plays with the audience's expectations. I love that feeling of having your mind blown and not being able to explain what you just experienced. Witnessing a trick always makes me reconnect with a childlike sense of wonder.

I try not to take the magical things in my life for granted. Seeing a seed sprout into a plant that has a flower that turns into food is magical. Yes, we can explain it with science, but that doesn't take away from how magical that is. Coincidences can probably be explained by probability *or* we can let it feel magical. Math is a lot more magical than we choose to see. Music, a thing that can unite us, move us and make us feel something that we can't put into words is completely ruled by math. Meter, time, the distance between notes and the vibrations of sound waves are all mathematical, yet what it produces is a magical feeling. We see the same math in the beauty of nature and art too, from the Fibonacci sequence to the rule of thirds.

I think one of the things that drew me to finance was an element of magic. It seemed like people somehow made something from nothing; like there was sleight of hand inherent in how the financial world operated. I choose to study finance because I wondered how it all worked behind the curtain. Where does the money go? If a bank lends a dollar that I deposited, did the bank just magically create two dollars out of one? How can these seemingly stupid, fast-talking salespeople in nice, slick suits get so rich? How do they take other people's money and use it to magically make more money? Who are they tricking? Are they tricking us?

Unfortunately, some folks in the financial world use illusion and deceit because the system can incentivize that kind of behavior. There are instances where it's nefarious and instances where it's benign. Knowing the math behind the magic is the first step in differentiating between the two.

So, let's first take a look at the truly magical concept of compounding. Compounding is like a patch of mushrooms that appears overnight; fascinating but freaky. The good news is that the magic of compounding can work for you in the case of investing. But with debt, compounding interest can potentially work against you. If you've ever borrowed money only to end up owing multiples of what you originally borrowed, you've experienced the kind of Criss Angel dark magic of compounding interest.

## COMPOUNDING INTEREST IS MAGIC

When you borrow money, you will always pay back more than you originally borrowed since you're paying interest. But there are instances where high interest compounds over time and the monthly payments aren't enough to keep the balance from growing. We see this most often with credit cards and payday loans. As we just learned in Part 3, credit cards and payday loans are designed to get the borrower trapped in a cycle of debt. This happens because of the magic of compounding interest.

In the same way that something negative in your life can show up in another area in positive manner, compounding can either be a force of good or evil, depending on how it's applied. When compounding is applied to debt, it grows what you owe. But when it's applied to your investments and your assets, it grows what you've got. Words do no justice for explaining the incredible power and mysterious magic of compounding interest, so let's just let the math do the talking by looking at an example.

Here's one example. Would you rather have $1 million today or would you rather have the total amount of a penny doubled each day over a month? Let me explain the second option. It starts with one cent on day one. Then it's doubled on day two to two cents. Then two cents gets doubled to four cents on day three, and so on and so forth for a month. If this sounds like a trick question, it's because it kind of is. Here's how the math shakes out:

THE TOTAL AMOUNT OF A PENNY DOUBLED EACH DAY OVER A MONTH

If you choose option two, you'd end up with a lot more than the million from option one. This is an extreme example of how compounding works. Here's another very crude and simple way of understanding what's going on: the snowball effect.

# THE SNOWBALL EFFECT

THIS SMALL SNOWBALL IS YOUR INITIAL INVESTMENT

TIME PASSES AND THE INVESTMENT COMPOUNDS

AND COMPOUNDS...

AND COMPOUNDS...

OVER A LONG TIME YOUR INVESTMENT GROWS THANKS TO THE POWER OF COMPOUNDING.

A growing balance due to compounding interest is like a cartoon snowball rolling down a mountain. The original amount of money you invest is represented by the snowball. Father Time is represented by the mountain. And the money your investments make through dividends and interest is represented by the snow accumulating on the snowball as it rolls down the mountain.

If you accumulate more interest without touching either the amount you invested or the amount you earn, what you earn ends up growing the balance. A bigger snowball has a larger surface area, which means it can grow bigger, faster.

Okay, how about a real-world example? Let's say Alice starts saving $438 a month at age twenty-five and continues to do so over the next forty-two years, until she reaches retirement age at sixty-seven. She saves a total of $220,752 because $438 a month x twelve months x forty-two years = $220,752. But during that time, her investments had an average annual return of 6 percent. So at age sixty-seven, her retirement account balance has grown to $1 million. Damn, Alice—way to grow a million.

These examples are meant to show you how powerful compounding is. And that you are tripping your balls off if you don't take advantage of this insane, human-made phenomenon of using money to create more money. However, if it seems too good to be true, in a way it kind of is. Here's what I mean.

The messed-up thing about all of this is what it's all built on. Where does all this growth come from? For simplicity's sake, let's say you buy stock in a company. As a shareholder your investment grows from both an increase in stock prices and from getting paid dividends. Ultimately both the stock price and dividends are a reflection of the company's growth. Yes, the company can be growing because people are consuming more and that leads to more sales, but another way to increase profit is to cut costs. And oftentimes the biggest costs a company has is paying workers.

Between the years of 1948 and 1971, wages for American hourly workers and worker productivity grew relative to one another. But ever since 1972, we've been witnessing a phenomenon where productivity continued its upward trajectory while wages did not. Between the years 1979 and 2018, we've seen workers' productivity increase by 69.6 percent, while wage growth has only grown by 11.6 percent. In other words, productivity has grown six times more than wages.

If workers are more productive, where does that extra productivity, in terms of dollars, go? It could get invested in a variety of ways. It can get invested back into the company. It can go into a pension fund that the worker benefits from later. It can go into a profit-sharing plan that the owners and the workers benefit from.

Alternatively, and more commonly with public companies (companies that sell shares of ownership on the stock market), that extra productivity gets paid to the shareholders, owners and management. If you own company stock, you benefit.

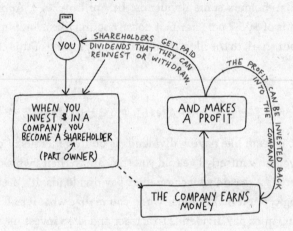

AN EXTREMELY SIMPLIFIED EXPLANATION OF ONE WAY INVESTORS MAKE MONEY

START

YOU

SHAREHOLDERS GET PAID DIVIDENDS THAT THEY CAN REINVEST OR WITHDRAW.

WHEN YOU INVEST $ IN A COMPANY, YOU BECOME A SHAREHOLDER (PART OWNER)

AND MAKES A PROFIT

THE PROFIT CAN BE INVESTED BACK INTO THE COMPANY

THE COMPANY EARNS MONEY

This is how we are able to profit from the stock market. Corporations create a profit by spending less than they make. One way to do this is to keep wages the same while revenue increases. Which means the people working in the company are undervalued and underpaid while the value they create through their labor gets passed on and up to the owners and shareholders in the form of dividends or interest.

When a company can issue stock that gets traded on the stock market, this means they're a public company. A public company is similar to a person who has a public life, like the Queen of England or John Legend. When you're a public person, the public has expectations of your behavior. You can't be ignorant and harm people if you're a public person; it's just part of the job and the social contract.

Corporations that are public also have to live up to some expectations. Wall Street, or professional investors and the people in that industry, expect these public companies to make money and grow and do so well that they pay their shareholders dividends.

For example, Apple sells even more iPhones, cuts costs and makes more money in the current quarter than the previous one. When they make more money, there is a good chance they'll pay their shareholders some dividends. In April of 2020, Apple paid dividends of $0.82 per share.[1] It doesn't sound like a lot, but please refer your snark to the illustrations at the beginning of this chapter.

## WHY DO COMPANIES PAY DIVIDENDS?

Doesn't it seem like paying dividends is oddly generous of companies given how miserly I've told you they are to their own workers? But there is a reason why companies pay dividends. It's pretty circular logic, but it makes sense when you realize what it's all about.

Companies pay dividends to attract and keep investors and because it's good for the stock price. Oftentimes, after dividends get paid out to investors and shareholders, the company's stock price goes up because there is an expectation that the company is doing well since it can afford to pay dividends. Wall Street wants the stock price to go up over time because it's another way that the value of investments grows. If something you own goes up in value, what you own becomes more valuable. The folks at the top of public companies most likely get some of their compensation in the form of stock or stock options. So they are incentivized to maximize shareholder profit because they themselves tend to be shareholders.

And so, the logic goes, if investors can expect dividends, they'll invest in your company. When a lot of people buy a stock, it tends to push up the price. Corporations can issue more stock, which means they can raise money that they put back into their company to grow it even more, which means they can make more money and then pay more dividends and watch their stock price go up. And on and on it goes.

How silly is this? I think it's very, very silly. When I see dividends going into my own investment account or when I see the value rise because the prices of what I own increase, I am still genuinely flabbergasted because I did not do one single thing and the value of what I own went up.

When I allow myself to really sit and think about it, it feels fake and stupid, but it's how investing and the modern economy work. It's not great for the Earth because it assumes that companies can just grow and grow and grow and grow and grow without consideration for how bad all that growth is for the environment. If it were up to me, I'd say, let's all stop buying into this idea that limitless growth is possible, but a lot of people who are benefiting from this system aren't quick to dump it for something new. The undeniable truth is, as my participation in this system grows, so does my potential to benefit. And I am not so virtuous as to not participate in this alchemy of making more money with the money I've got. I told you this was some dark-magic wizard shit.

I think our expectations of economic progress have to change before the mechanisms that promote this behavior change. Here is an incredibly simplistic prescription to help makes things less goddamn exploitative: take the profits a worker creates and allow them to benefit from it instead of extracting it and reallocating it to the owners, shareholders and managers. Many companies do this by reinvesting in their workers, providing a profit-sharing program, structuring their company as employee-owned or giving the employees some ownership through stock. Some start-up founders are even starting to reorient their goal from "Let's build a company that sells for a billion dollars" to "Let's build a company that is valuable for a community of people." Blockchain as a technology is also starting to show how society can build platforms that are decentralized so the concentration of who benefits from something is spread among many. While it's easy to feel bad about how all this works, I feel optimistic that inclusive change will happen; it will just take time to bring these ideas into existence in a meaningful, large-scale way.

Until then, one way to bring the impact of our investing into our circle of control is to choose socially responsible investments (SRIs). An SRI is a way to invest in companies and portfolios that strive to both generate a return for the investor and to make an impact by putting money into companies that make a sustainable or societal impact. Renewable energy or companies that invest in their workers are great examples of companies that fall into the SRI space. Another reason why I feel hopeful is because of the big change in attitude and returns from SRIs within the last ten years. When I first started in finance, there were very few options for SRIs, and industry veterans would, as noted before, arrogantly laugh in my face whenever I asked about them. Today, these funds do generate comparable (and sometimes better) returns for investors and they are much more widely available and easy to access.

My hope is that this is one step in the journey to giving many, many fucks about workers and the world. While perhaps I am optimistic to a fault, I believe humanity has the imagination and ingenuity to retool the social contract between corporations, people and the planet. It starts here, by learning about the underpinnings of this system. So thanks for doing your part.


## HOW TO START INVESTING: THE BASICS

The universe of investing is vast. This is not the book that will take you on that very long journey. We're not going to cover things like futures or cryptocurrency. This book is the first step in your journey of investing, so I'm only going to give you the basic things that you need to know so you're ready for that first step. Buckle up, kids, you're about to hit a dense patch of information.

When it comes to investing, there are three main concepts to grasp that all center around managing the risk of losing your shirt. The good news is you don't need to know *how* to execute the concepts. When you set up your investment accounts, the tools to execute on these concepts are built in. They are built in in the form of questionnaires about your own feelings towards risk (risk tolerance) and what you'll use the money for and when (investing timeline). They're built in because laws force it to be built in, but it's good to know what the hell is going on as you're answering the questions and looking at the pie chart that it spits out for you.

## Concept 1: Risk in Terms of Time. When Do You Need the Money You're Investing?

At its core, investing is very simple. It's basically a risk-reward relationship. The amount of risk you should take with your investments is determined by how long you can afford to take said risk. In other words, the amount of risk you take depends on when you'll need the money you're investing.

For example, if you are twenty-four and you're investing in a retirement account that you don't need to access for at least forty years, you can take a lot of risk now so you can reap returns, and then slowly take on less risk as you get older. But if you're investing money for a down payment for a home that you plan on purchasing in the next ten years, you probably won't take on as much risk because you don't have forty years to ride the ups and downs. And if you need the money in your checking account for rent next month, you won't invest it at all because you can't afford to lose it.

When you go to invest your money, you can tell the application you're using—or the person if you're analog like that—when you need the money. For some people, the hardest part isn't how to invest the money, but what are they investing it for?

## Concept 2: Asset Allocation

Managing risk can also be done through asset allocation. An asset allocation is how investments are put together based on the inherent risk of each asset class. Think of it like putting together the flavors, textures, aromas and layers in a dinner or minding the elements in a photographic composition.

Stocks (ownership shares in a company), bonds (like a loan, but where the company that issues the bonds is borrowing money from investors) and cash are all different asset classes. These are three of many types, but let's just keep it simple for now.

Different asset classes have different characteristics about how they work and how inherently risky they are. In general, stocks are inherently riskier than bonds and bonds are inherently riskier than cash. It's like how riding a bike with one eye closed and only one hand is just inherently riskier than riding a bike with both eyes open and with both hands.

Asset allocation is a way to choose the type of asset classes to have in an investment portfolio that takes into account how much risk an investor can tolerate. The concentration of each asset class is also important to manage risk. An investor that owns one stock, one bond, one dollar and one house appears to have a balanced asset allocation, because there is one of everything, but it doesn't take into account the value of each asset class. This is also why asset allocation is often expressed as a pie chart. Pie charts make it easy to understand asset allocation in terms of ratios and how much of what you have relative to another thing.

## Concept 3: Diversification

Diversification is not just having diversity across asset classes, but diversity within each asset class. For example, if different fruits were different classes—stone fruits are stocks, berries are bonds and melons are cash—there are a variety of different types of fruits within each classification.

Within the category of stone fruits, there are nectarines, peaches, apricots, plums, mangoes and cherries. There are strawberries, blueberries, raspberries, gooseberries, blackberries, boysenberries, bananas and more within the berry family. And watermelon, cantaloupe and honeydew are just a few variations of melons. Each variety has different characteristics, like what part of the world they come from. This helps spread risk. For example, owning foreign stocks, or let's say gooseberries, can help hedge against risks that only impact the market in your home country, where nectarines come from.

Don't worry, you will not need to be picking foreign stocks. Most investing is done through buying shares of funds.

### Investing for Most People Is Putting Their Money into a Fund

A fund is like an already diversified grocery basket full of fruits; the fund is the basket and the various products in the basket are the various types of investments. Investing in a fund allows investors (like you and me and your work BFF) to pool their money together. Pooling our money gives us access to more investments than we could buy on our own. Having more access is a way to diversify what we're invested in so it's a lot less risky.

With pooled money, each investor gets access to investments that they might not be able to afford on their own. For example, if you wanted to invest in Tesla, you could buy one share, but there are two problems with that. The first problem is cost. At the time of this writing, a share of Tesla is just north of $600. If you don't have $600, you can't invest in one share of Tesla. Although you are still able to buy fractional shares with certain investment platforms, there's also the cost of time and energy that go into researching each individual stock you'd like to purchase. The second problem is risk. Buying one individual stock is risky. It's like putting $600 on a single number on the roulette table.

A FUND IS A BASKET OF INVESTMENTS

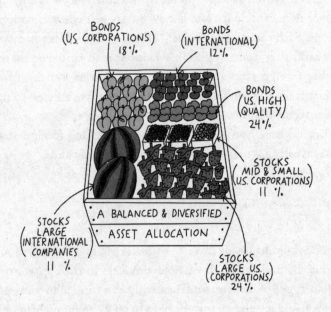

But if you bought into a fund that holds Tesla stock, you're still getting to invest in a smaller amount of Tesla, and it's a lot less risky because you're also investing in other companies too. Investing through a fund is like pooling $60 with ten friends and then placing multiple small bets all across the roulette table.

Sometimes a fund is full of other funds. And when you invest, you'll more than likely invest into an index fund or an exchange-traded fund (ETF).

## Investing Is Not Picking Stocks

The financial media that exists might confuse you into thinking that all investing involves picking and choosing stocks. The dog and pony show that is the financial media is pretty damn weird. One very popular TV show is basically some old, bald white dude with his button-down shirtsleeves aggressively rolled up past his elbows. Why doesn't he just wear a shirt without sleeves? Throughout each episode he talks about economics, individual companies and individual stocks. Which might lead you to believe that investing involves picking individual stocks. This type of financial media, and most financial media, is not for the everyday investor looking to invest in their retirement account. It's for people who are looking to speculate (gamble) with extra money and it's for the professional investor who actively picks stocks to hold in a portfolio or fund that they manage. While investing can involve picking individual stocks, for the average, everyday investor, you don't have to choose individual stocks. You have the option to buy into an index of exchange-traded funds (ETFs).

Picking stocks might be fun for some people the way camping is fun for some people. For other people, camping just feels like needlessly subjecting themselves to things they've tried to avoid their whole life: sleeping outside, being cold, pooping in a community outhouse and being dirty. You don't have to pick stocks or camp if you don't want to. You have other options.

## Index Funds and ETFs

Index funds and ETFs are funds that bundle together a bunch of investments into one single fund that you can invest in. They are both passively managed, meaning a human or team of humans doesn't pick the investments in the fund. The investments within the fund are based on an index, like Standard and Poor's 500, also known as the S&P 500 for short—which is an index that measures the stock performance of 500 large companies listed on stock exchanges in the U.S. Indexes can either represent the market as a whole or a specific sector, like retail or energy.

There are a few benefits of investing in an index fund or an ETF. It's a lot cheaper than investing in a fund that is actively managed by a portfolio manager. In an actively managed fund, humans actively pick stocks and that's mostly what you pay for. Index funds and ETFs are passively managed since you invest in whatever the index holds. The main difference between ETFs and index funds are how they are bought and sold, which doesn't really have a major impact on how most people will operate. ETFs are bought and sold during the trading day, while index funds are bought and sold at the end of the trading day.

Another major difference is that sometimes index funds have a minimum investment requirement and ETFs don't. For example, if you opened up an account through the investment advisory Vanguard, and you wanted to invest in index funds, there is a minimum investment of $3,000 for most of its index funds. With ETFs, you don't need thousands to get started. In fact, when you use an investment platform like Betterment, there is no minimum to get started. If you have an employer-sponsored retirement plan, you can get started right away. There are no minimums and it's easy to start investing.

## YOUR RETIREMENT ACCOUNT IS THE GATEWAY DRUG TO INVESTING

If you have access to an employer-sponsored retirement plan, like a 401(k) or 403(b), it should be pretty easy to get started investing. To get started, reach out to HR or whoever you think would know the answer to the question, "How can I start participating in the company's retirement plan?" They'll probably have you fill out some paperwork and choose how much of your paycheck you'd like to invest, and that's all it takes.

With an employee-sponsored retirement plan, your investing is done automatically. The money gets taken from your paycheck before you have the chance to spend it. It's a forced savings plan that removes your need to make a decision from the equation. It's a way to protect yourself from yourself. Some companies are now having employees opt out of their retirement plans instead of opting in. This is a move to make retirement savings even easier than asking to sign up and having to fill out a form.

If your employer doesn't offer a retirement plan, then you're probably eligible to contribute to an Individual Retirement Account, also called an IRA. And if you're self-employed or run a small business, you have the IRA option and more to choose from, like the SEP IRA and the Solo 401(k) to name a couple. Your small business accountant would be the perfect guide to walk you through your options, to give you the pros and cons and to help you decide what kind of retirement account works best for your unique tax situation.

## Most Retirement Accounts Have Target-Date Funds

A target-date fund is an index fund that invests your money based on when you plan to retire. Hence the name *target-date*; your retirement is the target date. A target-date fund takes into account when you need the money and it creates an asset allocation and diversification strategy based on your retirement date. It handles the three main considerations and it automatically makes sure everything is invested accordingly each year. So, as you get closer to retirement age, the investments in the fund shift to less risky investments. You don't have to do anything. This is the idea of "set it and forget it."

Here is a small detail that sometimes gets overlooked by investing newbies: make sure when you sign up for your employer-sponsored retirement account or set up your IRA that you choose the target-date fund you'd like to invest in. If you don't choose the fund to invest in, it won't get invested. This is a small but crucial detail. Other platforms make it hard for you to make this mistake, but I've heard stories of folks who thought they were investing because they were making contributions to their account, but they never actually elected the investments they'd like to purchase with each contribution.

These days, this is usually done automatically, but be sure that it is. You can see it on the investment statements you receive, you can log into your account to see what you're invested in or you can call the financial advisor who manages your company's retirement plan to confirm.

## How Much Should You Save and Invest for Retirement?: The Theory

There are a lot of different ways to look at this. One approach is a nebulous, maximalist perspective: save as much as you can for retirement. For some people that might mean contributing the maximum amount they can to their retirement account(s) each year. Alternatively, most financial experts like financial planners recommend saving 10 to 15 percent of your income starting in your twenties. Another rule of thumb for a target savings amount is having a nest egg that is twenty to twenty-five times your annual salary. An online calculator is also a great way to find out how much you should aim to save. I really like the one made by SmartAsset.[2]

Projections and online calculators use assumptions to generate their projections, but these projections are not guaranteed. The crazy truth is that nobody has a damn clue what the markets will do. So many people who eventually do retire not only did all the right things, like saved enough, but are also the beneficiaries of some good fortune. Good fortune could be getting the right internship early on that jump-started their career. Good fortune could be graduating into a strong economy. Good fortune could be not having student loan debt or never having to care for a terminally ill family member.

I have no clue what the future or fate of retirement will be. I don't know what social security will be like when I'm of retirement age.

Retirement as we currently know it is a relatively new concept. Prior to the invention of modern pensions in 1889, most instances of pensions were for troops and veterans. Pensions really started out as way to compensate veterans for their service and not so that workers could eventually retire.

Historically, the concept of pensions and retirement beyond veteran compensation was introduced by German Chancellor Otto von Bismarck in 1889, but not because he gave any fucks about old people not working. It was a preemptive move to prevent a growing socialist movement in Germany from getting any stronger. After this, pensions spread across Europe and then to the United States.

Over time we've seen pensions disappear. A pension is what is known as a defined-benefit retirement plan because typically the benefit was defined. Companies would invest on behalf of employees and they would define the benefit the employee would receive in retirement. For example, a defined-benefit pension might guarantee that they pay their retired workers $2,200 a month.

In contrast to that, we have the defined-contribution plan. This is what most companies have switched to. A defined-contribution plan doesn't have a guarantee of what a retiree gets in retirement. Instead, the company defines what they'll contribute to an employee's retirement account now. For example, a company may match up to 3 percent of the employee's contribution to their account. This change shows how the onus of securing one's retirement has shifted from employer to employee.

Retirement is an experiment in process. The 401(k) was invented in 1978. We're just starting to uncover when it works, when it doesn't and what assumptions about it might be flawed.

The concept of retirement is changing and being redefined constantly. A lot of folks are resigned to the concept that they'll just work forever. As much as I think I'll "always work," I know that at some point society might not want to employ me and I'll be irrelevant. But retirement in the traditional sense of not doing any work for the last chunk of your life preceded by working for forty years doesn't seem normal or attractive to me.

So, my take on retirement is that I'll aim for it by continuing to build assets, like a profitable business and intellectual property that I can sell or license, saving and investing a portion of everything I earn, making assessments along the way and hoping for the best—which is probably not unlike the strategy of so many folks before me.

## How to Save and Invest for Retirement?: The Practice

For folks who are traditionally employed and have access to an employer-sponsored retirement plan, saving automatically each time you get paid is simple in theory. The hard part is getting it set up so you can put it into practice. If you haven't yet started saving and investing for retirement for whatever reason, you can start where you are. Remember, sometimes the most important thing to do is start small, just so long as you start. Even if you can only invest 1 percent of your paycheck now, start where you are.

Investing a portion of what you earn each time you earn money is a systematic way to invest. No matter what the market is doing, as long as you're earning, you'll invest. This is another way to eliminate investment risk because you are buying shares of funds at various price points and not having to time the market. This is called dollar-cost averaging.

Finding the money to save and invest comes back to balancing the personal finance equation. I feel like I've gone over this an irritating amount of times, but just in case you think I haven't, here it is again. The money you use to save and invest can come from diverting funds used to pay for expenses. Another great way to "find" the money to invest with is by continuing to invest the amount of money you were putting into your emergency fund after you've already funded it. You can also do this with a loan payment you were making each month. If you had a $350 monthly payment for a student loan, when it's paid off, take that $350 a month and invest it. I know the $350 a month would be sweet to have and spend as you please, but remember the hedonic treadmill. At first spending that $350 might feel good, but eventually that pleasure will wear off. The same goes for investing it. At first, it might hurt, but eventually that hurt will level off.

You can also find the money to invest by investing any additional increases in your income. Any of these methods on their own works, but so does employing any of them in tandem. Once again, the freelancers and self-employed folks have an edge here since they tend to have much more autonomy and agency when it comes to increasing income almost on demand. Investing an additional few hundred (or thousand) a month can be done by taking on more work or hiring someone to take it for you.

Freelancers and self-employed folks do have an added layer of complexity because of the likelihood of having an income that fluctuates. This means investing can't be done entirely automatically. But you can invest using the same "do it your damn self" method I outlined in Chapter 4. Here's a refresher on how: You can make small retirement contributions automatically and then contribute more as you earn. For example, you might have an automatic weekly contribution of $50, but during the first weekly finance time of the month, you contribute 10 percent of what you earned in the prior month.

Another strategy for those with fluctuating income is to save a certain amount of income, like 25 percent, into a savings account throughout the year. Then you can make a retirement contribution at the end of the year or, if the type of retirement account allows it, you can make a contribution when you file your taxes. This strategy means you miss out on the ups and downs of the market during that year, but the trade-off is you have cash on hand if you need it during the year. Of course, the big drawback is that you might spend it instead of investing it. Do what works best for you.

I truly don't care what strategy you use, as long as it works for you and helps you get closer to what you're trying to accomplish.

**DO THE WORK**

## Start Investing and Keep On Investing

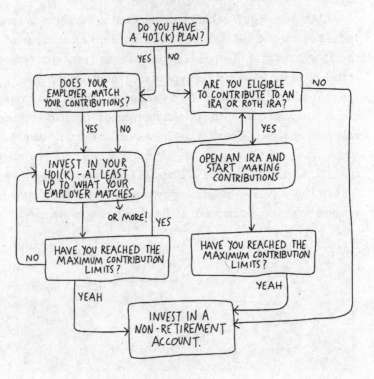

WHERE TO START INVESTING FOR RETIREMENT?

- **Let's talk strategy. Do you have a plan to start investing in the next twelve months? What is it?**
- **What's your investing plan look like in the next five years?**
- **What's your investing plan look like in the next ten years?**

## CHAPTER 16

# So You Wanna Hire a Financial Advisor?

I feel the same way about paying for professional financial services as I do about steamed broccoli. Depending on when you ask me for my opinion, I might reply with something innocuous like, "They both have their place and their value in the world." On other days, maybe if I'm cold or particularly hungry, I might snap at you and tell you how I think both of those things are pointless and boring. When it comes to my opinions on hiring financial help, my feelings are complicated.

On the one hand, most people truly don't need to hire anyone to help them with their personal finances. Most folks can figure it all out without ever hiring a financial planner or an investment advisor. The average person can pretty much learn everything they need to know on their own. Between all the books, blogs, podcasts, videos and online courses, the information is more available than ever. And in some cases, like for folks living paycheck to paycheck, those with a lot of debt or anyone who already knows what they're doing, they don't need to pay someone to validate what they probably already know about their financial plan and their financial life.

But on the other hand, I am a proponent of hiring professionals to help you take your life to the next level. Good financial planners and advisors truly add value to their clients' lives, but not just in the area of investments. Since nobody can predict the market and most advisors can't beat the market, a good advisor or planner must be valuable outside of investing. Especially when you first start working with a planner or advisor, they should spend time listening to you speak. They need to understand where you're at and where you want to go. Then they have to educate you, so you understand what it takes to reach your financial goals. They have to know what to focus on and what to ignore. And sometimes they have the unpleasant job of pissing in your cornflakes; telling you what goals might be possible but not probable and all the ways you must prepare against the possibility of misfortune.

I come from the world of traditional financial planning, where working with a financial planner requires that you have complexity in your financial life, a certain amount of wealth and the commitment to sign up for yearlong engagements. That's not how all financial planners work. You can hire someone to create a plan for you, to review a plan you created or to consult with at various times in your life. For example, if you're newly divorced, received an inheritance, got a big fat raise, are close to retiring, have gone through some other major financial milestone or think you need to hire an actual professional to get your crap together, you can get someone to be your temporary guide as you move through these different circumstances in your life.

Whether you decide you want to hire a financial planner or advisor (or any other kind of financial professional), here are the things you should consider and the questions you need answered to help you decide which person is right for you.

## BUT FIRST, WHAT'S THE DIFFERENCE BETWEEN A FINANCIAL PLANNER AND A FINANCIAL ADVISOR?

Financial planners can also be advisors and vice versa. But they can also just be planners or just advisors. The difference is similar to the way that squares and rectangles can both be classified as parallelograms, but are different shapes when you take a closer look. Financial planners are generally trained to help you come up with a comprehensive plan to help navigate your entire financial life, whereas financial advisors might be more limited to giving you advice on investments.

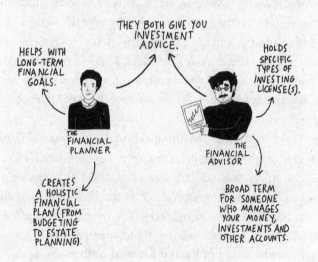

THE DIFFERENCE BETWEEN A
FINANCIAL PLANNER AND A FINANCIAL ADVISOR

HELPS WITH LONG-TERM FINANCIAL GOALS.

THEY BOTH GIVE YOU INVESTMENT ADVICE.

HOLDS SPECIFIC TYPES OF INVESTING LICENSE(S).

THE FINANCIAL PLANNER

THE FINANCIAL ADVISOR

CREATES A HOLISTIC FINANCIAL PLAN (FROM BUDGETING TO ESTATE PLANNING).

BROAD TERM FOR SOMEONE WHO MANAGES YOUR MONEY, INVESTMENTS AND OTHER ACCOUNTS.

Financial planners are great if you're looking for someone with a holistic perspective who can help you with your entire financial life—which is why my bias is in favor of financial planners over advisors. Financial advisors are good for people who are looking for specific help in the area of investments. Generally, I have observed advisors to be product pushers—salespeople—because their compensation is often tied to commissions. Since they make money by selling you financial products, it's a good idea to be cautious when dealing with advisors who aren't also planners.

So far I've been duped into two separate meetings with two different people for the same life insurance pyramid scheme. Both of them told me they were financial advisors when in reality they were life insurance salespeople who were participating in a pyramid scheme and calling themselves advisors.

The first guy approached me after I gave a talk to a group of people at a co-working space in the suburb of Costa Mesa, California. He told me he was a financial advisor. This guy said something along the lines of, "I've been attempting to manifest meeting the right person to partner with and I think you're the person." He was just vague enough and complimentary enough to my ego to pique my interest. So, like a naive dum-dum, I agreed to exchange cards and planned to connect more on the subject later. In the next few days, we arranged a meeting at my favorite neighborhood coffee shop.

He told me about the financial advisory "business" he was "building," even though his most recent professional experience was in an unrelated industry like production or something completely and entirely different from finance. I told him I left the traditional financial services industry for a couple of reasons: First, I realized I truly loathed talking about investments. I also didn't come from the world of having a casual million-dollar, inherited net worth, so trying to find clients who did was not as natural and easy for me as for other folks who were born into that world. He agreed with me and said he wasn't trying to build a roster of super wealthy clients and that his strategy was to instead build a big list of clients. That's when I realized that this guy was trying to bull-shit me.

Anyone who knows anything about managing money knows that being an independent planner and having a big book of business with a lot of little clients is a recipe for a needlessly stressful lifestyle. Because an independent advisory business based on volume, without the right support or technology, will grind you into the ground and turn you into a shell of a human being. There are only so many clients you can serve in a day, a week, a month and a year.

I told him what I thought—that his approach is not a smart thing to do if you do not want to have a life where your thousand clients can text you any time of the day, any day of the year. And that's when he began to explain that his business was much less about managing investments; that there was actually the potential to make more money by recruiting and building a business rather than signing more and more clients.

And in that moment I felt like the biggest idiot in the world because I was a financial professional that had been duped into a meeting with some random dude who was trying to get me to join a pyramid scheme! The company he was involved with is called World Financial Group. I told him he was involved in a scam, because any time you can make more money recruiting people than serving your clients, you are most definitely involved in a pyramid scheme. Instead of pausing and thinking critically, he insisted it wasn't a scam and tried to prove it by drawing tick marks on a napkin. You know the drawing—it vaguely resembles the top of a pyramid. I can't remember how the meeting ended, but it generally doesn't end well when you tell someone to their face that they're trying to get you involved in a scam.

The next time I got bamboozled by someone trying to rope me

into a similar company's scheme, it happened through a DJ I met at a creative conference I spoke at. He slid into the Instagram DMs and said he wanted to introduce me to one of his former DJ friends who was now in finance. Maybe that should have been a red flag for me, but I'm still learning how to be good at setting boundaries so I set up a lunch with this guy. While dining al fresco in the lovely courtyard of a downtown Los Angeles restaurant on a perfectly sunny day, the realization slowly came to me. I was mostly mortified that I was once again not smart enough to have seen this coming. And once again, I was having a conversation where I'm telling this dude that he's involved in a scam and I have to listen to him parrot back the same answers as the last poor soul. Thankfully, the napkins at this establishment were cloth.

Listen, I'm not trying to make the case against hiring help and I'm not saying these are bad people; they're just mixed up with a bad company within a system that creates incentives to sell products even if people don't need the product. Great financial planners and advisors can add a lot of value to your life, but for every great one, I'm sure there are a countless number of clowns and bozos strutting around town trying to sell you some bullshit. The financial industry is just fertile ground for it. To prevent yourself from getting roped in and agreeing to buy some insurance disguised as an investment, this chapter will help you arm yourself with some information to go into any meeting well prepared and with enough knowledge to keep these clowns at bay.

# WHOEVER YOU HIRE MUST BE AN INDEPENDENT FIDUCIARY WHO NEVER RECOMMENDS PRODUCTS UNDER THE "SUITABILITY STANDARD"

Let's define some key terms.

- A **fiduciary** is a person or organization that acts on behalf of another person to manage assets. A fiduciary is legally and ethically required to put their client's best interests before their own. But here's the kicker: not all financial advisors are fiduciaries! How could this even be a possibility? Because some sales people just need to abide by something called the suitability standard.

- The **suitability standard** is a regulation that says a broker must make "reasonable efforts to obtain information" on a client's financial life when determining whether a financial product is deemed "suitable" for a client.[1] Suitability doesn't sound sketchy, but it can be. For example, if you hired a dietician whose food recommendations only needed to meet a suitability standard, they could argue that it's suitable for you to only eat vitamin-infused Pop-Tarts. What is suitable for you is not what is in your best interests. That's the trick with this language.

- When advisors are **independent**, this means they are free to recommend financial products from different companies. Someone who is not independent would be a "wealth manager" who works at Wells Fargo; they are usually only allowed to sell you Wells Fargo products, which might not be the best product for you but is the only product they can sell.

- **Products** are types of investments, securities and financial instruments like annuities or life insurance policies.

Let's look at an example. Let's say Jake, the financial advisor, has two product options for his client, Jane. The first product is an investment that is the best option for Jane and that happens to be less costly for her, but it only pays Jake a 3 percent commission. The second investment is not the best option for Jane and it happens to be more expensive, but it meets the suitability standard and pays Jake a 10 percent commission. The problem with the suitability standard, and with commission-based fees in general, is that it can create a conflict of interest between the advisor and the client.

You might be thinking, why did she specifically say, "Whoever you hire must be a fiduciary that never recommends products under the suitability standard"? Maybe you're thinking, "If a financial advisor is a fiduciary, how could they possibly recommend products using the suitability standard?" Sadly, it's because advisors who are fiduciaries are still finding ways to work around their legal

and ethical obligation to put their client's best interests before their own.

Here's how: it's all in the technicality of the type of firm they work for (or set up themselves). All financial advisory firms have to register their companies as either a brokerage firm or a registered investment advisor (RIA), or they can be both by becoming a hybrid.

- A **brokerage firm** only needs to abide by the suitability standard.

- A **registered investment advisor (RIA)** is legally required to act as a fiduciary.

- A **hybrid firm** is registered as both registered investment advisors and as a brokerage firm. This means certain things that this firm does are done under the fiduciary obligation, like managing money for a fee. But there are other times, like when selling certain products, where they can also act as a brokerage firm, only beholden to the suitability standard. A hybrid firm is like when you visit the border of two states and you can stand in both of them at once and make a dad joke about being in California and Nevada. It's the best of both worlds . . . for the advisor.

WHAT'S THE DIFFERENCE BETWEEN THE DIFFERENT
TYPES OF FINANCIAL ADVISORY FIRMS?

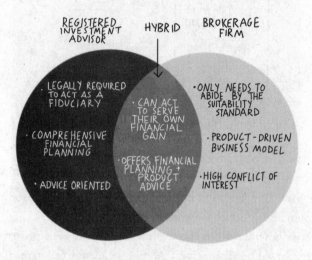

REGISTERED INVESTMENT ADVISOR    HYBRID    BROKERAGE FIRM

- LEGALLY REQUIRED TO ACT AS A FIDUCIARY
- COMPREHENSIVE FINANCIAL PLANNING
- ADVICE ORIENTED

- CAN ACT TO SERVE THEIR OWN FINANCIAL GAIN
- OFFERS FINANCIAL PLANNING + PRODUCT ADVICE

- ONLY NEEDS TO ABIDE BY THE SUITABILITY STANDARD
- PRODUCT-DRIVEN BUSINESS MODEL
- HIGH CONFLICT OF INTEREST

Ultimately, it's not enough anymore that the financial planner or advisor you hire is a fiduciary. They also should never, ever recommend financial products using the suitability standard. And while they might be able to boast about the benefits of setting up a hybrid firm over only an RIA, realize that there is this little loophole that can be exploited to their benefit and possibly to your detriment. I'm not saying they will, but you should know that it's a possibility. It might be best for you to work with someone where that possibility just doesn't exist.

# KNOW ALL THE WAYS YOU PAY WHOEVER YOU HIRE—BEWARE THE HIDDEN COSTS IN THE PROMISE OF RETURNS

There are generally two ways financial professionals get paid. There are client fees and commissions on selling financial products. Client fees can be structured in a variety of ways. There are asset management fees, hourly fees, retainers, quarterly fees or flat-rate fees.

When hiring someone to help you with your money, it's important to know how they make theirs because it comes at your expense—literally. There is nothing inherently wrong with people getting compensated for their work, but that doesn't mean we shouldn't be critical about potential conflicts of interest or critical of the value you receive compared to the price you're paying.

## Fee-Only

If you interview a financial planner, ask them to tell you all the ways they get paid and if their response is that they are a fee-only practice, this means their compensation comes directly from the clients they serve. Fee-only planners and advisors are almost always fiduciaries that act in the best interests of their clients.

Since their pay comes directly from their clients and not from third parties like mutual funds or insurance companies, these planners and advisors can keep their focus on their clients' needs and best interests. When a fee-only advisor or planner recommends financial investments products, you can feel confident knowing that they are truly recommending the best product for you since the recommendations are not in competition with commissions.

The fee paid to advisors and planners can be structured in a number of different ways. There are annual retainers, monthly subscriptions, a fee to deliver a comprehensive financial plan and different service packages with different options. There are planners who charge an hourly rate or a fee per session. An asset management fee has been a popular fee structure in the industry, but it can end up being a lot costlier for the clients in the long run.

## Assets Under Management

An assets under management (AUM) fee can be fee-only, but it can also be a part of fee-based compensation if the advisor also gets paid commissions. It's tricky, which is why it's important to get these questions answered when considering hiring someone.

In my first week working at the financial planning firm, my new boss sat me down and explained to me how the industry worked. He explained how our firm can charge an annual financial planning fee and a 1 percent asset management fee. This means that 1 percent of the client's investment account balance is paid as a fee. So, a client with a million dollars invested with us would pay us $10,000 per year and a client with $10 million would pay us $100,000 a year. At first, this seemed totally fine and a 1 percent fee may not sound like much, but it ends up being very expensive in the long run. It could cost investors 25 percent of their returns over forty years—or nearly half a million dollars![2] Ouch.

For some people, paying this fee is worth it because they use their financial planner to help them analyze all sorts of investment options or financial opportunities, from businesses they might invest in to publishing and licensing deals they're considering. But for a lot of folks, this fee is not worth it because they aren't getting services to justify the fee. Most people don't need to be giving away that much of the returns they could be generating themselves by investing in index funds and ETFs.

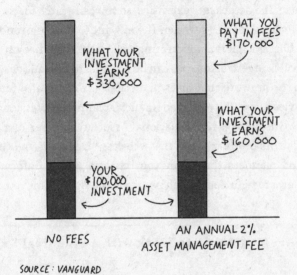

UNDERSTANDING THE LONG-TERM COST OF ASSET MANAGEMENT FEES

WHAT YOUR INVESTMENT EARNS $330,000

WHAT YOU PAY IN FEES $170,000

WHAT YOUR INVESTMENT EARNS $160,000

YOUR $100,000 INVESTMENT

NO FEES

AN ANNUAL 2% ASSET MANAGEMENT FEE

SOURCE: VANGUARD

## Commissions on Products

If you ask a financial advisor how they get paid and their answer is that their compensation is fee-based, this means that they can get paid both from fees paid by clients *and* from commission on the financial products they sell. Why do they call it fee-based when it sounds misleading and so similar to fee-only? To confuse you, maybe? I don't know if that's the answer, but it probably is because it would be way more straightforward to call this payment structure "fees *and* commission."

## WHERE TO FIND FEE-ONLY ADVISORS AND PLANNERS

The XY Planning Network is a wonderful database to find fee-only advisors.[3] The database is extensive, so you can search for the things you're looking for in a planner. If you want to find someone who is local, charges a flat rate for creating a plan and specializes in socially responsible investments, you can do a search to find all the advisors within the network that meet that criteria. You can also find other fiduciaries like a CFP (certified financial planner) professional or an advisor who belongs to the National Association of Personal Financial Advisors on their respective websites.[4] Once you find the advisors and planners that meet your criteria, set up informational interviews to figure out which person is the right fit for you.

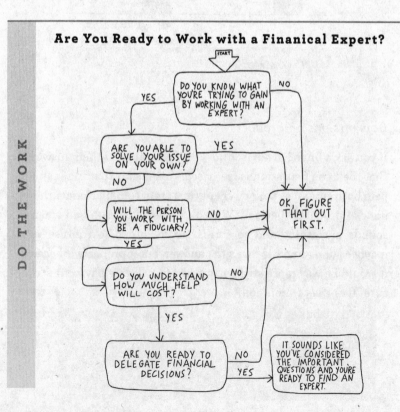

**Are You Ready to Work with a Finanical Expert?**

START

DO YOU KNOW WHAT YOU'RE TRYING TO GAIN BY WORKING WITH AN EXPERT?

YES — ARE YOU ABLE TO SOLVE YOUR ISSUE ON YOUR OWN?

NO — OK, FIGURE THAT OUT FIRST.

YES — OK, FIGURE THAT OUT FIRST.

NO — WILL THE PERSON YOU WORK WITH BE A FIDUCIARY?

NO — OK, FIGURE THAT OUT FIRST.

YES — DO YOU UNDERSTAND HOW MUCH HELP WILL COST?

NO — OK, FIGURE THAT OUT FIRST.

YES — ARE YOU READY TO DELEGATE FINANCIAL DECISIONS?

NO — OK, FIGURE THAT OUT FIRST.

YES — IT SOUNDS LIKE YOU'VE CONSIDERED THE IMPORTANT QUESTIONS AND YOU'RE READY TO FIND AN EXPERT.

DO THE WORK

**CHAPTER 17**

## How to Build Wealth

### Know Your Net Worth

We can trace the pursuit of wealth in modern life to some unsavory, fucked-up events. The pursuit of more wealth is what drove European countries to colonize other parts of the world. The Atlantic slave trade and the origins of Wall Street are intertwined. The origin of wealth in our modern world sprouted from these seeds. It's no wonder the trope of the immoral, greedy wealthy person persists. It's because the world as we know it was shaped and continues to be shaped by these principles of scarcity over abundance, extraction over sacred exchange and the violence of colonization.

Recognizing how these ideas are present in the principles behind wealth building can help us understand ways we can approach and possibly reshape our relationship with wealth. Facing our history allows us to choose an intentional way of participating in building wealth.

Wealth is a megaphone for our values, ideas and voice. Someone who has wealth has the freedom and resources to work and create the things they want to see in the world. Wealth is power. Anyone who feels strongly compelled to impact society realizes that wealth is an ingredient to accomplishing this. You don't need to have extreme wealth to support radical ideas that you want to see in the world. Even at modest levels of wealth, you can still impact communities while investing in relationships. Poet, activist and author Sonya Renee Taylor created a project called Buy Back Black Debt. It's a local project of interracial, spiritual and economic relationship building. Groups of five to ten people pool economic resources and commit financial support to Black people in their local community who are experiencing the impacts of institutional racism via debt. This is a radical idea and an extremely literal example of how wealth can amplify our values, ideas and voice in the world.

What is wealth anyway? It's not all caviar and first-class flights. In fact, for most people building wealth requires that they often must go without those things. Wealth isn't the amount of money that you spend, contrary to every episode of *Gossip Girl*. Wealth is what you keep, it's what you own.

I remember the first time that the concept of wealth really clicked for me. I was sitting in my boss's office and he was teaching me about life insurance applications. On the application, you had to choose a benefit amount and give some justification about the calculation that was used to determine the amount. Figuring this out was kind of like doing geometry; there were different ways you could solve the theorem.

That day I learned about a simple rule of thumb that my boss used for all his clients. Life insurance, which we'll cover more in depth in the next chapter, was insurance that would replace someone's income if they died while they were covered by the policy. He said that for each $50,000 of income that would need to be replaced, they'd need a million dollars' worth of term life insurance. The rationale behind this was that if you had a lump sum of one million dollars and invested that million at that time, you could reasonably expect to generate a 5 percent return each year. This is how you'd make the $50,000 of income that needed to be replaced. The million dollars was invested, and those investments generated a return that was the income that could then be spent for living expenses.

What blew my mind was the underlying assumption that the beneficiaries of the policy wouldn't just get a million bucks and slowly spend it over time like the majority of all lottery winners. The assumption that they'd invest it and live off its earnings meant that there is the potential that the lump sum is mostly preserved in the form of owning investments.

While this is theory and not practice—like, I'm one hundred percent not saying that life insurance is a tool for building wealth— this lesson made me realize that I'd been thinking about income, spending, investing and wealth all wrong. It made me realize that folks who had a million dollars could keep their million dollars if they could live off of the $50,000 it generated in returns. And by doing this, you can pass wealth on to the next generation. It illustrated, again, that wealth isn't what you spend, it's what you own.

When you're truly wealthy, your financial security doesn't depend solely on the income you get from a paycheck. This is what independent means in the term "financially independent." Your financial security is independent of a paycheck from a job. When you're genuinely wealthy, earning money isn't dependent on working. The whole point of saving and investing is this idea that at some tipping point, your income will actually come from your wealth instead of your wealth being built by your income.

This was something that my family never taught me. I only came by it and internalized it after repeated exposure to the inner workings of the finance industry. For many people, thinking about building wealth in this way isn't a natural instinct. We have to be taught and shown this perspective. And if you're like me, you need to see this concept illustrated in various ways in order for it to really make sense.

Wealth is sometimes hard to grasp because it's often conflated with income. I didn't get a degree in finance because I wanted to learn how to quietly build wealth while living frugally. I wanted to learn how I could spend money like an asshole while working as little as possible. This is embarrassing to admit, but I doubt anyone gets a degree in finance for any other reason. I don't think I'm alone in this conflation of wealth and income. We tend to think people are wealthy because they have a high income.

Society often views actors and athletes who sign multimillion-dollar deals or doctors with seven-figure private practices as wealthy people because of their income level. While income and wealth are most definitely related, they are not the same thing. Income is how much money you earn over a period of time and wealth is owning valuable things. And while you can have a high income, if you spend the million you earn because you're trapped on that hedonic treadmill, you'll never truly be wealthy because you have to go out and earn that money all over again.

## INCOME ≠ WEALTH
## BUT WEALTH CAN CREATE INCOME

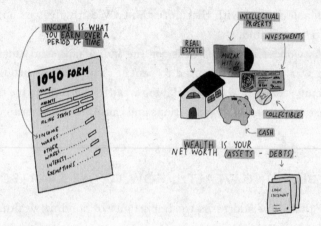

Unfortunately, it's not uncommon to see this play out among professional athletes. According to a 2009 *Sports Illustrated* article, 60 percent of former NBA players are broke within five years of retirement. And 78 percent of former NFL players have gone bankrupt or are under financial stress within two years of retirement.[1] These are athletes who earn more in one year than most people do their whole lives, but manage to spend it all, with no wealth to show for it. I've seen this phenomenon up close, but instead of athletes, it's Angelenos.

As a financial planner, I worked with couples who earn nearly a million dollars a year, but also spent nearly every dollar earned. I quickly saw that high earnings don't guarantee wealth. Building wealth often requires earning an income but creating wealth requires a shift in perspective.

Creating wealth is a financial goal that is often assumed but not always talked about. Wealth can represent freedom and security, but it also allows you to be financially resilient as opposed to financially fragile. When you're financially fragile, you feel all the little economic shocks and bumps in the road. Remember, economic and financial shocks are routine, we should expect them like we expect the tides to come in. Wealth can leave us feeling like we're able to deal with that uncertainty. Wealth gives us options and peace of mind.

As wonderful as wealth is for the individuals who amass it, their wealth can also be used to benefit communities through financing economic activism. Having wealth gives us the means to invest in the people, organizations and causes that matter to us.

## BUILDING WEALTH: HOW TO GET STARTED

Now that we've addressed the importance of building wealth, let's look at how to get started.

### Investing in the Market

A very common, traditional and, frankly, easy way to multiply your money is through what we've discussed in the prior chapters: investing in the stock market. The most common way folks do this is through a retirement plan or retirement account, but it can also be done through brokerage accounts. A brokerage account is an account where an investor can buy and sell investments like different kinds of funds or even individual stocks. It's like a retirement account, but you can sell your investments and use the money any time, without penalties for taking funds out before retirement age since it's not a retirement account. The trade-off is that any gains and income that you have within your brokerage accounts don't have tax benefits the way retirement accounts do. When you earn interest and dividends, or you realize a gain from a sale because you bought it at a lower price than when you sold it, you'll have to pay taxes on these increases. This is why retirement accounts are called tax-sheltered accounts. The government tries to encourage us to save for our own retirement by creating tax incentives.

## Real Estate

Another common and traditional way people like to invest is by buying an investment property, like a house that generates rental income. This way of investing requires a lot more energy and capital compared to the stock market. If you want to do this, educate yourself on how to run it like a proper business and learn about the market you're getting into. And realize that when you do this, you are giving yourself the job of becoming a landlord, unless you contract it out to a management company. However, at the end of the day, the property is still your responsibility as the owner. Alternatively, some people view their primary residence as an investment.

A home *can* be a smart investment, but, on average, its expected return is about equal to investing in stocks.[2] The return on your investment varies from city to city and by the timing of when you buy and sell your home. Historically, primary residences have been a way for many people, regardless of socioeconomic status or income, to create wealth. However, it's important to note that housing data, which doesn't account for that many years in the grand scheme of humans on Earth, may convince us that a bet on our primary residence is a sure thing, but it might require a much more nuanced approach instead.

Buying a home is usually the largest purchase anyone makes in their life, and it requires you to have a sum of money between five and six figures for a down payment. So just like everything else in your financial life, knowing whether home-buying is the right thing for you is a personal decision that only you can sort through.

The *New York Times* has a really great calculator[3] that can help you determine whether or not renting or buying is better in terms of pure economics. But that's the challenge with these things; the numbers can only tell the story of monetary costs. It's your job to explore how these monetary costs translate to second-order consequences that impact your whole life.

## Create and Own Valuable Things

The wealthiest people own valuable things. Owning assets is key. This has always been true throughout history. Whoever came up with the scheme of owning land had the power and the means to create wealth. These days, for better or for worse, the financialization of everything means that there are many ways to buy assets. Assets can be intellectual property. They are ideas that get monetized. They are art, fractional shares of art and even digital art in the form of non-fungible tokens. They are sneakers! They are the means of production; they are businesses.

They are a catalog of songs or a screenplay or an additional dwelling on your property that increases the value of your home or creates rental income. You can even find ownership if you work for an employee-owned company. Yes, you'll have to meet the requirements so that you eventually have ownership in it, but it's a way to correct the misalignment of values between employees and employers that I mentioned in Chapter 5. There are also corporations that compensate their workers with stock options. This is another path to owning something valuable, albeit a less traveled and less commonly available path.

Ownership is imperative to build wealth, but it's also valuable beyond individualistic advancement. Building wealth won't solve all of our problems in society, but for marginalized groups, it certainly helps. At the individual level, someone who works a modest job can amass six figures by the time they are middle aged or even younger. This can be life changing for people. It might not be enough to retire early and fuck off traveling the world at thirty-five, but it's enough to feel secure, safe and abundant. It's enough to give someone options and to take away the stress so that they aren't trapped in a loop of anxiety-induced bad decisions.

On a larger scale, if you're interested in building power structures that exist outside of a capitalist structure, you have to participate in building and owning things. When more people can control the means of production, as opposed to a concentrated few, we have the power and means to impact communities. We can create, support and choose business models that coexist in capitalism and community. Imagine if you and a few of your friends were the landlords in a gentrifying neighborhood; you could find a way to help people stay in a community that they are being quickly priced out of. We can take radical action that will eventually build bridges to new ways of organizing society. We can create alternative power structures because we control the asset. When you create assets, you create a concrete expression of an idea in the world. That is power.

## A Balanced Approach

Different folks will approach building wealth in different ways. Some folks will quietly save and invest for thirty to forty years. Some folks will start businesses or create other valuable things. Others may choose to go the real estate route. And many will take a balanced approach, owning and investing in many things—creating a business, investing in the market and buying real estate.

Creating wealth through a balanced approach is traditional, but it can be a very practical way to diversify your wealth. Diversifying how you hold your wealth is a way to hedge, or manage, risk, just like with investing in the market. As an example, if most of your investments were concentrated in a few apartment buildings in one county of the country, the lack of diversification means you run the risk of a natural disaster or some kind of regional shock potentially impacting the bulk of your assets. The same goes with having most of your wealth invested in the stock market. During the inevitable downturns, the value of your wealth goes down. Risks like this are also why saving cash in an emergency fund is a priority ahead of creating wealth. Without it, you're forced to use your assets, which is like taking one step forward in building wealth only to take two back. Diversifying what you own is a way to make sure that you don't run the risk of losing all your eggs because they're in one basket.

Whatever mix of assets you choose to invest in, please keep in mind that it will behoove you to learn all about how that investment works. In other words, if you want to invest in a business, you should spend some time learning about business. At the very least read a few business books. If you want to buy an apartment, study real estate and learn about what it's like being a landlord. If you want to create an asset, you'll want to have knowledge to draw on. Leverage your experience, connections and insider knowledge to create an asset.

# SOME GARDEN VARIETY ASSETS

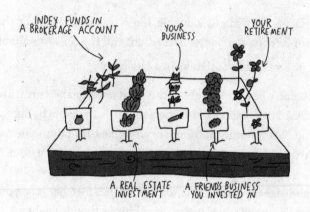

INDEX FUNDS IN A BROKERAGE ACCOUNT

YOUR BUSINESS

YOUR RETIREMENT

A REAL ESTATE INVESTMENT

A FRIENDS BUSINESS YOU INVESTED IN

## THE MEASURE OF YOUR WEALTH IS YOUR NET WORTH

Calculating your net worth is really easy. You just add up all your cash and the value of your assets, then you subtract the total balance of all your debts and, voila, you'll have your net worth.

Here's generally what's included in your personal asset category:

- All your cash in your various checking accounts
- All your cash in your various savings accounts
- Investments, including 401(k) plans and other retirement plan balances
- Real estate
- Furniture

- Jewelry
- Art
- Other stuff that's valuable, like a guitar or violin or that bit of Bitcoin you bought to see what all the fuss was about
- The value of your stake in a business

You don't have to go into detail with jewelry and furniture and all of that stuff, especially if it's not worth that much. But just in case you have a family heirloom or a Michael Jordan rookie basketball card that is actually worth a lot, you might want to account for it.

Liabilities are your debts, or money you owe because you borrowed it. Here are some examples of things that are debts:

- A mortgage or home equity line of credit
- Student loan balance
- The balance you owe on your credit cards
- Car loan
- Personal loans
- Anything you may have financed that you're making monthly payments on

Your net worth number can help you gauge where you are relative to your financial and life goals. Even if your goal right now is simply to have a positive net worth, it's still important to know where you are relative to your goal because that will drive your strategy and decisions. Your net worth is a data point that guides what actions you take.

# WHAT SHOULD YOUR TARGET NET WORTH BE?

In the short term, net worth matters because it's a way to understand how stable and resilient your finances are. Folks with a positive net worth, folks who have cash on hand and investments, have the space to breathe. They have options; they might have the ability to quit their jobs without another one lined up.

In the long term, net worth is the underlying mechanism that allows people to retire. When you take the traditional approach to retirement, as we discussed in the previous chapter, there's a simple, quick and dirty method for coming up with your target net worth. The method gives you a target based on a multiple of your pretax income based on your age. Of course, there are much more complicated calculations you can use to find your target net worth, but for now, let's keep it simple. There's plenty of time to nerd out on retirement calculators later.

I had reservations about including this chart in this book because I know it will freak a lot of people out if they are very far away from "where they should be." On the one hand, being freaked out and feeling behind and stressed is not a good state to be in. It's so hard to think clearly when you're in that state. But on the other hand, if you are interested in the kind of financial well-being that allows you to afford life without having to work, this chart is a great tool for understanding what that will take and if it's something you'd like to pursue.

# USE THIS CHART TO FIGURE OUT WHAT YOUR NET WORTH SHOULD BE

| AGE | OK | BETTER | GOOD | GREAT | 🔥🔥🔥 |
|-----|-----|--------|------|-------|--------|
| 22 | Ø | | | | 0.1 |
| 25 | Ø | 0.1 | 0.25 | 0.4 | 0.5 |
| 28 | Ø | 0.25 | 0.4 | 0.5 | 1 |
| 30 | 0.5 | 0.75 | 1 | 1.5 | 2 |
| 35 | 1 | 2 | 3 | 4 | 5 |
| 40 | 2 | 4 | 6 | 8 | 10 |
| 45 | 3 | 6 | 8 | 10 | 13 |
| 50 | 4 | 7 | 9 | 12 | 15 |
| 55 | 5 | 8 | 11 | 14 | 17 |
| 60+ | 6 | 9 | 13 | 16 | 20 |

STEP 1: FIND THE AGE CLOSEST TO YOURS.

STEP 2: MULTIPLY YOUR ANNUAL TAKE-HOME PAY BY EACH NUMBER IN EVERY CATEGORY.

STEP 3: COMPARE YOUR NET WORTH WITH YOUR TARGET NET WORTH NUMBERS.

| AGE | OK | BETTER | GOOD | GREAT | 🔥🔥🔥 |
|-----|-----|--------|------|-------|-------|
| 22 | 0 | | | | 0.1 |
| 25 | 0 | 0.1 | 0.25 | 0.4 | 0.5 |
| 28 | 0 | 0.25 | 0.4 | 0.5 | 1 |
| 30 | 0.5 | 0.75 | 1 | 1.5 | 2 |
| 35 | 1 | 2 | 3 | 4 | 5 |
| 40 | 2 | 4 | 6 | 8 | 10 |
| 45 | 3 | 6 | 8 | 10 | 13 |
| 50 | 4 | 7 | 9 | 12 | 15 |
| 55 | 5 | 8 | 11 | 14 | 17 |
| 60+ | 6 | 9 | 13 | 16 | 20 |

FOR EXAMPLE, JESS IS 30 AND HAS AN
ANNUAL TAKE-HOME PAY OF $45,000.
SHE HAS THE FOLLOWING TARGET NET WORTH:

$45,000 × 0.5 = $22,500 ⟶ OK

$45,000 × 0.75 = $33,750 ⟶ BETTER

$45,000 × 1 = $45,000 ⟶ GOOD

$45,000 × 1.5 = $67,500 ⟶ GREAT

$45,000 × 2 = $90,000 ⟶ 🔥🔥🔥

JESS HAS AN ACTUAL NET WORTH OF $38,950,
WHICH LANDS BETWEEN "BETTER" AND "GOOD."

The chart has a range because some people will want to know how much they should be saving to live a traditional, normal retired life after forty to fifty years of working and some people might be curious about building a large pile of wealth that would allow them to free themselves from relying on a paycheck much sooner. The latter are interested in building a pile of Fuck-You Money.

Fuck-You Money is exactly what it sounds like. It's a giant pile of money (cash and assets) that gives you the freedom to walk out of your job, *Half-Baked* style, middle fingers blazing. Of course, you can be more graceful, up to you. But the chart illustrates a range and lets you see how much more you'd have to save to retire sooner than regular retirement age. The range just gives you options. Or it might give you permission to aim your sights on a life you didn't think you could have.

You'll notice on the chart that the older you get, the higher the multiple gets. The reason for the increase is twofold. First, you're closer to retirement so you need to have accumulated more. Second, we're assuming your wealth has been compounding, which means it has been growing exponentially.

## PICK A GOAL AND DECONSTRUCT THE HABITS THAT PRECEDE REACHING YOUR GOAL

There are plenty of parents who couldn't rely on their own parents for financial support so they want to create wealth that can benefit their children. There are also plenty of folks who are not interested in passing their wealth on to their heirs. They're interested in enjoying it, spending it and then directing it to organizations they want to support.

You don't have to have the goal of creating a giant pile of wealth that you hope to one day pass on to your children. There are plenty of wealthy people who have publicly committed to donating the majority of their wealth to charity. And at the time of this writing, organizations that allow people to invest in other people and communities are starting to pop up. I expect to see more of these kinds of platforms that allow people to build wealth for beneficiaries outside of themselves to become more prominent over time. However, this kind of thinking isn't necessarily new. Benjamin Franklin bequeathed $2,000 to be divided between the cities of Boston and Philadelphia. But the catch was that much of that money couldn't be drawn on for 100 years, and the majority of it would not be distributed for 200 years. In 1990, his gift was worth $6.5 million.[4] This is both a fascinating example of the power of compounding and an untraditional way to direct wealth. Whatever you choose, I hope you'll allow your net worth target to reflect what feels right for you and what you value.

When you decide on a target net worth, you have a new financial goal to work towards. Now you'll need to determine what regular actions you need to take to get you closer to your goal. Not everyone's plan of action will look the same.

If you are a new business owner that wants to have a $3 million net worth, you'll have to examine all the options you have to make reaching this goal a reality. Maybe one option is building a business that will sell for $3 million in ten years—or five years. Another option is creating a business that is profitable enough to support the owner's salary and profits so they can be both invested in retirement accounts and in real estate over the next ten years.

Someone with different circumstances and different goals might have a different approach. A young, single employee who wants to amass $100,000 by the time they're forty has different paths to building that wealth. They can find a well-paying job, choose to live with roommates or choose to live with family or in a van. They can decide to take on additional work as a freelancer and live as frugally as possible. Once you have a goal, you can start to see that many paths can lead to the same destination.

It's valuable to have clear goals and a clear strategy for how you'll grow your net worth. But remember the concepts we went over in Chapter 4. Goals are great at pointing you in a direction, getting you started, giving you structure and allowing you to see how far you are from where you need to be.

There will always be things outside of our control that will get in the way of what we are trying to achieve. The things within our circle of control are the habits we can build that often precede reaching a goal. For example, investing 30 percent of any income, bonuses, gifts or windfalls. What are the behaviors and habits that will precede you reaching your goals? And can you commit to them consistently?

Don't underestimate your personal power. I'm serious here. Don't underestimate what you can do. And maybe this sounds really cavalier and sort of out of touch because, again, there is so much outside of our control. But once you start to see what happens when you maintain focus on things within your circle of control, you start to see more ways that you have agency. All these little areas of agency compound. It's a long game of consistency.

## BUILDING WEALTH IS A LONG GAME

Building wealth requires the kind of consistency that waves exert on a cliff, eventually causing a beautifully eroded cliffside. Day in and day out, the waves are a constant force, not necessarily working hard, just doing their thing. This is how you build wealth. By consistently saving, investing and creating valuable things that you own. There is absolutely nothing glamourous about what it takes to have a consistent focus on building wealth. It's really quite boring, but that is so often the case with any sort of achievement or reaching of one's goals. The outcome might be sexy, but the low-grade grind that gets you there is quite unsexy. It's this ability to put your energy towards something through the tedium and boredom of it all that can be really hard to do sometimes.

But by the time you're at the level in the Pyramid of Financial Awesomeness where you're building wealth, you've worked through a lot of layers of tedium. You've seen how powerful you are. You've spent time setting up systems for spending and saving. You've funded your emergency fund. Maybe you've gone through years of paying off credit card debt and slowly building a business. By now, this high up on the pyramid, you'll start to see that building wealth is the natural result of having gone through the processes that come before this one.

## USE THIS TOOL: RETIREMENT PLANNER

As your net worth starts to grow, you may want to take a closer look at your plan by running a retirement projection or using a retirement planner. A retirement planner is an online tool you can use that both tracks your net worth and helps you project your net worth into the future. The tool I use personally and often recommend is made by the company Personal Capital.[5] Personal Capital is a web-based tool that has an accompanying application for your phone. It aggregates data from your various financial institutions, pulling in the balances from asset accounts and debt accounts, giving you an at-a-glance view of your net worth. The planning section of the website will ask you questions about your current earnings, savings, investing and desired date of retirement. The tool will make assumptions about investment returns based on the data you feed it. And these assumptions will help give you a ballpark range for whether or not you will meet your retirement goal.

Smart Asset also makes a free retirement tool that you can use to run a retirement projection.[6] The site will guide you through a series of questions about your earnings, savings, investments, spending and when you'd like to retire. While a projection and planner aren't always 100 percent guaranteed, they are a good tool for seeing how your investments can potentially grow over time.

## USE THIS TOOL: THE REVERSAL OF DESIRE

Inevitably as you begin to build wealth, you'll have to learn new things, embrace discomfort and change your behavior as you seek to accomplish your financial goals. Throughout this process you'll be met with fear and resistance. This is natural. Everyone you know has these kinds of fears. From the most accomplished people to the most easygoing folks, we all have to contend with our fears. If you want to deal with fear, you cannot avoid it. You have to surrender to it, you have to let it in and you have to move through it.

There are a couple of ways you can move through fear. When you feel the sensation pop up, you can simply pause what you're doing, recognize it in your body and take a few deep breaths. Feeling it is one way to work through it.

The same coach who taught me grateful flow taught me an exercise called the Reversal of Desire, also created by Phil Stutz, MD, and Barry Michels, JD, LCSW.[7]

The Reversal of Desire is a tool that invokes visualization to help you move through fear or face something painful that you are avoiding. There are two cues for using this technique. The first is whenever you notice you feel uncomfortable because of resistance or fear. The second cue is whenever you think about doing something difficult, challenging or scary. For example, when you are feeling full of fear just before a salary negotiation or avoiding a difficult project or conversation. Use this tool and it will help you act in the face of your pain and fear. It will allow you to move forward.

Just a note that although this tool is great for confronting fear, you'll see the use of the word *pain*. This is because we avoid doing things that are painful, uncomfortable or that inspire dread and fear. The words *pain* and *fear* will be used interchangeably.

1. Close your eyes. Focus on the pain you are avoiding. Visualize the pain as a cloud, appearing in front of you. In your mind, say to yourself, "Bring on the pain." You're doing this because your pain has great value and you want it.

2. Next, visualize yourself moving forward and stepping into this cloud of pain and fear. Say to yourself, "I love pain!" as you continue to move through the cloud. While you're doing this, allow yourself to accept the fear and pain. Don't fight it.

**3.** As you walk out of the cloud, say to yourself, "Pain sets me free!"

Listen. I know this sounds crazy, but earnestly try it and it might work for you. And if it does, you have a real-life shortcut to working through fear and pain that will undoubtedly change your life for the better and in ways you'll never know until it does. I use it all the time, especially in my creative practices, when I spar or have to be around people who trigger my trauma. It helps me relax and move through my fears so I can take action and not make an ass out of myself because I'm full of uncontrollable dread.

## Calculate Your Net Worth

**Use the form below. Enter the total value of each category as of today.**

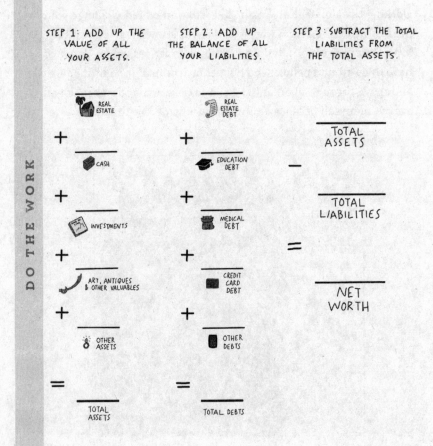

STEP 1: ADD UP THE VALUE OF ALL YOUR ASSETS.

STEP 2: ADD UP THE BALANCE OF ALL YOUR LIABILITIES.

STEP 3: SUBTRACT THE TOTAL LIABILITIES FROM THE TOTAL ASSETS.

REAL ESTATE

REAL ESTATE DEBT

TOTAL ASSETS

+

+

–

CASH

EDUCATION DEBT

TOTAL LIABILITIES

+

+

INVESTMENTS

MEDICAL DEBT

=

+

+

ART, ANTIQUES & OTHER VALUABLES

CREDIT CARD DEBT

NET WORTH

+

+

OTHER ASSETS

OTHER DEBTS

=

=

TOTAL ASSETS

TOTAL DEBTS

DO THE WORK

- **What is your target net worth? And when would you like to reach it?**

- **What are the details of your target net worth? What is your strategy for landing as close to your target as possible? For example: A $3 million net worth in thirty years through selling my business for $1.5 million. Investing $11,000 a year over thirty years to hopefully land at around $600,000. Owning real estate valued at $900,000. You may want to use a retirement calculator or planner to help you understand how your current investments may grow over time.**

- **What are the behaviors that precede reaching your goal?**

- **Why is this goal meaningful?**

- **What kinds of attitudes and beliefs does a person who has reached your target net worth goal have, embody and exhibit?**

- **What kind of decisions have you made in the last twelve months that have gotten you closer to your target?**

- **What kind of decisions have you made in the last twelve months that have set you back further from your target?**

- **What kind of decisions will you make in the next twelve months to move you closer to your target?**

## PART 5

# Protecting
# What You've Got

The higher you go up the Pyramid of Financial Awesomeness, the bigger your potential fall.

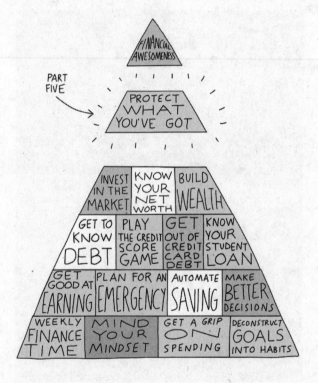

While there isn't a sure way to avoid the risk of loss entirely, let's explore the role of insurance in protecting what you've got.

**CHAPTER 18**

# Protecting Your Assets

*You best protect ya neck!*

—Wu-Tang Clan

A s you progress in your financial life, building and work-ing your way up the Pyramid of Financial Awesomeness, you might start feeling a sense of worry that you didn't have before. It's a bit like getting older; you worry about risks that didn't faze you when you were young. In your youth, you could quit your crappy part-time job because you didn't have very many obligations and finding another crappy part-time job might've been easy. You could jump off a twenty-foot cliff into a freezing cold lake because you weren't too worried about getting sick or hurt. In fact, you wouldn't even consider that you could get hurt. But as you get older, worries that you never gave any attention to suddenly stop you. When I was twelve, snowboarding was, like, totally cool, dude. But at thirty-five, it's, like, totally cool with an opportunity to break a bone or two.

Climbing the Pyramid of Financial Awesomeness might make you acutely aware that from higher up, there is a bigger tumble down. Backsliding is a natural fear that comes with progress of any kind. As you grow your assets and wealth, as you shrink your debt, you start to realize that you have a considerable amount of coin that would feel painful to lose. Even when we are cautious, our lives are full of risks, financial and otherwise. This chapter is all about how we can use insurance as a tool to protect us from losses that result from risks becoming reality.

Insurance is weird and probably one of the most misunderstood products a person can buy. It's unlike most products or services you buy in your life. Normally, when you buy something you have a reasonable expectation that either you or someone you know will use or consume what you've purchased. If you order a tuna fish sandwich, you have a reasonable expectation that you'll see a tuna fish sandwich appear in front of you in the near future. When you hire a plumber to provide plumbing services, you have a reasonable expectation that the plumber will plumb. There is a feeling of gaining something when you buy most things. Insurance is not like this. With insurance, one important feature people don't really grasp is that insurance is a tool to protect against loss and not a tool for gain. The nature of an insurance purchase is not to gain anything, but to prepay now so that if you were to have to pay for a loss later, you wouldn't lose as much. The fact that humans have created this tool is amazing and ridiculous. It's pretty abstract.

What's also weird about insurance is that many of us buy it hoping we'll never need to use it. Actually having to use the insurance means something went awry. Isn't it weird to buy a thing and secretly hope we won't need to use it to its full extent? Perhaps that reveals a bit of denial that bad things will happen to us.

That bit of denial may prevent us from ever purchasing insurance in the first place. Because to take insurance seriously, especially considering life and disability insurance, we're forced to confront the realities of life. That loss happens and that there are risks whose consequences we can't always predict. To take insurance seriously is to surrender to and confront the ideas that we're vulnerable, we're not always in control and that the worst-possible scenarios can happen to us. To say this is uncomfortable is an understatement. For some, it's paralyzing. The simple act of purchasing insurance requires us to rationally react to an imagined emotional catastrophe. I can't say I blame anyone for avoiding insurance and the inevitable contemplation that goes along with it.

But forgoing insurance isn't just choosing willful ignorance, it's letting your fears have undue influence over you and shrinking from the responsibilities that you've created for yourself. If you are feeling resistance and fear as you got through this chapter, use the Reversal of Desire tool from the last chapter to help you move through it. It only takes a minute to do the exercise, so you literally only have a minute to lose and the protection of insurance to gain.

Fear isn't the only reason why we avoid purchasing insurance. Our human brains are just plain bad at understanding risk in terms of probability and severity. While purchasing insurance is a gamble, forgoing certain types of insurance is also a gamble. The challenge is knowing which odds are better. To the make a decision about insurance, we may want to first understand the different ways we can manage risk in our lives.

## INSURANCE IS ONE OPTION YOU HAVE TO MANAGE RISKS IN YOUR LIFE

There are four ways to manage the risk in our lives. There is avoiding the risk altogether by not engaging in the activity that can result in the potential loss. If you attempted to make alligator wrestling your new career choice, this would open you up to the potential for all kinds of catastrophic losses. You might choose to avoid that activity altogether because you want to keep your fingers and your limbs and your life.

Accepting risk is another way to deal with risk. We usually accept the kinds of risks that have a low probability of occurring and that result in a minimal amount of loss. For example, instead of wearing shoes in your home to protect you from stubbing your toes on any furniture, we all realize that this is a normal life "risk" that we all accept to be comfortable at home. It doesn't happen that often and it doesn't usually result in more loss than a minute of cursing and feeling like an idiot.

The third way to deal with risk is to mitigate it. The decision to microchip your dog is a way to mitigate the loss of losing your dog because if they do run away or get lost, the microchip increases the likelihood that they'll be returned home.

The fourth way to deal with risk is to transfer it. When you buy insurance, what you're really buying is the transference of risk. Transferring risk makes sense when the risk you're taking can potentially have a severe and devastating loss, but a low likelihood of occurring. Renters insurance is a great example. In the unlikely event that all the stuff you own in your apartment or home gets stolen or completely ruined, there is the potential for a severe economic loss because you'd have to replace everything. Buying renters insurance is a way to transfer the risk of loss that has a low likelihood of happening, but a severe impact if it does.

# FOUR WAYS TO DEAL WITH RISK
## (TRANSFER, AVOID, ACCEPT OR MITIGATE)

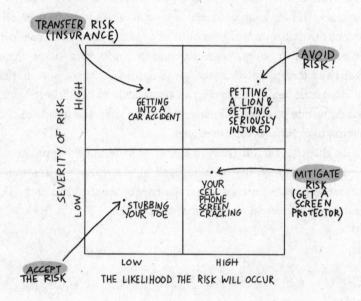

## HOW TO THINK ABOUT INSURANCE

If you have never had to use insurance, you might feel like you're a sucker because you're paying premiums that you have yet to recoup. But when you buy insurance, you are pooling your money together with a bunch of other people. Everyone pays into insurance and when someone needs it, the money is there.

Insurance is also a way to pay now to potentially limit your misery later. The nature of the kinds of risk that you would insure are ones that have the potential to change the quality of your life, but not in a good way.

Health insurance—in theory—limits the amount of money you can spend out of pocket each year on health services. Long-term disability insurance limits the amount of income you can lose if you are too sick or injured and unable to work. Life insurance limits how much of your income your dependents can lose. Homeowners insurance limits your potential losses in repairs or replacement costs. It can also limit the amount of personal assets you can lose because of an accident. Renters insurance limits your losses if you ever need to replace your stuff. And automobile insurance limits your losses if you're involved in an auto accident. In all these cases, the downside of these risks is much worse than the upside of not having to pay insurance premiums.

In this chapter, I'll give you a brief overview of the types of insurance mentioned in the paragraph above. These are the most common types of insurance that many people use to transfer risk, limit their losses and protect what they've got.

## HEALTH INSURANCE

The modern American health care system was created through a series of historical accidents. For a very long time, health care was stuck in the relative Middle Ages and it was cheap because it kind of sucked. Most people associated hospitals with death instead of health care. But in 1909, the very first drug that cured a disease, syphilis, set the stage for modern health care. In the 1910s and 20s, people's expectations changed. They began to believe their doctors could cure them.

As hospitals went from a crapshoot where people went to die to places that actually helped people heal, more people started to seek out health care. The increase in demand drove up the cost of care. Then the Great Depression hit and, given the higher cost, most people avoided going to the hospital until it was absolutely unavoidable.

An official in Baylor, Texas, noticed the decrease in patients in the hospital and came up with a harebrained idea that had a profound impact on how health care works in America today. He basically figured out a way to market and price health insurance so that it could be paid for over time in the form of a monthly payment—like a subscription. The hospital started this deal by offering it to a group of public-school teachers. As the depression's economic impact ravaged the country, other hospitals started to notice their unoccupied hospital beds. Suddenly the Baylor group plan seemed attractive and innovative. Plenty more hospitals began adopting it and eventually the Baylor plan became Blue Cross. Blue Cross started marketing the insurance to groups of workers. This was the initial reason why health care started to get tethered to employment, but two particular things helped solidify the connection: first war and then the IRS.

During World War II, there was a huge demand to produce the materials needed to fight and, in turn, a huge demand for workers to help produce these materials. Companies got desperate and began finding different ways to attract workers. One way was to offer fringe benefits, like health insurance. And in the same way people expected their syphilis to be cured, they began to expect employers to offer health benefits.

But the final nail in the coffin of health care that wasn't linked to employment came from our old pals at the IRS in what was likely a routine ruling. The ruling stated that, in some cases, employers could deduct health insurance premiums they paid on behalf of their employees. Business owners and accountants got wind of this and accountants started to file business tax returns that took this rule into account. Eventually, employers and business owners demanded that this rule become a law, and in 1954, it did. And, voila, that's how we ended up with this flaming crap bag we call the American health care system.

It is no wonder that a health care system that wasn't thoughtfully designed has a lot of flaws. I sure hope economists will work with policy leaders to change our system, which may as well be held together by a piece of gum and a Band-Aid, but until then, this is what we've got, kids.

In many ways health insurance is the reason why health care sucks in this country, but you need health insurance so you limit how much the system can screw you. Health insurance can limit the amount you might pay for both unexpected, high-cost health care as well as routine, preventative care. Access to preventative care has financial protection in that it keeps you healthy and screens for potential health issues or risks that could become problems later on. Without insurance, preventative care, which can help save money in the long run, might be cost prohibitive in the short term. Health insurance will typically protect you from paying more for essential and high-cost things like emergency services, prescription medications and maternity care. Your health insurance provider will pay for some or all of the costs provided that they are covered services and within your health care provider's network.

MOST HEALTH INSURANCE POLICIES HAVE AN INVERSE RELATIONSHIP BETWEEN THE MONTHLY PREMIUMS & THE ANNUAL DEDUCTIBLE

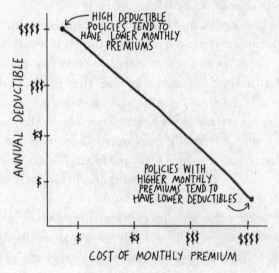

Even if you end up purchasing a policy that has a high deductible and low monthly premium, you can still limit the amount of money you spend on health insurance in a given year if your medical costs are all within the network.

A study of bankruptcy filings in the United States showed that 66.5 percent were due, at least in part, to medical expenses.[1] This is a very sad and unfortunate feature of our market-driven health care system. What's even more disheartening is that it's not just the folks without insurance who are filing for bankruptcy. It also includes folks with insurance who still get saddled with expenses that they can't afford despite having insurance. In a way it does feel like you're damned if you do and you're damned if you don't. But focusing on the things within our circle of control is literally the only thing we can do. Navigating and surviving in a broken system like the one we have in the U.S. means taking responsibility for ourselves because our government is not equipped to do it for us.

Besides having good fortune, here are some things you can do to stay out of medical debt:

- Call your insurance company to verify that a health care provider is in-network. Some insurers will pay 70 to 80 percent of costs for providers that are in their network. That's huge.

- Research services online so you can understand costs ahead of time and try to plan for them.

- You can also ask your doctor to give you an estimated cost for a procedure before you schedule it.

- Learn and ask about your options or generic alternatives for medication.

- Some doctors also give a discount for cash payments of services. If you're in the position to do that, ask if that's an option.

- Make sure to scrutinize your medical bills to ensure there aren't any billing errors and cross-reference that with your insurance policy.

- You can always negotiate with your doctor's office and set up payment plans if you find yourself in need of managing medical bills.

## How to Choose Health Insurance

You can get health insurance in the U.S. if your employer offers it as a benefit to their employees. In lieu of this, some employers offer a monthly health care stipend. If you need to purchase an independent insurance policy, head over to www.healthcare.gov to see what your options are, ways to enroll and details about various policies.

Before you decide on a plan with an insurance company, you'll need to sort through the various combinations of deductibles, premiums, co-payments and co-insurance.

- Monthly premiums are what you and all the other members pay each month to your insurance provider. This is the cash that goes into paying for health services that you and your fellow insured folks use when you use your insurance.

- The deductible is what you pay for before the insurance company shells out a buck for your health services. If your deductible is $1,000, that means you'd pay for the first $1,000 of health services. After you meet that deductible for the year, the insurance will start to pay for some services.

- Co-payments are what you pay for doctor's visits, hospital visits and prescription drugs. You pay 100 percent until the deductible is reached.

- Co-insurance is the percentage that you pay for procedures and hospital stays. If your health insurance plan's allowed amount for an office visit is $100 and your co-insurance is 10 percent:

- If you've reached your deductible, you pay 10 percent of $100, or $10, and the insurance company pays the rest.

- If you haven't met your deductible, you pay the full allowed amount, $100.

## LONG-TERM DISABILITY

We aren't talking about short-term disability because, generally, an emergency fund can serve as your short-term disability policy. Long-term disability insurance is a separate insurance policy you can purchase that will pay you part or all of your income if, in the long term, you can't work because you are too sick or injured. Your employer might offer disability insurance or you can purchase your own policy directly from an insurer.

Here are some things I know you don't want to hear, but since I care so much about you, I'm going to be that real, real friend who tells you the things you don't want to hear. Your biggest asset is your ability to earn income. If that gets taken away because of an injury or an illness, and you don't have a giant pile of cash to cushion the blow, you're going to have a tough time financially. I know what you're thinking. "Paco, that would just never happen to someone like me." Well, at the risk of being the kind of person who doesn't get invited to parties because I cite disability statistics, I'm going to cite them for you because, again, I care about you.

- More than one in four of today's twenty-year-olds can expect to be out of work for at least a year because of a disabling condition before they reach the normal retirement age.[2]

- Although there is the Social Security Disability Insurance (SSDI) federal insurance program available to disabled workers, it generally takes three to five months from the time of application for SSDI benefits to get an initial decision.[3] If you needed to appeal a decision, the backlog of appeals cases was more than one million in 2017. The associated processing time averaged more than eighteen months![4]

- As of February 2021, the average SSDI benefit was $1,279 a month, or $15,348 a year.[5] Not that you need to reference the poverty guideline to know how little that amount of income is, but in 2021, it was $12,880 for a one-person household and $17,420 for a two-person household.[6]

## How Does Long-Term Disability Insurance Work?

- First, you sign up for a disability insurance plan. The plan details depend on your income and how much you want to receive monthly if you're unable to work for a long period of time. The premium you pay is scaled to the size of the monthly benefit you'd receive, so a higher premium for a higher monthly benefit.

- Then hopefully you never have a serious injury and you live happily ever after. But for the sake of example, let's say you suffer a serious illness or an accident and you're unable to work. The next step is to make a claim.

- After a waiting period called an elimination period (generally thirty to ninety days), you receive biweekly or monthly checks that replace approximately 50 to 80 percent of your income (dependent on your income and premium).

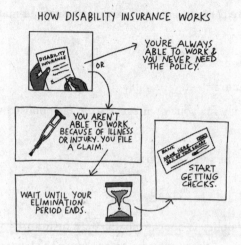

HOW DISABILITY INSURANCE WORKS

- Depending on your plan, the checks continue for months to years and stop when you return to work or reach retirement age, although some group policies stop paying out at age sixty-five.

## How to Get Long-Term Disability Insurance

■ **Option 1:** Sign up for an employer-sponsored plan through your work. Some employers will pay for coverage. If they don't, you might still be able to purchase coverage at your employer's group rate.

■ **Option 2:** Buy a policy through a trade or professional association. For example, Freelancer's Union offers disability insurance at a group rate for freelancers. Group rates are great because there are no penalties for profession or gender. You get the same rate as everyone else even if you have a higher risk of sustaining a long-term disability.

■ **Option 3:** Get an individual policy through a broker or insurance company. Guardian, MassMutual, Northwestern Mutual and Principal are big insurance companies in this space.

There are three important features you should make sure your disability policy has:

- It's noncancellable
- It's guaranteed renewable
- And it's for your own occupation (as opposed to any occupation)

Let's define some key terms.

### Noncancellable Insurance

A disability policy is noncancellable if an insurance company can't cancel, increase the premiums on or reduce the benefits as long as the customer pays the premiums.

### Guaranteed Renewable

A guaranteed renewable policy requires the insurer to continue coverage as long as premiums are paid on the policy. Insurability is guaranteed, but the cost of premiums can increase as long as they impact numerous policyholders and not just one customer.

### Own Occupation

An own-occupation insurance policy covers individuals who become disabled and are unable to perform the majority of the occupational duties that they have been trained to perform at their own occupation. For example, if an artist can no longer paint or make ceramics because of a hand injury, an own-occupation policy would still pay a benefit even if the ceramist could find work as a freelance writer. If they can't continue working in their own occupation, they are eligible to receive disability benefits. This type of insurance policy is contingent on the individual being employed at the time the disability occurs.

## HOMEOWNERS INSURANCE OR RENTERS INSURANCE

If you buy a home by borrowing money with a mortgage, there is virtually no chance that you'll get approved for a mortgage without homeowners insurance. Homeowners insurance limits the amount of money you would have to pay if your home was damaged and needed to be repaired, or if there was theft or loss and possessions needed to be replaced, and limits your personal liability for harm to others.

There are essentially three types of homeowners insurance: actual cash value, replacement cost and guaranteed (or extended) replacement cost/value. Actual cost coverage pays you what your house and belongings are actually worth, not what you paid for them. Replacement cost covers what you paid for your house and possessions so you can repair or rebuild your home to the original value you purchased. And guaranteed replacement cost takes inflation into account and will cover the costs to repair or rebuild your home—even if it's more than the policy limit.

YOU PURCHASED THIS TV FOR $1,000 THREE YEARS AGO. TODAY IT IS VALUED AT $500.

YOU'RE FILING A HOMEOWNERS INSURANCE CLAIM AND THIS TV IS ONE OF THE BELONGINGS ON YOUR CLAIM.

HERE'S WHAT EACH TYPE OF COVERAGE WOULD PAY

| COVERAGE | AMOUNT | WHY? |
|---|---|---|
| ACTUAL COST | $500 | IT'S THE ACTUAL COST TODAY. |
| REPLACEMENT COST | $1,000 | IT'S THE ORIGINAL COST YOU PAID. |
| GUARANTEED REPLACEMENT COST | $1,300 | IT'S WHAT IT COSTS TO REPLACE THE SAME TV TODAY. |

## How to Get Homeowners Insurance

If you need to get homeowners insurance, it's smart to shop around and do some research before committing.

If you already have insurance, check to see if that insurance provider also offers homeowners insurance. Insurance companies often give discounts to customers who purchase multiple insurance policies from them.

You might want to do some research online to find out an insurance company's reputation in handling claims. If you're in the unfortunate position of having to use your homeowners insurance, the last thing you want is an insurance company lowballing how much they'll pay out to cover the cost of home repairs.

An independent insurance agent or broker can be very helpful during the insurance shopping process. If they are independent, that means they don't have a loyalty to one insurance company. They can get you quotes from various companies and guide you through which provider and policy would be the best fit. The benefits of working with a licensed broker or agent is that they are insurance experts. All day long they help people with insurance, so they know what to look for and what to avoid in a homeowners policy.

## How Much Renters Insurance Should You Get?

You should get a renters insurance policy in the amount equal to the value of your stuff. Just like a homeowners policy, you can choose between actual and replacement cost coverage. Your policy premiums will likely range between $5 to $25 a month. If you have super valuable shit you wanted covered, like a Picasso or really special Magic the Gathering cards, you might need to either list these special things out on your policy or get an entirely different policy to cover your special, weird things.

IF YOU DUMPED EVERYTHING YOU OWN
INTO A PILE OF CRAP, THE VALUE OF THAT
CRAP PILE IS HOW MUCH RENTERS INSURANCE
YOU SHOULD GET.

## AUTOMOBILE INSURANCE

It's pretty amazing how human beings can compartmentalize the risk of driving a two-ton death trap machine also known as an automobile. Driving a car is hella risky business and not having the right insurance can be the beginning of a bankruptcy story, so it's important to understand the types of coverage there are.

- Liability for people you injure and property you damage. This coverage is not for your own medical bills or your own property.
- Collison
- Comprehensive
- Uninsured and underinsured liability

## Liability Coverage

The liability part of your auto insurance pays for other people's costs and protects your assets if you are ever found at fault in a car accident. Bodily injury liability will cover other people. And property damage liability will protect other people's property. When you buy auto insurance you can set the limits for this coverage. Limits are the maximum amount your insurance will pay out for medical costs and property damage. Almost every state has a required limit that each driver should have, but sometimes those limits are really low and when you get into an accident, your coverage could come up short.

Liability limits are generally expressed as three numbers like this: 50/100/100. These numbers are actually in thousands. The first number, 50, means that the maximum amount the insurance company will pay for injuries for a single person after an accident is $50,000. The second number, 100, means the total amount the insurance company will cover for everyone's injuries, except yours, in an accident is $100,000. And the third number is the maximum limit that the insurance company will pay for property you damage. Property is anything that isn't a person, and coverage pays for other people's property, like other people's cars or a building, and not your own property.

Unlike bodily injury limits that have per person limits, property damage only has the one accident limit. So if you're at fault for hitting a Tesla, a school bus and a hotel in one accident, the limit of property damage maxes out at $100,000 if we're using our example numbers from earlier. The limit is the maximum amount your insurance company will pay out for damages and the hope is that the limit will be enough to cover any damages.

Liability insurance limits the amount of personal assets you can lose if you cause an accident. In other words, it protects your finances. You should make sure that your liability coverage equals the total value of your assets. Net worth worksheet for the win.

## Collision Coverage

Collision insurance will pay for damage to your car if it's involved in a car accident. This type of coverage is generally not required by states, but some lenders or leases might require it. In most cases, there is a deductible and some insurance companies require you to buy comprehensive insurance when you get collision insurance, and vice versa. Collision insurance makes sense if your car is still pretty valuable. Compare what your car is valued at to the cost of the deductible plus the total you pay in insurance premiums for six to twelve months. If your car is worth a lot more than that total, it's probably worth keeping your collision coverage.

## Comprehensive Coverage

This covers the repairs to your car if it is damaged by something other than another vehicle. Things like a fire, a burglar, hail, a flood or a bear ripping the side of your car door off to get to emergency Lärabars are likely covered under comprehensive coverage. This type of coverage is generally not required by states, but some lenders or leases might require it. And like collision coverage, it makes sense if your car is still pretty valuable relative to the cost you pay for comprehensive coverage and your deductible cost.

## Uninsured and Underinsured Motorist Liability Insurance

If someone is driving around without insurance and causes an accident that results in damage to your vehicle or your person, who pays? You do, unless you have uninsured and underinsured motorist coverage. If it sounds like you're paying for more insurance for people who don't have insurance, it's because you are. Some states require this type of insurance. If the state you live in doesn't, you still might want to consider it because it's another type of liability insurance. Remember, liability insurance is meant to protect your assets. Adding this type of coverage isn't free, but it is generally worth the cost for the amount of coverage and the peace of mind.

### Bonus Liability Insurance: Umbrella Insurance

If you have a healthy net worth, like $700,000, you might discover that your auto insurance doesn't offer liability limits that high. They might only offer a limit as high as $500,000. In that case, when you need more insurance to protect your assets, there is a type of policy called an umbrella policy. These policies expand your auto and home liability beyond the normal limits that insurers provide. If you ever hit your limit on your auto or home policy, then your umbrella coverage kicks in to cover the rest. It's like having a dinner table that has an extendable leaf so that you can go from seating six to seating eight. Those tables are clutch, just like umbrella insurance, and you should only get either of those things if the numbers make sense. In other words, if you plan on having eight people over for dinner or if you have significant wealth.

## HOW TO THINK ABOUT LIFE INSURANCE

Before we jump right into the life insurance pool, first we must dip our toes into the realness that life ends for all of us. Yep, talking about life insurance means we are going to be talking about our inevitable fate. I just wanted to warn you in case you were reading this right before going to your best friend's birthday party and you aren't trying to have death on the noggin. I know thinking about your mortality can be tough, but the truth is it's a very important reminder that we only have a short time to love who we love and do what we want and need to do.

## So Who Needs Life Insurance?

A life insurance policy is used to replace the economic support or salary of a loved one when they pass away. If you have anyone in your life depending on your financial support, like a spouse or a litter of children or aging parents, you might want to consider getting life insurance. Especially if you have a mortgage, privately held student loans or other kinds of debts that your loved ones will become responsible for in your stead.

Even if you don't earn any income, but you're the main caretaker for your children, you still may consider a policy to cover childcare expenses in your absence. If you don't have anyone relying on your income, you technically don't have a need for life insurance. You might consider a small policy that would cover funeral expenses that your family and relatives would otherwise have to pay for.

Life insurance brings peace of mind knowing that your family will be cared for if you can't be there.

## Insurance Is a Tool to Protect Against Loss, Not a Tool to Gain

I mentioned this at the beginning of this chapter, but it's worth mentioning again: Insurance is first and foremost a tool to protect against loss and not a tool for gain. I'm bringing this up because there are types of life insurance policies that life insurance sales folks sell by making the case that the policies are more than just insurance. The problem with these kinds of policies is that most people just need the insurance.

## There's More Than One Type of Life Insurance, but Most People Just Need Term Insurance

There are many types of life insurance and it can be confusing to navigate, but the good news is, for the majority of people, term life insurance is the way to go. This type of life insurance gets its name because of how it works.

The premium (the amount you pay to the insurance company for the policy) is fixed for a certain term, hence the name. The typical flavors of term insurance are between five and thirty years. So, for twenty years, you pay the same, fixed premium every year. You can pay your premium for the year in one fell swoop or you can set up monthly or quarterly payments. Usually, you decide this when you apply for insurance.

If you kick the bucket within the term period, the insurance company will pay a predetermined amount (you determine this amount when you apply) to your beneficiary. You name your beneficiary or beneficiaries during the application process, but you can still change it once the policy is placed.

If you're still alive and kicking when the policy expires, you outlive the policy, and the insurance company wins the bet and they keep your money. Simple, right?

Term is the most popular kid at school because it's the simplest and cheapest way to meet your life insurance needs. It's the bucket-of-chicken deal. It gets the job done and it's the most bang for your buck. Really though, the most important thing it will give you is knowing that your loved ones will not become destitute if you prematurely bite the dust.

In case you're a rebel who is curious about the thing I told you to avoid—whole life insurance—here's something to keep in mind. Yes, it's a popular type of insurance that agents like to sell by saying it's like having the best of both worlds: an investment and insurance. Unlike term insurance, that's great at one thing (being

insurance), whole life policies are mostly mediocre as an investment and an insurance policy.

Each person's finances are a set of unique circumstances. In
general, financial advisors will recommend whole life insurance
policies for resource-rich people who are already putting the maximum amount of money they can into tax-sheltered savings accounts (retirement savings accounts, kids college savings accounts,
and health savings accounts). If you're one of those people flush
with cash, just reading this book to feel good about all the things
you're doing right, maxing out contributions to those accounts I
listed, then you may consider adding a permanent insurance policy
to your strategy.

## How Much Term Life Insurance Do You Need?

Many roads lead to the same destination. In other words, there are
different ways to calculate how much term insurance you need. One
simple rule of thumb is multiplying your annual salary by ten. This
is a crude rule that doesn't take your financial details into account.

A better calculation is the DIME rule, which stands for *debt*, *income*, *mortgage* and *education*. This is a much more detailed method.

- **Debt and final expenses:** Add up all your non-mortgage
  debts, plus an estimate of your funeral expenses.

- **Income:** How many years will your family need support?
  Multiply your annual income by that number.

- **Mortgage:** Calculate the amount needed to pay off your
  mortgage.

- **Education:** Estimate school and college costs for your
  children.

You can choose whether or not you want to subtract your assets
from the number that you land on. If you don't, you'll have a bit

more insurance than you need, but that may change as you get older. If you buy term life insurance while you're young, your income is modest, and your family hasn't grown into its full size yet, you can always buy more. While it's true that every day that you get older, life insurance gets more expensive, buying just enough insurance today ensures you aren't overspending right now.

### How to Buy Term Life Insurance

You can buy life insurance through an independent local insurance agent, from an independent online broker or directly from an insurance company.

An independent agent or broker can present you with options and quotes from more than one company. This is great so you can compare prices and your options.

Knowing what you want is another way to prevent being taken advantage of. Remember that 85 percent of you will just need term insurance. Knowing this before you work with an insurance agent, should you choose to, is a smart move. Insurance agents as people are not bad people, but the system they are working in creates a situation where their incentives are not aligned with what is in the best interests of their clients. If they are compensated through commissions only, just be aware of this if they come back to you with way more insurance than you thought you needed. This is an unfortunate reality of the industry. So if you can get a referral from a trusted source, that's a good start.

Policy Genius is a really great online broker.[7] And most of the time you don't have to get a medical exam when you apply, so if you were using that as a mental hurdle you couldn't get over, it shouldn't be one. If you didn't know medical exams were involved, don't worry too much because often you won't need one to get a policy.

The first part of the application process is completing your application online. Then, an agent will call you to verify details, walk you through options and help you decide on the company you will apply for insurance with. The agent will send you documents to sign. Then you wait to get approved. Once you're approved, you pay your premium. The process can take up to several weeks if you have to have a medical exam done.

## Here Are Some Pro Tips and Considerations About Life Insurance

• **Policies that you get from your job are great, but if you stop working at that job, your policy doesn't go with you.** A life insurance policy that is a benefit through your current employer is not a portable policy. Independent term life insurance policies will be in force (that's the life insurance technical term for active and in good standing) as long as it's within the term and your policy payments are up to date. I like independent policies for this reason. But, I'm not totally against group policies. Since they are offered to a group at group rates, you might be able to get access to cheaper, additional insurance that you couldn't independently. I guess you can think of a group policy as extra insurance, if you can afford it.

• **Don't miss a payment!** If you miss a payment, your coverage will lapse. That means you'll lose coverage and you'll have to reapply to get it back. And since you're getting older every day, your premiums might go up when you reapply. Usually, if you make the payment within a thirty-day grace period, your policy won't lapse, but please make sure that's the case with your insurance provider.

- **The contestability period.** The contestability period is the two years after you get the policy. If you die within that period, the insurance company can investigate the claim and deny the claim, which means your beneficiaries may not get the benefit.

- **Don't lie on your application.** Taking a drag off of a friend's cigarette at a party in the last twelve months and not reporting it on your application is a little different than omitting your pack-a-day habit. Either way, please don't lie on your application so that your premiums will be lower. It's fraud, yo. The insurance company could investigate your claim and if they can prove you lied, because you posted daily pictures on Facebook of you smoking, that can impact whether or not your family receives the death benefit. Yes, they might look at your Facebook. Insurance companies are petty so be honest so you don't make things difficult for your family.

- **You need a policy for as long as you have dependents.** This can be hard to predict because you could have adult children or aging parents who you help support. But know as a general rule of thumb, the term policy should last as long as you have dependents. And in a perfect world, when you're older, you've built your wealth so you don't need insurance to replace your income because your assets have.

---

DO THE WORK

### Protect Your Neck, Get Insured

**Researching your insurance options, comparing quotes and revisiting your spending plan to see how it all fits in is a multilayered process. It's totally reasonable to break up all these tasks across multiple weekly finance times.**

**If you don't have health insurance:**

☐ **Find out about your health insurance options.**

☐ **Are you able to participate in a group plan offered by your employer?**

  • **If yes, how much will it cost you monthly?**

  • **When is the next open enrollment when you can begin your coverage?**

  • **Make sure to put a reminder on your calendar for open enrollment.**

☐ **If you don't have the option of participating in a group plan, start researching your options.**

  • **Do you belong or can you join a trade association like Freelancers Union that offers group health insurance?**

  • **Check out Healthcare.gov for options.**

☐ **Revisit your spending plan and explore your options to make sure you can afford health insurance.**


**If you don't have long-term disability insurance:**

☐ **Find out about your disability options.**

☐ **Are you able to participate in a group plan offered by your employer?**

  • **If yes, how much will it cost you monthly?**

  • **When is the next open enrollment when you can elect for disability?**

- • Make sure to put a reminder on your calendar for open enrollment.

☐ If you don't have the option of participating in a group plan, start researching your options.

- • Do you belong or can you join a trade association like Freelancers Union that offers group long-term disability rates?

- • Does your auto or renters insurance offer disability?

☐ Revisit your spending plan and explore your options to see how you can afford long-term disability insurance.

**If you don't have renters insurance:**

☐ Get some or make sure your homeowners insurance is adequate.

☐ Revisit your spending plan and explore your options to see how you can afford renters insurance or any increase in your homeowners policy.

**If you drive, make sure your auto insurance includes:**

☐ Liability for people you injure and property you damage. This coverage is not for your own medical bills or your own property.

☐ Collison

☐ Comprehensive

☐ Uninsured and underinsured liability (optional, but recommended)

**Do you need umbrella insurance?**

☐ If so, start shopping around. Start with the insurance company you use for your auto and/or homeowners insurance.

**Do you need life insurance?**

☐ Calculate how much you need.

☐ Check out Policy Genius to run some quotes. You can run with them or use this information if and when you decide to use a broker.

☐ Apply for life insurance.

☐ Make sure your policy is in force and you stay up to date with your premium payments.

# Conclusion

## A State of Financial Awesomeness:
## Mind Your Relationship with Money

*Even though overarching systems of oppression are the primary cause of the world's ills, combatting injustices and dismantling violent structures start with a single act.*

—Yesi Taylor Cruz[1]

A rriving at the top of the Pyramid of Financial Awesomeness is not an easy feat. Congratulations on getting there. It means you've put a considerable amount of time and energy into contemplating and shaping your financial life. Now that you have arrived at a moment of achievement, I hope you'll appreciate the feeling of accomplishment. I hope you'll also recognize that in a lot of ways, your journey has just begun.

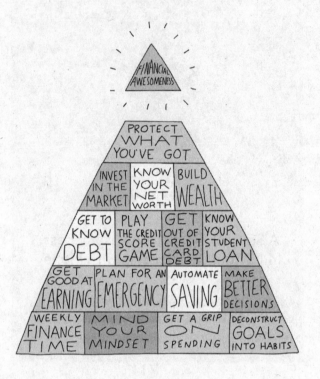

Your relationship with money is just like any other relationship in your life. Your relationships are dynamic, they evolve and change as you do and as the world does. As you continue to navigate your financial life and as you face financial decisions, don't forget about all the different tools you have at your disposal. And that having a good relationship with your finances is as much about how to practically and rationally make good decisions as it is about feeling emotionally aligned with ourselves and our actions.

As you continue to foster a healthy relationship to money, I hope that you will remember that minding our relationship with money isn't just about amassing wealth for wealth's sake. It's not just about deepening our dependence on capitalism for the sake of material gain. This work is one single yet powerful way for us to exercise power in a world that is hell-bent on denying power to many folks. It's a way to use currency to amplify the values and ideas we want to see exist in the world. It's one single area of our lives that we can practice the struggle of trying to change what is into what should be while realizing the paradox of this struggle. Minding your relationship with money is a radical and revolutionary act.

But what does a revolution look like anyway? Sometimes it's resisting and protesting and other times it is quietly reading the written word in the pages of a book, sowing the seeds of new ideas. There are probably many roads that lead to revolution. But one requirement regardless of the path we take is to recognize and come into our personal power.

As you go off and take what you've learned and express it in the world, I'd like to offer you some closing thoughts on things to keep in mind as you continue to foster a healthy relationship with money and power in your life.

## RECOGNIZE THAT YOU HAVE THE POWER TO CHOOSE ABUNDANCE OVER SCARCITY

Even when circumstances are tough and when the economy shrinks, there are ways in your life that you can expand and appreciate abundance. This is not a call to live outside of reality. It's a reminder that there are a multitude of perspectives in any circumstance. Being able to see things from many perspectives reveals your options and it takes away your powerlessness. We can always choose to see the good in the bad and the bad in the good. You have so many tools to calm your nervous system and to help you navigate financial decisions. Many of them are free to use and to access.

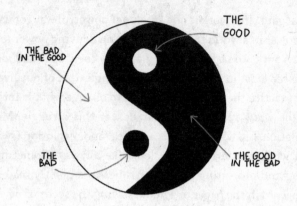

## KEEP INVESTING IN YOURSELF

What you've done as you've read through this book, contemplated, completed the exercises and taken action is you've invested in yourself. Please keep investing in yourself. You are worth it. You deserve it. Remember that progress can be slow and it requires time and space. Space to breathe and space to expand. This book was never about trying to blanket over your negative feelings about money and the world; it's about giving yourself the space and focus to experience growth. Growth isn't about eliminating all the ways we suffer; it's about being willing to dance with our suffering. It's about asking yourself what you are unwilling to feel and trusting yourself to feel it. That is where the good stuff is—in life, in relationships— and it's where we'll find solutions to big problems—in the shit, in the suffering.

## DON'T BELIEVE EVERYTHING YOU THINK

Your relationship with money is about money, but it's about a lot more than money. By reassessing it and working on it, you demonstrate to yourself just how powerful stories can be. The stories we tell ourselves end up creating rules in our lives, and those rules impact how we act and behave. If you've read through this book and you were able to unearth hidden rules and stories you've told yourself and change them, you must also realize that you can do that with the stories you tell yourself in other areas of your life. That all these areas of your life are not compartmentalized; they don't line up neatly at their edges. The stories you tell yourself are interwoven. What you believe about your worth doesn't limit itself to your financial decisions; what you believe about your worth creates rules everywhere in your life. So many of the tools in this book can be applied to other parts of your life. I hope you'll see that.

I hope you'll see the ways you've improved your relationship with money as a blueprint for ways that you can improve relationships in all areas of your life, especially your relationship with yourself. You deserve it; the world deserves it because everything and everyone is connected.

# Acknowledgments

It's been a privilege and an honor to be able to put the time, care, energy and thought into creating this book, none of which would have been possible without the support of the many people involved in its creation.

I'd like to thank the folks who have been reading, supporting and sharing my work over the years. Thank you to all of the clients who I've had the distinct pleasure of working with—you inspire me every day.

To the Hell Yeah Group team: Randy, Traci, Jon, Evan and Alex. Thank you for having my back while I took the time to work on this book.

I owe a huge debt of gratitude to my agent, Jenny Stephens, and the fine team over at Sterling Lord Literistic. Thank you so much for taking a chance on me and encouraging me to take on the crazy task of writing a book.

Thank you to my editor, Emily Wunderlich, for guiding me throughout this process, shaping this book into a book and for being so patient all throughout this journey. Thank you to Nidhi Pugalia for your enthusiasm, insight and support. And to the entire Penguin team, I'm so grateful to have worked with such a thoughtful group of pros.

Thank you to my family, my parents and my sister, Al, for always encouraging me to be my full weird self, to follow my curiosity, for fostering my independent spirit and never questioning whatever thing I decided to throw myself into.

Mordechai, you were the person who really showed me how this world of money works. And you were the first person who really wanted to know what I thought about it. I haven't stopped sharing my opinion ever since. I'm forever grateful to you.

Thank you to Sonja Rasula. The community of small business owners and creative weirdos that you brought together to make magic has forever changed my life. Thanks for bringing me into your world.

Thank you so much to Kristan Sargeant. I don't know if this book would ever have gotten written, let alone pitched, if you hadn't helped me face my biggest obstacle: myself. The work you do is life changing; words literally do not do justice to how transformative it is, and I'm forever grateful that our paths have crossed.

Thank you to my friends for their endless support, limitless love and the hours of their time that they've generously given me listening to my ideas. I hope that I can expand your life as much as you have expanded mine. Thank you to Jenna, Andrew, Bryan, Anne, Emma, BK, Casha, Chris, Michelle, Shaun, Aye, Karen, Roja, Noel, Junko, Frosti, Dina, Nico, Alyx, Cathy, iO . . . and so many of you who have been champions of my work and my writing. Thank you all so much.

And thank you to my wife, Jenn. Your unconditional love and support have shaped me into who I am today. Thank you for teaching me how to believe in myself, for your endless patience with helping me work through my fears, for your imagination and for your relentless push for me to put my work into the world.

# Notes

## CHAPTER 1: Why We're Weird About Money

1. Adam Curtis, dir., *The Century of the Self*, episode 1, "Happiness Machines," aired April 29, 2002, on BBC Two, https://www.youtube.com/watch?v=DnPmg0R1M04.
2. Edward. L. Bernays, *Propaganda* (Brooklyn, New York: Ig Publishing, 2004), 71.
3. Robert M. Sapolsky, "How Economic Inequality Inflicts Real Biological Harm," *Scientific American*, November 1, 2018, https://www.scientificamerican.com/article/how-economic-inequality-inflicts-real-biological-harm.
4. Carl Gustav Jung, *The Wisdom of Carl Jung* (New York: Citadel Press, 1960), 81.

## CHAPTER 2: How to Think About Spending

1. Leon Festinger, "A Theory of Social Comparison Processes," *Human Relations* 7, no. 2 (May 1, 1954): 117–40, https://doi:10.1177/001872675400700202.
2. B. L. Fredrickson, "Gratitude, Like Other Positive Emotions, Broadens and Builds," *The Psychology of Gratitude*, eds. R. A. Emmons, M. E. McCullough (New York: Oxford University Press, 2004), 145–66.

**CHAPTER 3:** Protect Yourself from Yourself: Get a Grip On Spending

1. Alan S. Waterman, Seth J. Schwartz, Byron L. Zamboanga, Russell D. Ravert, Michelle K. Williams, V. Bede Agocha, Su Yeong Kim and M. Brent Donnellan, "The Questionnaire for Eudaimonic Well-Being: Psychometric Properties, Demographic Comparisons, and Evidence of Validity," *Journal of Positive Psychology* 5, no. 1 (January 2010): 41–61, https://doi: 10.1080/17439760903435208.

2. World Bank, "Poverty and Shared Prosperity 2020, Reversals of Fortune," Washington, DC: World Bank, https://openknowledge.world bank.org/bitstream/handle/10986/34496/9781464816024.pdf.


**CHAPTER 6:** In Case of Emergency, Save

1. Walter Mischel and Ebbe B. Ebbesen, "Attention in Delay of Gratification," *Journal of Personality and Social Psychology* 16, no. 2 (1970): 329–37, https://doi.org/10.1037/h0029815; Angel E. Navidad, "Marshmallow Test Experiment and Delayed Gratification," *Simply Psychology*, November 27, 2020, https://www.simplypsychology.org/marshmallow -test.html.

2. Celeste Kidd et al., "Rational Snacking: Young Children's Decision-Making on the Marshmallow Task Is Moderated by Beliefs About Environmental Reliability," *Cognition* 126, no. 1 (January 2013): 109–14, https://doi:10.1016/j.cognition.2012.08.004, https://pubmed.ncbi.nlm .nih.gov/23063236.

3. U.S. Bureau of Economic Analysis, Personal Saving Rate [PSAVERT], retrieved from FRED, Federal Reserve Bank of St. Louis; accessed June 2021, https://fred.stlouisfed.org/series/PSAVERT.


**CHAPTER 7:** How to Be in Control When You're Not in Control: Automate Your Savings

1. David T. Neal, Wendy Wood and Jeffrey M. Quinn, "Habits—A Repeat Performance," *Current Directions in Psychological Science* 15, no. 4 (August 2006): 198–202, https://doi.org/10.1111/j.1467-8721.2006.00435.x.

2. Bankrate, "Best Money Market Accounts," Bankrate, LLC, accessed September 20, 2021, https://www.bankrate.com/banking/money-market /rates.

3. High-liquid means a type of financial instrument that can be turned into cash quickly, or what the industry calls cash equivalents. I know, I'm sorry it's like this.

4. Assets are things that are valuable and can be exchanged for money.

5. For example, if you contribute 3 percent of every paycheck to your 401(k), your employer will also contribute 3 percent.

6. B. L. Wisner, "An Exploratory Study of Mindfulness Meditation for Alternative School Students: Perceived Benefits for Improving School Climate and Student Functioning," *Mindfulness* 5 (2014): 626–38 https://doi.org/10.1007/s12671-013-0215-9.

## CHAPTER 9: Reframing Debt

1. Tara Isabella Burton, "The Protestant Reformation, Explained," *Vox*, November 2, 2017, https://www.vox.com/identities/2017/11/2/16583422/the-protestant-reformation-explained-500-years-martin-luther-christianity-95-theses.

2. Olivia Schwob, "The Long History of Debt Cancellation," *Boston Review*, November 13, 2019, http://bostonreview.net/class-inequality-politics/olivia-schwob-long-history-debt-cancellation.

## CHAPTER 10: How Credit Scores Work and How to Play the Game

1. Louis DeNicola, "How Long Do Late Payments Stay on Credit Reports?," Experian, January 14, 2020, https://www.experian.com/blogs/ask-experian/how-long-do-late-payments-stay-on-credit-reports.

2. For more info on how to dispute errors on your credit reports, check out https://www.consumer.ftc.gov/articles/0151-disputing-errors-credit-reports.

## CHAPTER 11: How to Get Out of Credit Card Debt

1. "1958," Morris County Library, accessed September 20, 2021, https://mclib.info/reference/local-history-genealogy/historic-prices/1958-2.

2. "The Fresno Drop," *99% Invisible*, January 19, 2016, https://99percentinvisible.org/episode/the-fresno-drop.

3. Elizabeth C. Hirschman, "Differences in Consumer Purchase Behavior by Credit Card Payment System," *Journal of Consumer Research* 6, no. 1 (June 1979): 58–66, https://doi.org/10.1086/208748.

4. Rick Weiss, "Study Has Tips for Waiters: Credit Card Logos Serve Them," *Washington Post*, September 21, 1996, https://www.washing tonpost.com/archive/politics/1996/09/21/study-has-tip-for-waiters -credit-card-logos-serve-them-too/2f13b12f-86d9-4e46-b27d -5d52e96a4619.

5. Here is a company that specializes in refinancing credit card debt: https://www.payoff.com.

6. Here's a relatively new company that offers personal loans: https:// www.sofi.com.

7. For peer-to-peer lending options, check out https://www.lendingtree .com, https://www.prosper.com.

8. For more info on understanding the difference between debt settle-ment and debt management programs, check out https://www.ex perian.com/blogs/ask-experian/debt-settlement-vs-debt-manage ment-programs.

9. To get help with a NFCC Certified Financial Counselor, check out https://www.nfcc.org.

**CHAPTER 12:** To Borrow Money or Not to Borrow Money?: How to Think About the Debt Decision

1. Matt Levine, "Fed Day, Junk Bonds and Unicorns," *Bloomberg*, Decem-ber 16, 2015, https://www.bloomberg.com/opinion/articles/2015-12 -16/fed-day-junk-bonds-and-unicorns.

2. Here's a simple online loan calculator to help you understand what your monthly payment will be for your loan: https://www.bankrate .com/calculators/mortgages/loan-calculator.aspx.

3. "What Is a Debt to Income Ratio? Why Is the 43% Debt to Income Ratio Important?" Consumer Financial Protection Bureau, last modified November 15, 2019, https://www.consumerfinance.gov/ask-cfpb/what -is-a-debt-to-income-ratio-why-is-the-43-debt-to-income-ratio -important-en-1791.

4. David Brooks, "The Wisdom Your Body Knows. You Are Not Just Think-ing with Your Brain," *New York Times*, November 28, 2019, https:// www.nytimes.com/2019/11/28/opinion/brain-body-thinking.html.

## CHAPTER 13: Spend a Long Weekend with Your Student Loans

1. Here are some of my favorite tools for tracking your debt balances and comparing different monthly payment plans: http://www.personalcap ital.com; https://unbury.me; https://www.tillerhq.com/solutions/get -out-of-debt.
2. Zack Friedman, "99% of Borrowers Rejected Again for Student Loan Forgiveness," *Forbes*, May 1, 2019, https://www.forbes.com/sites/zack friedman/2019/05/01/99-of-borrowers-rejected-again-for-student -loan-forgiveness/#7c9060c0b16b.
3. These are great email newsletters you can subscribe to in order to stay up to date with student loan info: https://studentloanhero.com/subscribe and https://askheatherjarvis.com/blog. Please be warned, every now and again Student Loan Hero will send out emails pushing financial products.
4. For more info on consolidating your federal loans, check out https:// studentloans.gov/myDirectLoan/index.action.

## CHAPTER 14: How to Think About Investing

1. Melissa Rayner, "Happy National One Cent Day: So What Could a Penny Buy You 100 Years Ago?," *Gale*, March 31, 2015, https://blog .gale.com/happy-national-one-cent-day.
2. Kimberly Amadeo, "Consumer Price Index and How It Measures Inflation," *The Balance*, updated April 15 2021, https://www.thebalance .com/consumer-price-index-cpi-index-definition-and-calculation -3305735.
3. If you're curious about historical CPI rates, you can see them all here: https://www.usinflationcalculator.com/inflation/consumer-price -index-and-annual-percent-changes-from-1913-to-2008.

## CHAPTER 15: How to Stock Market

1. "Dividend History," Dividend History, Apple, last modified April 2021, https://investor.apple.com/dividend-history/default.aspx.
2. Here's a good calculator to help you understand how much money and assets you should aim to have in order to retire: https://smartasset .com/retirement/retirement-calculator.

## CHAPTER 16: So You Wanna Hire a Financial Advisor?

1. "Suitability," Rules and Guidance, FINRA, https://www.finra.org/rules-guidance/key-topics/suitability.
2. Dayana Yochim and Jonathan Todd, "How a 1% Fee Could Cost Millennials $590,000 in Retirement Savings," NerdWallet, April 27, 2016, https://www.nerdwallet.com/blog/investing/millennial-retirement-fees-one-percent-half-million-savings-impact.
3. This database can help you find a fee-only financial advisor or planner: https://www.xyplanningnetwork.com.
4. For a CFP or advisor who belongs to the National Association of Personal Financial Advisors, see https://www.letsmakeaplan.org and https://www.napfa.org.

## CHAPTER 17: How to Build Wealth: Know Your Net Worth

1. Pablo S. Torre, "How and Why Athletes Go Broke," *Sports Illustrated*, March 23, 2009, https://vault.si.com/vault/2009/03/23/how-and-why-athletes-go-broke.
2. Nick Holeman, "Is Buying a Home a Good Investment?," Betterment, November 19, 2016, https://www.betterment.com/resources/buying-home-good-investment.
3. This rent vs. buy calculator can help you decide whether you should rent or buy: https://www.nytimes.com/interactive/2014/upshot/buy-rent-calculator.html.
4. Fox Butterfield, "From Ben Franklin, a Gift That's Worth Two Fights," *New York Times*, April 21, 1990, https://www.nytimes.com/1990/04/21/us/from-ben-franklin-a-gift-that-s-worth-two-fights.html.
5. For the Personal Capital retirement planner tool, see https://personalcapital.com.
6. For the Smart Asset retirement planner tool, see https://smartasset.com/retirement/retirement-calculator.
7. For more info on the Reversal of Desire tool, check out https://www.thetoolsbook.com/the-reversal-of-desire.

## CHAPTER 18: Protecting Your Assets

1. David U. Himmelstein, Robert M. Lawless, Deborah Thorne, Pamela Foohey and Steffie Woolhandler, "Medical Bankruptcy: Still Common

Despite the Affordable Care Act," *American Journal of Public Health* 109 (2019): 431–33, https://doi.org/10.2105/AJPH.2018.304901.

2. Johanna Maleh and Tiffany Bosley, "Disability and Death Probability Tables for Insured Workers Born in 1997," Table A, Social Security Administration, October 2017, https://www.ssa.gov/oact/NOTES/ran6/an2017-6.pdf.

3. "What You Should Know Before You Apply for Social Security Disability Benefits," factsheet, Social Security Administration, https://www.ssa.gov/disability/Documents/Factsheet-AD.pdf.

4. "State-by-State Disability Backlog," Allsup, May 2017, https://www.allsup.com/media/files/stateby-state-backlog-2017.pdf.

5. "Monthly Statistical Snapshot, February 2021," Table 2, Social Security Administration, March 2021, https://www.ssa.gov/policy/docs/quickfacts/stat_snapshot/2021-02.html.

6. "Poverty Guidelines 01/15/2021," Office of the Assistant Secretary for Planning and Evaluation (ASPE), 2021, https://aspe.hhs.gov/poverty-guidelines.

7. Here's a great online insurance broker: https://www.policygenius.com.

## CONCLUSION: A State of Financial Awesomeness: Mind Your Relationship with Money

1. Jesi Taylor Cruz, "Composting Food Waste Is an Act of Resistance," *ZORA*, July 8, 2020, https://zora.medium.com/composting-food-waste-is-an-act-of-resistance-f5ba3425394a.